# Cloud-Based Microservices

## Techniques, Challenges, and Solutions

Chandra Rajasekharaiah

Apress®

*Cloud-Based Microservices: Techniques, Challenges, and Solutions*

Chandra Rajasekharaiah
Suwanee, GA, USA

ISBN-13 (pbk): 978-1-4842-6563-5          ISBN-13 (electronic): 978-1-4842-6564-2
https://doi.org/10.1007/978-1-4842-6564-2

Managing Director, Apress Media LLC: Welmoed Spahr
Acquisitions Editor: Susan McDermott
Development Editor: Laura Berendson
Coordinating Editor: Rita Fernando

Cover designed by eStudioCalamar

Cover image designed by Pixabay

Distributed to the book trade worldwide by Springer Science+Business Media New York, 1 New York Plaza, New York, NY 10004. Phone 1-800-SPRINGER, fax (201) 348-4505, e-mail orders-ny@springer-sbm.com, or visit www.springeronline.com. Apress Media, LLC is a California LLC and the sole member (owner) is Springer Science + Business Media Finance Inc (SSBM Finance Inc). SSBM Finance Inc is a **Delaware** corporation.

For information on translations, please e-mail booktranslations@springernature.com; for reprint, paperback, or audio rights, please e-mail bookpermissions@springernature.com.

Apress titles may be purchased in bulk for academic, corporate, or promotional use. eBook versions and licenses are also available for most titles. For more information, reference our Print and eBook Bulk Sales web page at http://www.apress.com/bulk-sales.

Any source code or other supplementary material referenced by the author in this book is available to readers on GitHub via the book's product page, located at www.apress.com/9781484265635. For more detailed information, please visit http://www.apress.com/source-code.

Printed on acid-free paper

*For my daughter Tanya, the world's greatest nine-year-old coach, critic, and chum.*

# Table of Contents

About the Author ............................................................................................ xi

About the Technical Reviewers ................................................................... xiii

Acknowledgments ........................................................................................ xv

Introduction ...............................................................................................xvii

Chapter 1: Case Study: Energence........................................................... 1

    Managing Energy Production and Distribution.................................................... 3

    Hardware and Software Infrastructure ............................................................... 5

    Monolithic Software Solutions .......................................................................... 5

    Growth Opportunities and Objectives ............................................................... 8

    Next Steps...................................................................................................... 10

    Summary......................................................................................................... 11

    Points to Ponder............................................................................................. 11

    Further Related Reading ................................................................................. 12

Chapter 2: Microservices: What, Why, and How? ................................. 13

    Origins............................................................................................................ 13

    Microservices Architecture ............................................................................ 15

        Implementing Microservices ....................................................................... 16

        Communication–Orchestration and Choreography ....................................... 19

    Microservices Migration Plan for Energence ................................................... 21

        Breaking a Monolith into Modules ............................................................... 21

        Breaking Modules into Submodules.............................................................. 24

        Establishing Microservices Architecture ..................................................... 27

    Transition Architectures ................................................................................. 28

Microservices-Native Architecture ....................................................................... 30

    The Approach in a Nutshell ........................................................................ 30

    Defining Top-Level Domains ....................................................................... 31

    Deciding Interdomain Communication .......................................................... 32

    Toward Subdomains ................................................................................. 33

    Designing Microservices ........................................................................... 34

Architectural Advantages and Gains ................................................................... 35

    Scalability .............................................................................................. 35

    Elasticity ............................................................................................... 37

    Agility ................................................................................................... 38

Energence's Monoliths as Microservices ............................................................. 39

Summary ........................................................................................................ 39

Points to Ponder .............................................................................................. 40

Further Related Reading .................................................................................... 40

**Chapter 3: Architectural Challenges ............................................................. 41**

Identifying and Classifying Challenges ................................................................. 42

AC1: Dispersed Business Logic .......................................................................... 44

AC2: Lack of Distributed Transactions ................................................................. 47

    Orchestrated Domains .............................................................................. 48

Choreographed Domains ................................................................................... 49

AC3: Inconsistent Dynamic Overall State ............................................................. 50

    Challenges in Data Exchange ..................................................................... 51

    Problems with Sharding ............................................................................ 52

AC4: Difficulty in Gathering Composite Data ........................................................ 53

AC5: Difficulty in Debugging Failures and Faults ................................................... 54

AC6: The v2 Dread—Difficulty in Evolving ........................................................... 56

Summary ........................................................................................................ 57

Points to Ponder .............................................................................................. 57

Further Related Reading .................................................................................... 58

**Chapter 4: Overcoming Architectural Challenges.................................. 59**

Service Catalog.......................................................................... 59

Sagas (Long-Running Transactions)............................................. 62

    Ignoring Errors................................................................... 63

    Compensating Errors Inline ................................................. 64

    Compensating Errors Offline ............................................... 64

    Implementing Sagas........................................................... 65

Maintaining the Global States..................................................... 65

    The Scenario of Dynamic Overall State ................................ 66

    Intermittent-Peek Option.................................................... 68

    Always-Listening Option...................................................... 70

    Larger Questions ............................................................... 71

Centralized View ...................................................................... 72

Observability............................................................................ 74

Contract Testing ....................................................................... 76

Summary.................................................................................. 79

Points to Ponder....................................................................... 79

Further Related Reading ............................................................ 80

**Chapter 5: Process Changes........................................................... 81**

Continuous Integration............................................................... 84

    Non-production Environments............................................... 85

    Automated Testing............................................................. 87

    Performance Testing.......................................................... 87

    Ephemerality and Equivalence of Environments .................... 89

Continuous Delivery .................................................................. 90

    Infrastructure as Code........................................................ 90

    Delivery Techniques........................................................... 90

DevSecOps............................................................................... 92

Changes to Energence ............................................................... 94

Summary.................................................................................. 94

Points to Ponder ............................................................................................. 95

Further Related Reading ................................................................................. 95

**Chapter 6: Cloudification: Strategy ................................................... 97**

The Allure of the Cloud .................................................................................. 98

    Financial Gains of Moving to Cloud ........................................................ 98

    Business Opportunities in Moving to Cloud ........................................... 100

    Technological Gains of Moving to Cloud ................................................ 101

Prerequisites to a Cloud Journey ................................................................. 102

Overall Setup for Microservices in Cloud ..................................................... 103

Networking and Connectivity ........................................................................ 104

    Regions and Zones .............................................................................. 105

Compute ...................................................................................................... 106

Integration .................................................................................................... 108

Databases and Traditional Datastores .......................................................... 108

Special-Purpose Datastores .......................................................................... 109

Cost Analysis ............................................................................................... 110

    Billing .................................................................................................. 111

    Cost Factors ........................................................................................ 112

Energence on Cloud ..................................................................................... 114

Summary ...................................................................................................... 117

Points to Ponder ........................................................................................... 117

Further Reading ............................................................................................ 118

**Chapter 7: Core Cloud Concepts: Compute ..................................... 119**

Containerization over Virtualization .............................................................. 120

    Containerizing Microservices ................................................................ 123

Container Orchestration ................................................................................ 125

Service Meshes ............................................................................................ 131

    Traffic Control, Traffic Management, and Traffic Shaping ....................... 134

    Establishing and Securing Communication ............................................ 135

Building Overall Observability..............................................................136

Challenges and State of the Art of Service Meshes ...........................138

FaaS aka Serverless ..................................................................................138

PaaS ...........................................................................................................141

Integration Services..................................................................................141

MaaS: Messaging Services ...................................................................142

Point-to-Point Messaging....................................................................143

Publish-Subscribe Messaging .............................................................145

Streaming and Distributed Commit Logs...........................................147

Energence's Cloud Setup for Compute .....................................................150

Summary.....................................................................................................152

Points to Ponder........................................................................................152

Further Related Reading ...........................................................................153

**Chapter 8: Core Cloud Concepts: Storage...................................... 155**

DBaaS .........................................................................................................155

Classifying DBaaS by Data Type .........................................................156

Classifying DBaaS by CAP ...................................................................161

DataStores for OLAP..................................................................................171

Data Warehouses on Cloud.................................................................172

Data Movement on Cloud ...................................................................174

Summary.....................................................................................................176

Points to Ponder........................................................................................177

Further Related Reading ...........................................................................177

**Chapter 9: Securing Microservices on Cloud ................................. 179**

Securing Microservices .............................................................................180

Reducing the Attack Surface ...............................................................181

Securing Services..................................................................................182

Securing Outgoing Communication .....................................................183

Securing Microservices on Cloud ...................................................... 183

    Virtual Private Clouds ................................................................ 184

    API Gateways and Load Balancers ......................................... 187

    IAM of CSPs .............................................................................. 191

    Securing Inter-Service Communication .................................. 192

Processing Integrity ...................................................................... 193

    Trusted Binaries ....................................................................... 193

    Trusted Execution .................................................................... 194

Availability ....................................................................................... 197

    Disaster Recovery (DR) ........................................................... 198

    Multi-region Solutions ............................................................. 199

Summary .......................................................................................... 201

Points to Ponder ............................................................................. 201

Further Related Reading ............................................................... 202

**Chapter 10: Microservices, Here and Beyond ....................... 203**

Forecasts and Trends .................................................................... 204

    Integration of Microservices ................................................... 205

    Automation of Support and Operations ................................. 205

    Standardization of Compute Options ..................................... 206

    Cloud-Bursting, Multi-Cloud, Cloud Agnosticism ................ 206

    Changing Security Landscape ................................................ 207

Alternate Thoughts ........................................................................ 207

    Monoliths are Dead; Long Live the Monolith ........................ 208

    HCI or the Comeback of On-Prem .......................................... 208

In Closing ......................................................................................... 209

**Appendix: Comparison of Cloud Service Providers ............. 211**

**Bibliography ................................................................................ 215**

**Afterword ..................................................................................... 221**

**Index ............................................................................................. 223**

# About the Author

**Chandra Rajasekharaiah** has led multi-million-dollar enterprise initiatives in cloud-based microservice development. For the past five years, he has also migrated giant enterprise monoliths to microservices-based applications on the cloud and multi-data centers. His career of more than 20 years in the software engineering industry has posed him in various capacities in multiple Fortune 500 companies. He has been a principal, enterprise architect, solutions architect, and software engineer. His experience of working with multiple domains—retail, ecommerce, telecommunications, telematics, travel, electronic payments, and automobile—has given him a broad base to draw parallels, abstract problems, and create innovative solutions. He enjoys architecting, delivering, and supporting enterprise products. Continue the learning after reading the book; learn cloud-based architectures on the website `https://cloudbooks.info`.

# About the Technical Reviewers

**Mark Schaefer** is a Principal Software Engineer for Risk Management Solutions (RMS). He has written REST microservices in Node.js, Scala, Java and C#.NET, containerized using Docker, deployed in Mesos and Kubernetes clusters on Azure and AWS clouds. This work followed the typical trajectory of initial lift-and-shift operations for monolithic applications, followed by strategic refactoring into container-based solutions leveraging cloud-based storage and microservices. He is a graduate of Massachusetts Institute of Technology, holding masters' degrees in EECS and Management. Prior to RMS, Mark worked for Viavi Solutions and General Motors / OnStar.

**Erick Rosas** has worked in large enterprises for over 10 years and has successfully led transitions from monoliths to microservices. His experience is focused on building storage solutions and APIs optimized for low latency. He enjoys working on distributed data structures and has built several distributed storage layers to serve telematics and IoT use cases. He is currently working on distributed tracing at Amazon Web Services.

# Acknowledgments

This book would not have been possible without the love, support, and encouragement from my family. I'm deeply indebted to my wife Binita and my son Milind, both technophiles; without their support and input, this book would not have been possible. Many thanks to my uncle Dr. Huliyar Mallikarjuna, for his guidance and counsel.

Sincere acknowledgments are due to the technical reviewers, Mark Schaefer and Erick Rosas, without whose stern reviews and invaluable insights the book would not have been complete.

Special thanks to the Apress team: Susan McDermott, for believing in this project and making it possible; Rita Fernando, for tenaciously following up and ensuring we bring this to a conclusion.

I'd like to acknowledge Raghunath Krishnamurthy and Nivas Ramanie for peer-reviewing the content on microservices early on; your inputs are appreciated.

# Introduction

Microservices architecture, as a general paradigm, is a gradual evolution of software development. The various concepts of microservices have changed and shaped the software engineering landscape, and continue to do so. The recent surge in popularity of microservices is primarily due to the agility it brings and its readiness for the cloud. Enterprises continue to reap the benefits of cloud computing, and the combination of microservices and cloud computing has become a de facto architecture standard. This mandates architects and engineers need to learn the field of cloud-based microservices—either to confidently enter the domain or to undertake more significant challenges. This book intends to be a field guide for people who are in any phase of the transformation and accompany them along.

Owing to the proliferation of microservices and cloud computing, the knowledge of cloud-based microservices architecture is now essential for architects and engineers. It is no longer sufficient to know small portions of this topic, but command over the field is necessary. This book shares ideas with individuals in their journey toward attaining such mastery over the field.

## What This Book Is

**A technology-agnostic discussion.** There is no focus on a single technology other than discussions about a class of similar technology options. The concepts discussed in the book are implementable with any technology adopted by enterprises.

**An architecture-specific discourse.** The book focuses on the ideas of architecting microservices landscape in an enterprise. The discussed topics include engineering principles, theoretical work, industry techniques, practical challenges, and potential solutions.

# What This Book Is Not

**A technology choice guide.** The intent of the book is not to provide choices in a particular technology stack. Some technology references are used to illustrate a point, or due to the popularity of that technology in the industry.

**A software development process guide.** This book does not discuss project management, program management, or people management necessities. The content does delve into engineering aspects of software development, but strictly from the perspective of technical aspects of management.

**A microservices programming guide.** Any engineering effort in computing science requires in-depth design and development knowledge. This book does not teach or provide a detailed description of how to build microservices in a particular language.

# Layout

We begin our discussion on the topic of cloud-based microservices with a case study. A fictional energy distribution company that has a software stack of monoliths, but has goals of being agile, incredible growth, and going global. This chapter sets the stage of why monoliths running in traditional data centers hamper them from achieving their goals.

The first part of the book focuses on microservices. We discuss how to turn monolithic software into microservices and, with an example, also discuss the theory behind microservices. The next chapter focuses on the challenges that microservices transformations pose. Subsequent sections discuss mitigation options of overcoming challenges, along with introducing various architecture concepts.

The second set of chapters discusses cloud architecture. We begin with understanding the process changes required in a microservices architecture and how to prepare for transitioning to a CSP—a cloud service provider. We discuss how CSPs offer their services and how to choose from their a la carte of options. We divide our discussions into parts—how to plan for a cloud journey with relevant cloud concepts, select resources from the wide variety of service options, and finally, how to ensure our microservices architecture is secure.

Readers of the book will gain an apt understanding of all the concepts required to transform into cloud-based microservices. Chapters also recommend follow-up reading for those who wish to further their knowledge of a particular domain. I sincerely hope the book results in increasing the proficiency of architects and broadening the field of cloud-based microservices.

# CHAPTER 1

# Case Study: Energence

To understand the journey to the microservices world, let us take a hypothetical case study and apply our various learnings along the way. First, we will explore multiple business use cases from the company and how their software solves the issue. Next, we will attempt to understand the growth path of the company and how it plans to expand its operations in the next few years. Finally, we will focus on how the current IT operation—both software and hardware infrastructure—needs to change to support the company's growth.

Energence is an alternative energy company that focuses on supplying eco-friendly energy to households and factories. Its goal is green production and efficient distribution of power, and it works to reduce carbon footprint in the process. To do this, Energence is generating power only through renewable energy resources. Its goal also is to make energy use efficient, for which it is installing smart meters in every factory and household they serve. Energence acts as energy manufacturer, DSO (distribution system operator), and energy retailer. As an energy distributor, it manages infrastructure to supply power to households and factories. As an energy retailer, it has software infrastructure to read meters, manage consumer's usage, and bill them. As an energy manufacturer, it has made great strides by producing energy based on advanced demand monitoring and planning.

Energence had a great 2019 and is now powering thousands of households in the three states: California, New York, and Florida. Being a modern enterprise, Energence relies on technology to gain efficiency in their network (see Figure 1-1).

© Chandra Rajasekharaiah 2021
C. Rajasekharaiah, *Cloud-Based Microservices*, https://doi.org/10.1007/978-1-4842-6564-2_1

As an energy manufacturer, Energence has built capabilities to manage their manufacturing systems efficiently. The fundamental abilities are

- **Ability to plan and forecast energy requirements and manufacture accordingly**: It is vital to have precise forecasts to control the manufacturing of energy. Energy storage is an expensive solution, and also, for being green, it is essential to reduce excess energy generation and balance consumption with production.

- **Ability to change load over time distribution to avoid grid overloads**: It is important to have resilience against power overloads in the grids. Energence continually monitors the power grids and injects power into the energy network to balance consumption.

- **Ability to find flexible consumers and offer them incentives**: Finding consumers who are flexible in power usage allows moving loads to different parts of the day to reduce peaks and crests in demand and have a stable consumption.

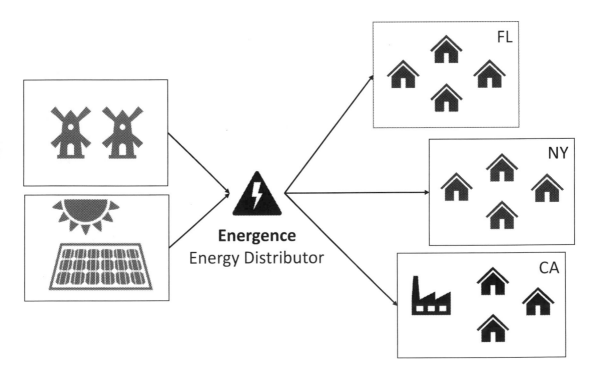

***Figure 1-1.*** *Energy distribution setup of Energence*

As an energy retailer, Energence can

- **Read devices and collect data regularly**: Gathering data at regular intervals aids in understanding the usage patterns of various appliances.

- **Monitor meters for usage; take meter readings frequently**: Repeated meter readings during the day help understand the overall consumption of users, forecast usage, and bill accurately.

- **Monitor smart meters and connected smart devices for failures and faults**: Detecting failures in devices aids, and moving them out helps in averting hazardous outcomes. It increases safety and decreases energy wastage.

- **Periodically send bills, usage reports, and energy recommendations**: Energence finds it essential to educate the consumer about their part in greener earth. Energence can help the consumer get detailed information on their usage and better control their consumption.

# Managing Energy Production and Distribution

An energy retailer needs to watch usage across its power grid. They must monitor usage of every device in every household and consuming entity and collect data from the devices. Most houses today already have appliances that can communicate using Internet protocols and can send various usage metrics. In order to collect usage data from older houses, Energence also installs a smart monitor into electric panels. Apart from collecting the usage data, it is possible to monitor and manage the smart appliances and smart devices remotely. Specialized hardware devices, termed edge routers, are capable of constantly monitoring and managing these appliances and various devices in a house. Edge routers are located inside the houses and create a dedicated home network, termed on-premises-network, based on communication technology such as 802.15.4, wi-fi, or powerline. Apart from routers, energy retailers attach metering devices, called smart meters, which collect data on usage of power across various lines and over time. It is natural that energy retailers such as Energence tap into such a setup for gaining efficiencies in energy distribution.

Energence has built systems that collect usage data from all the registered consumers' devices (Figure 1-2). The edge routers situated in houses and factories which are powered by Energence collect data from every device and smart meter from every household and send it to Energence's servers periodically. Edge routers are programmed to compress every data packet generated before sending data. Compression enables higher data throughput and efficient data uploads. Energence systems collect nearly half a billion reads so far from half a million devices, totaling roughly 2TB of data. Energence systems see a throughput of almost 250kbps. The collected data is used to

- Monitor and learn household usage patterns

- Look for anomalies in the behavior of devices

- Find opportunities to improve appliances' and devices' behavior

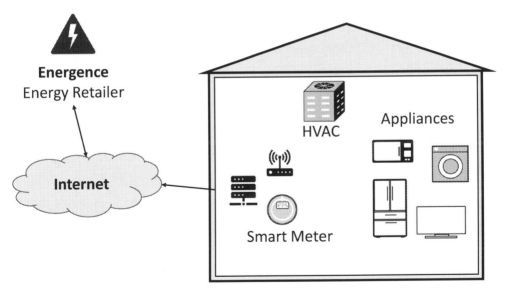

***Figure 1-2.*** *Data connectivity setup of Energence*

Energy retailers watch various smart devices, smart appliances and smart outlets in houses for failures, anomalies, and inefficiencies. Gathering usage information is a mutually beneficial activity for energy retailers and their consumers: retailers can ensure efficient consumption and improve distribution, because of which consumers will pay smaller bills.

# Hardware and Software Infrastructure

Energence hosts its software in a world-class data center located in Northern Virginia/ Washington DC area. This data center provides communication infrastructure, computing hardware, and storage needs. The Energence technology team, staying true to their vision of adhering to open-source, builds their applications on open source platforms. They also use open source datastores for their database, big data, and analytics operations. This combination of choices has allowed rapid development and deployment of the initial versions of their software platform.

Energence's software solutions segregate into four verticals, which squarely align with their software development departments:

- *Forecasting: **Energence Forecast Platform, Demand Planner*** Forecasting is the vertical that is responsible for identifying trends in usage and predicts demand patterns by analyzing historical data and usage projections.

- *Distribution: **Energence Home Platform, Energence Grid Platform*** Distribution is the vertical that has software and systems to control the distribution of energy—controlling both energy grid and energy distribution to consumers.

- *Manufacturing: **Energence Manufacture Platform*** Manufacturing deals with the energy manufacturing process.

- *Portals: **Consumer Portal, Partner Portal*** Portals are websites that enable self-servicing of consumers and partners of Energence.

# Monolithic Software Solutions

Energence has built applications that manage their software needs. Energence had the idea of monetizing their custom-built products for other energy companies. With this goal in mind, Energence's products are independently installable applications. Figure 1-3 shows the product suite.

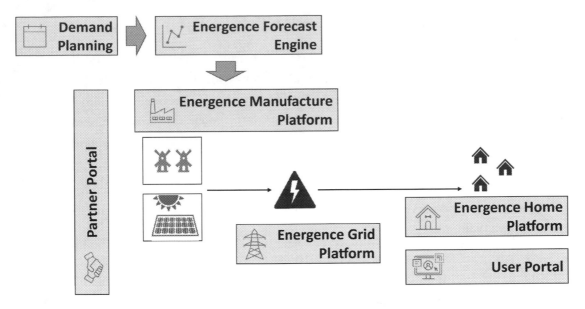

***Figure 1-3.*** *An overview of the Energence Product Suite*

Their **Demand Planner** allows planners to collate data from various partners and systems to generate an energy demand plan for different time slots. **Forecast Platform** analyzes past usage patterns, detects trends in usage, and accepts planning inputs to create a forecast model. Energence uses this forecast model across manufacturing and distribution software. Distribution software uses these inputs to distribute energy efficiently and to modulate the grid effectively. Manufacturing applications use these inputs to drive energy production, energy storage, and equipment manufacturing. **Consumer Portal** is a web front that handles consumer interactions, and **Partner Portal** manages partner interactions. These portals offer both a web front end and a mobile front end.

The most crucial application, and simultaneously the most massive, of Energence software stack is their middleware **Energence Home Platform**: a single system that does data collection, monitoring, billing, and a host of other activities that deal with smart homes (see Figure 1-4). Owing to rapid growth in Energence's business, its **Home Platform** is quickly evolving. Energence has earmarked a bulk of its hardware and labor capital for the coming years on this platform. Let us take a deeper dive into their Home Platform, focusing on its features and functionality.

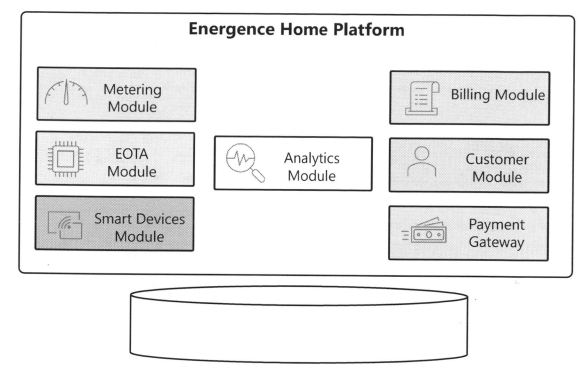

**Figure 1-4.** *Energence Home Platform*

**Data collection**: The **metering-module** receives data from smart meters and stores it into a database. The storage of data also triggers **analytics-module** to compute statistics, and **billing-module** to update billing tables. Many of these are transactional operations, ensuring the integrity of data across tables of all domains.

**Monitoring smart devices**: The **Smart-Devices module** maintains information about every smart device in the network and stores the data collected by **metering-module**. The data collection process includes every appliance in every household to which Energence is supplying energy. The **Smart-Devices module** module looks for changes in usage—this data can be used to learn usage patterns.

> **Managing smart devices**: **EOTA-module** (Energence over the air) manages various smart meters by applying software patches and updating configuration. It can also configure smart devices to optimize usage and performance (with homeowner consent). **EOTA-module** uses the **Smart-Devices module** to infer the best settings it can apply to the smart devices.

During the first architecture of the platform, sound design principles had led to separate the platform into various modules. However, these modules are not independent of each other and intertwine in functionality. These types of systems are termed **monoliths**, as their ***modules cannot execute independently***. Such systems suffer from complexities in maintenance, cross-dependencies between subsystems, and large runtime resource requirements (Dragoni, et al., 2017). Energence is beginning to realize this home platform is not agile enough to take on new business requirements quickly.

# Growth Opportunities and Objectives

Energence expects to grow to multiple states, enter hundreds of thousands of homes, and take on traffic from millions of smart devices in the next three years. Energence expects considerable backing from state governments in terms of subsidies, and support from eco-friendly citizens and corporations. The federal agencies' newer regulations are also fostering Energence's growth. To proactively address this—and prepare for the future—Energence had a focus group evaluate their various portfolios—production, energy generation, consumers, partners, and IT. The focus group has compiled a report on growth and challenges in every area.

IT organization received a report that listed the areas that need their attention. After pouring over the focus group's report, the technology group realized that a great opportunity lies ahead, but a great many architectural hurdles face them.

> **Systems need to handle a 10x increase in traffic**: The IT department needs to scale their systems to handle ten times its current traffic. Increasing customer bases and home automation pump in more data that requires processing. The next generation of smart-devices generate a lot more data as well. A significant burden lies on their Energence Home Platform, which needs to handle the extra traffic. There are some options, such as running

many platform instances in parallel to meet increased traffic. *The increased load may distribute unevenly on modules:* replicating systems result in *unnecessarily replicating all modules.* Replication also leads to increased hardware requirements. For instance, an increase in smart-devices data causes multiple instances of the entire platform to run, rather than running only numerous instances of the Smart-Devices module.

**Systems should be able to scale elastically**: Data from smart devices will change based on the season. For instance, usage data from HVAC systems and many home appliances will peak in summer but will reduce to a minimum in winter. The application instances should scale up and down based on seasonality and usage. A large technology company owns the data center where Energence runs its software. This company has a strict process in place in expanding to new hardware. High lead times in acquiring necessary infrastructure had slowed down Energence's rollouts earlier that year: on-demand elasticity might be a challenge. To mitigate this, *Energence is hoarding the hardware resources needed for such peaks throughout the year*; this has proven to be expensive.

**Systems need the ability to add new features quickly**: The platform will need to cater to an extensive pool of feature requirements arising from business needs. The business will need *quick turnaround time in rolling out features* to the platform. The tech team needs to devise a strategy for deployment cycles faster than the current monthly rollouts. These modules are bulky, and many dependencies are resolved at build time. For instance, the billing module's calls to the metering module require injecting service signatures into the other module. Also, communication technology is proprietary, making it hard to decouple them.

**Energence needs the ability to monetize their products**: Energence has learned that it is more beneficial to *offer their products as services*. Services add another layer of complexity to already challenging scaling needs. Any module of any of their products might need to be scaled out based on new sales.

**Systems should be capable of handling failures and disasters and be able to recover gracefully**: Growth of business and system requirements will create a varying intensity of system issues. The system failures could be partial—wherein a few servers are lost—or total—such as losing the entire data center. Energence solutions should be able to recover and continue business operations uninterruptedly. Engineers need a strategy for running services on a global scale.

**Systems need the ability to scale modularly**. Data volumes vary with the module, requiring independent scaling of modules. Growth in the metering module's data and processing grow faster than other modules. Also, Energence should use the right approach—for instance, stream processing—to handle scaling.

# Next Steps

Energence has excellent opportunities to grow as a leader in the energy industry. Globally governments and citizens are realizing the benefits of green and alternative energy and are pushing for regulations and investment in this sector, which will fuel Energence's growth. Note that Energence is also a technology-driven company, which presents them in a unique position, with significant future opportunities for monetizing their solutions. Energence can find smaller energy producers and retailers leveraging their services. Such occasions might arise locally, or globally, and Energence needs to be ready for that. As they expand, their software systems need to evolve and adapt to the changing business and technology space of the energy industry.

Their current systems can keep their business running but are not future-ready. The challenges seem to be in their first approach toward building applications. Energence built their applications as packaged products, which are single units with enormous functionality. Their idea was to install and configure the systems for customers. This model seems to be seriously affecting their speed of growth. To overcome this, they need to look at alternate ways of building and modeling their systems.

Let us start from this point, and chalk out a journey to a place where Energence has achieved all its goals. The rest of the chapters of this book attempt to capture such a transformation. We shall discuss how an alternate architecture such as microservices architecture is better suited to help them in their aspirations. We will walk through what microservices are and why enterprises choose them. Immediately following, let us look at the challenges enterprises face when they go on that journey and what are some of the actions to mitigate and overcome those challenges. We will also look at the process and automation changes needed to handle microservice architecture. We will follow up by discussing how to move microservice architecture to the cloud. The last chapter discusses the triad aspects of security—confidentiality, integrity, and availability—for microservices in the cloud.

> With many governments enforcing stricter privacy laws, cybersecurity—especially about collecting and retaining smart grid data—is an evolving topic. For this case study, we will assume that every customer has agreed to share their usage data.

## Summary

Energence is an emerging energy company that manufactures, distributes, and acts as a retailer of energy. Energence also aims to be a modern technology company, so it has invested heavily in its technology. They have built systems to manage their energy planning, drive their energy production, control efficient distribution, and allow users and partners to interact and self-service. Energence also aims to grow its energy business, as monetize their technology investments by selling their solutions.

With their updated vision, Energence realizes that their current software and hardware choices are limiting them from achieving their goals: they have issues in scaling, speed of change, being elastic, and recovery from failures/disasters. Their goal of monetizing their solutions as a product might be a difficult task at this point.

## Points to Ponder

1.  As the chief architect of Energence, what will be your plan to realize the vision? What changes will you bring about?

2.  Is there a way to quickly solve the problems of Energence?

3.  Are there any advantages of monoliths?

4.  How do capital-heavy enterprises differ from expense-heavy enterprises?

5.  Is Energence an energy company first, or a technology company first? Does Energence's vision and plan change in either scenario?

# Further Related Reading

**Method for an energy-oriented production control** by *Cedric Schultz et al. (Schultz, Braunreuther, & Reinhart, 2016)*

**Resilience of electricity grids against transmission line overloads under wind power injection at different nodes** by *Christoph Schiel et al.* (Schiel, Lind, & Maass, 2017).

**CHAPTER 2**

# Microservices: What, Why, and How?

*Can't nobody fly with all that shit. Wanna fly, you got to give up the shit that weighs you down.*

—Toni Morrison, Song of Solomon (1977).

A standard set of challenges face every enterprise with goals of modernizing. The usual suspects are their monolithic or legacy applications, their hardware and software infrastructure, and their software/service availability. Enterprises are usually in need of transforming their solutions to align with their long-term vision and goals. What differs is the urgency to act and the availability of funds. Modernization involves improving an enterprise's software architecture and making it nimble and agile. Such enterprise-level efforts introduce us to the microservices architecture, with the promise to enable quick and further progress.

In this chapter, we will examine what microservices architecture is and how it helps enterprises like Energence to meet their goals. First, we will review the origins, overview, and core concepts of microservices architecture. In the last two sections, we will explore how Energence systems can adopt microservices architecture and how this adoption will move them closer to their goals. The next two chapters discuss the challenges enterprises face during this transition and how to overcome those challenges. The final few chapters are for discussions focused on their journey to the cloud.

## Origins

Microservices architecture is a new concept, conceived in the early 2010s and gaining popularity throughout the decade. However, the principles that define microservices trace back to decades-old concepts in programming and architecture. Especially, ideas

© Chandra Rajasekharaiah 2021
C. Rajasekharaiah, *Cloud-Based Microservices*, https://doi.org/10.1007/978-1-4842-6564-2_2

from three computing science and software engineering areas—programming language concepts, systems architecture concepts, and software architecture concepts—have been quintessential in defining microservices.

Clean architecture concepts are direct derivatives of *pure programming* concepts. The history of pure programming begins from Dijkstra's cornerstone paper (Dijkstra, 1968) in the late 1960s that started the structured programming movement. It got engineers to start building code as functions and subroutines that are self-contained and idempotent. About a decade later, McCarthy's Lisp, a functional programming language, redefined programming as purely stateless mathematical expressions, thereby eliminating side effects and guaranteeing intent (McCarthy, 1978).

As computers became more commonplace and became end-user focused, software systems increased in complexity. For computers, operating systems were the user-facing software. Designers of Unix, the most popular operating system built in the 1970s, relied on layers of abstraction to simplify their design. User interactions were through commands, which performed a single function. Having a sole purpose ensured that commands are self-sufficient, are independent to run alone, and guarantee a predictable outcome in any scenario. These characteristics introduced shell programming: chaining commands as necessary, and to any scale.

New ideas in the design and architecture of software were conceived in the latter half of the twentieth century. *Object-oriented programming*, the concept of encapsulating data with operations that work on them, became a popular way of building maintainable and reusable code. Object-orientation has its origins in work done at MIT's AI lab, as early as the 1960s. The formal concept was proposed in the late 1960s with Simula 67. However, only in the 1990s were these concepts gathered, defined, and formalized. These concepts streamlined with the introduction of domain-driven design (Evans, 2004), which provided practical methods for abstraction. Object-orientation forced visualizing solutions as comprised of independent and self-contained units. Domain-driven designs led to creating a solution space as a composite of domains—concepts with contexts.

In parallel, over the past few decades, systems architecture has also seen a lot of evolution. The Web has become a prominent way of communicating, making HTTP the universal communication protocol. Roy Fielding's seminal thesis (Fielding, 2000), which described REST (representational state transfer), introduced a revolutionary architectural principle. With REST, systems manipulate resources with equivalent HTTP commands. REST enabled applications to talk over HTTP, thus allowing the same infrastructure that controls web traffic to control inter-application integrations, making REST a phenomenal success.

Many theorists spent time conceptualizing and defining SOA (service-oriented architecture), which allowed architecting any massive solution as a series of services. Consequently, SOA standardization described patterns and ideas for service definitions. The most critical factors identified were reusability, loose coupling, abstraction, autonomy, and statelessness (Erl, 2005, p. 291).

The amalgamation of decade-long ideas of self-sufficiency, independence, abstraction, and encapsulation brought about the microservices revolution. The popularity of HTTP, making it the transport protocol for all types of data exchange, also helped this movement immensely. Architects started building small, autonomous, self-contained services that communicate over HTTP, using JSON and other modern web technology. The standards and infrastructure that allowed the transfer of content to browsers also enabled the wide-ranging implementation of microservices. The term microservices as lightweight, well-defined applications with REST endpoints first appeared in 2010 (Iglesias & Garijo, 2010). It was only in the mid-2010s that several works standardized the concept of microservices (Newman, 2015) (Lewis & Fowler, 2014).

# Microservices Architecture

In an ideal microservices architecture, smaller and independent units of capability compose enterprise systems. These units, termed *microservices*, are built, supported, modified, improved, retired, and replaced without impacting the overall solution. Microservices are defined in a technology-agnostic way and use a standard communication model, allowing implementations to be in any technology. A significant side effect of technology agnosticism for enterprises is the opportunity to be polyglot, allowing access to a larger talent pool. The ubiquity of REST over HTTP resulted in the availability of adapters for legacy technology, enabling enterprises to bridge their application relics with modern systems.

> *"Well, I should like to be a little larger, sir, if you wouldn't mind," said* Alice: *"three inches is such a wretched height to be."*

> *"It is a very good height indeed!" said the Caterpillar angrily, rearing itself upright as it spoke (it was exactly three inches high).*

> —Lewis Carroll, *Alice's Adventures in Wonderland* (1865)

Though many traditional definitions of a microservices exist (Newman, 2015, p. 22) (Lewis & Fowler, 2014), we can identify the following characteristics as the most common:

- **Small and single purpose:** The scope of a microservice is kept small enough to have a single well-defined purpose.

- **Independent:** A microservice is not bound by any other service's logic or life cycle.

- **Isolated:** The microservice runs in an environment owned by itself, no sharing.

Designing microservices with these characteristics requires us to apply concepts from domain-driven design. I urge the readers to understand the relevant material and thoroughly comprehend the related concepts. For a quick primer on how to define microservices, let us walk through a design scenario. Pick a business domain of your choice. Assume that this business domain is a collection of capabilities/resources/functions. Limit this collection to less than a dozen. Divide each of the domains into smaller subsets using the same rule. Continue this exercise until you reach a point where the division does not make any sense. That smallest part is the realm of microservices. We will discuss the principles of what constitutes the "smallest division" later in this chapter.

---

The pivotal change to thinking for domain-driven design is that data is owned in isolation. One of them assume ownership, and the other domains rely on the owner for the data—the others only know the data through an identifier. The others ask the owner when the need arises and do not attempt to store the data.

---

# Implementing Microservices

Successful microservices architecture requires sticking to the following five principles regarding design, development, and architecture.

> *Microservices have a single purpose*: A microservice should focus on doing one thing and one thing only. Having a unique purpose makes microservices isolatable; they can separate and live on their own. Isolatable microservices are independently deployable. Other services know of the microservice's capability

and use it through its well-defined service endpoints, not worrying about its physical characteristics. Independence makes microservice testable, as the definition of the microservice is clear, concise, and unambiguous. It is possible to create a precise input set of data—and a mapping output set—to test the microservice comprehensively.

*Microservices are well-defined*: Accurately defining microservices contracts reduces coupling between systems, offering us the potential for composability. Having a well-defined service contract also better manages the evolution of software. New services can use the functionality and build on top of it. Such clients can also create definite stubs to test their implementations for correctness. Having well-defined microservices supports swapping in place. A newer or better version can replace an old one without affecting its clients.

Software upgrades are essential, for, against nature's laws, older systems never seem to die. Enterprises keep legacy systems alive because they "work in mysterious ways" and provide functionality that "might be needed." Enterprises sink an enormous amount of money on their support and maintenance. With well-defined services, modernization efforts such as technology refreshes become easy. A change in technology stack (such as a change in enterprise's standard programming language—from Go to Rust as an example, for the right reasons) can roll out with minimal impact. Enterprises with different technology benefit from this: the services (and engineers) in different technology can integrate and coexist without interference.

*Microservices are stateless*: A microservice should not "remember" the context in which it responds to a request—unless it refers to its persistent store, such as a database. Request to a single instance, or one among a million, should not change the response. Statelessness allows scaling microservices horizontally, transparent to the clients. It also ends the need for binding a client (or a session of consecutive requests) to a single instance.

More importantly, statelessness allows scaling out, where redundant instances share load without stepping on each other. Added to this, the ability to use any available instance, as opposed to a specific one, simplifies load distribution techniques. For microservices to be stateless, they need to store their states in persistent datastores only, not in-memory of their instances.

***Microservices are loosely coupled***: It is paramount that the microservices know others only by contract. Microservices should not share code describing any business logic, no matter how reusable it appears to be. Independent code bases ensure decoupled life cycles, where changes to common business logic do not affect multiple microservices. Code-sharing creates deployment dependencies, kicking us back to monolithic deployments. It is equally critical that microservices do not have a cyclical dependency. Cyclical dependency binds the involved microservices into a single life cycle. Cyclical dependencies also cause chattiness, where the associated applications call each other, which ends up affecting their performance.

***Microservices are discoverable***: A mechanism for clients to discover microservices should exist. This discovery must be dynamic, so it is vital to avoid specifying physical addresses. Any physical coordinates of a service, even of load balancers that front it, should be avoided. Physical addresses, such as IP or DNS addresses, bring in the knowledge of the ecosystem and binds down the microservice. Instead, a microservice should know its dependencies by resolvable names. Also, it should publish itself under a resolvable name. Such name-based registries offer advantages beyond decoupling. They allow traffic shaping—mirror traffic to multiple versions, wiretap traffic for observation, or piloting and testing against a small selected subset of clients—without extensive infrastructure overhauls.

When microservices are built with these five characteristics—single-purpose, well-defined, stateless, loosely coupled, and discoverable—we can see why they are a great way of designing large software systems. Complex system architectures turn into a controlled and hierarchical collection of functions. Such structures also provide a simplified, abstract, and trackable view of the solution space, allowing better control of the solution evolution. A lot of work has happened, and many techniques are published on realizing a microservices-based architecture. "Twelve-factor app" methodology (Wiggins, 2012), IDEAL design principles (*Isolated State, Distribution, Elasticity, Automated Management, and Loose Coupling*) discuss some of the excellent practices in implementing a microservices architecture. These factors touch upon most of the good practices required for designing, developing, and maintaining microservices.

## Communication–Orchestration and Choreography

We discussed how we could wire services together with standard web concepts (REST-over-HTTP, and JSON-payloads). Newer microservices use existing services by invoking their REST endpoints, wherever required. This method of integration—termed *orchestration*—is not the only way microservices can interact. There is an increasing drive toward integrating microservices asynchronously. In an asynchronous model, microservices emit messages upon completion, triggering one or more microservices. Processing a message might result in triggering more messages, which would result in more actions. This method of chaining services, termed *choreography*, is gaining momentum in many architectures.

Consider a typical enterprise, which consists of multiple organizations. Each organization is usually an entity of its own. When integrating these organizations, choreography fits the needs perfectly. Choreography technique allows organizations within an enterprise to maintain their independence, and preserve their logical separation as well. In the Energence example, the independent systems in Figure 1-3 show the top-level domains, which are potentially independent organizations. Planning, manufacturing, and distribution should be viewed as separate entities and integrated only through choreography.

It is essential to see why we do not want to bind organizations into a synchronous service call chain. Cross-organizational transactions are a strict no-no for three main reasons:

1.  Different organizations have different restrictions on software solutions. They could run a packaged software, or outsource to a third-party, or use a vendor service. There is no guarantee of a service-based integration.

2.  Engineering metrics such as transaction throughput, state change frequency, and availability agreements vary. Integrating them with orchestration percolates metrics across the enterprise without reason. Asynchronously integrating different systems prevents one system from bottlenecking the others.

3.  There is no "enterprise transaction." Transactions do not span across domain responsibilities. For instance, hospitals do not restrict admitting a patient until final billing and payment. At least, not always. Retailers do not hold customers on the place-order screen until their order is shipped. We will discuss these scenarios of long-running transactions in our sections on Sagas (Long-Running Transactions).

For instance, in the case of Energence, choreography is ideally suited for integrating planning systems with manufacturing systems. However, for the internals of planning and manufacturing systems, orchestration is the preferred method of integrating microservices. Within the boundaries of a system, we often find it required to maintain a call chain to provide functionality.

Choreography is possible in other forms, without an apparent async mode of communication. If integration between domains is through service calls, and any of the three earlier reasons apply, the service call should front an asynchronous mode of communication such as messaging infrastructure.

There are cases where choreography is advisable within an organization as well. The same three reasons act as our guidelines. If changes to a part of an organization's software stack are unforeseeable, it is better to choreograph that part into the rest of the solution. If a software system of an organization has a higher throughput requirement than the rest of the systems, it is best to asynchronously integrate with other systems, which process the data later. For instance, each of Energence's organizations—planning, manufacturing, distribution, etc.—should be integrated through choreography.

---

Architects need to thoroughly vet the domain boundaries and dependencies before choosing between orchestration and choreography.

---

One of the inevitable outcomes of moving to a microservices architecture is eventual consistency. It is important to note that data consistency and application performance are inversely related. When systems attempt to maintain congruency consistency of data across its multiple parts, it takes time to decide the final state, thus affecting performance. In such scenarios, it is best to resolve multiple parts separately and asynchronously.

# Microservices Migration Plan for Energence

Microservices offer a great many advantages such as clean architecture, polyglot development, and scalability, among many others, which we will discuss later in this chapter. Let's review a typical journey of evolving into the microservices world. Walking through that evolution process will help us better understand the scope of changes, how changes happen, and how these changes realize advantages. Such journeys are not simple or inexpensive. They tend to be multi-phased approaches, slowly segregating and chipping away at the monolith. However, there is a great benefit in taking up the task of moving to microservices, whose gains offset the cost of the journey. In many cases, as in the case of Eneregence, enterprises' monolithic systems cannot support their business opportunities. It is their best financial interests to fund the initiatives to break up the monoliths. Using Energence's use case, let's discuss evaluating system architecture of their systems, work involved moving them to microservices, a phased approach of doing so, along with the advantages each step brings.

# Breaking a Monolith into Modules

As a case study of transforming a monolith into modern architecture, let's focus on its Energence Home Platform. It is a monolith, composed of reasonably independent modules. A sample transformation of Energence's products begins with the monolith and ends with an architecture that meets their objectives. Their transformation journey should be comprised of three phases. The first phase in their journey will split/rework their platform into a collection of independent modules. The second phase will break individual modules further based on a smaller domain definition, standardize, and create services in every such submodule.

These services need to follow the five principles we discussed earlier. The third phase would be to carve out services defined earlier into independently deployable modules. These modules need their individual life cycles. The fourth phase will land them on the cloud, which will help them achieve most of their goals. In this chapter, we'll walk through a sample road map of how this platform can move to a microservices architecture—we will cover phases one, two, and three.

In the first phase, we can extract existing modules into independent, domain-specific, and self-sufficient systems. These self-sufficient systems (aka self-contained systems) are a collection of functionality centered around the data 'they own'. Such modularization requires knowledge of the domain, a vision of the future, and some excellent intuition. The simplest way to modularize any system is at the seams (Feathers, 2004, p. 31). A seam is a programming concept, which defines the boundary within which a subsystem is independent. However, splitting systems is more art than science. Breaking a system apart at seams works only if the modules were clearly separated from the beginning, as in the case of Energence Home Platform. There are many cases where monoliths are big balls of mud (Foote & Yoder, 1997); for those scenarios, there are a few useful concepts that will lead to a proper and futureproof decomposition. A brilliant technique in achieving clear demarcation of modules is to use *bounded contexts*. A bounded context allows for a clear and consistent definition of a system's boundaries, drawn from a particular business context. They form an excellent determining factor of what belongs within each independent system and what does not (Evans, 2004).

Some essential rules should govern these autonomous systems/modules:

1. **An autonomous system owns a domain and all the associated data:** No other system lays claim on the data. The other systems can query, change, or delete data only through the interfaces exposed by the owner system. The independent system holds all the necessary data and all the related logic that operates on it.

2. **Autonomous systems will own their infrastructure:** The running instance of the system holds the hardware and software it uses: VMs, databases, datastores, messaging brokers, or any other required infrastructure. A strict demarcation is mandatory; for instance, the VMs that run an independent system will not run anything that is needed by that system. Similarly, the database will host no data other than what belongs to that system.

3. **Autonomous systems will have disconnected life cycles:** They are built, tested, integrated, and delivered on a cadence and schedule that is entirely independent of other systems. We should view each separate system as a product that has its road map and release targets.

4. **An autonomous system will expose APIs or messaging endpoints that allow external entities to interact with it:** Here, external entities could be consumers of data or producers of data. The system chooses the right type of endpoint based on individual use cases. The internals—of how APIs process and deliver data, or what happens to the message when consumed by the system, or how they generate messages—are entirely invisible to other applications.

5. **Autonomous systems will not share code that details business logic:** It is essential to ensure that the independent systems are genuinely autonomous, with separate delivery plans and infrastructure. However, as architects, it is also crucial for us to promote reuse. When crafting autonomous systems, we should limit shared libraries. For instance, it is acceptable to share the library that verifies the security of the service call; for example, user authentication, such as JWT validation, or role-based access control validation. However, it is not okay to create shared libraries across all clients that parse a service's response. The former is a technology-related library, while the latter deals with knowledge of the domain.

At the end of the first phase, we break the monolith down into modules that are independent, domain-bound, well-defined products. Based on the size of the modules, these could potentially become a product with dedicated engineering teams. Such separation also requires choosing between synchronous vs. asynchronous communication ways of connecting these modules. We can thus make the right choice between choreography and orchestration—based on the immediacy of data propagation and needs for consistency and integrity. We discussed earlier that businesses are almost always eventually consistent: in many cases, asynchronous integration between modules is enough.

# Breaking Modules into Submodules

The second phase of the transformation is further refining modules into submodules and reapplying the earlier five rules. The submodules, which will go on to become independent systems, will have to define their service endpoints clearly. Phase one ends with the monolith becoming an aggregation of modules. At the end of phase two, the monolith will become a conglomeration of independent, maintainable, simple, and upgradable set of services. At this point, it is essential to ensure the smallest unit is cohesive. Any further decomposition will cause inconsistent definitions and states. By definition, aggregates are the smallest modules within which all data elements need to be consistent: aggregates are the best place to finish stage two of decomposition.

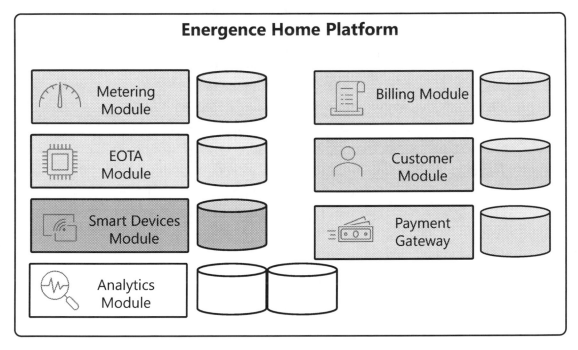

***Figure 2-1.*** *Phase 1a—breaking a monolith into self-contained-systems*

Let's explore a typical journey, considering Energence's platform. We'll start the first phase of breaking the monolith by converting modules into independent systems (Figure 2-1). We can break apart the single database and segregate tables that are related by domain boundaries into separate databases (or schemas). For example, the Smart-Devices module will become an independent system and will inherit all tables that deal with information about smart devices. No other system can hold any information about smart devices, apart from key identifiers about smart devices (e.g., device-IDs, device-class-IDs, etc.). If any other system needs information needed about a smart device, it can do so only by querying the Smart-Devices module.

The critical step in this phase is to ensure these modules are clean and have a well-defined hierarchy: we must identify interdependencies between modules (Figure 2-2). The first step is to ensure that we replace dependencies that create chatter between modules. We should remove all scenarios needing callbacks to complete a use case, or a business flow, or a transaction. We should replace such chatter with one-way calls, where data gets sent upfront. For instance, if the Billing module calls the Metering module to obtain meter readings, but the Metering module turns around and calls the Billing module for specifics of billing, causing a circular dependency between modules. That circular dependency needs to go—either eliminated by resolving data ownership, or synthesized into a separate subsystem used by both modules. An option to do so is by strapping on the required billing information to the query to the Metering module. This change removes callbacks from Metering module, thereby creating a clean one-way dependency.

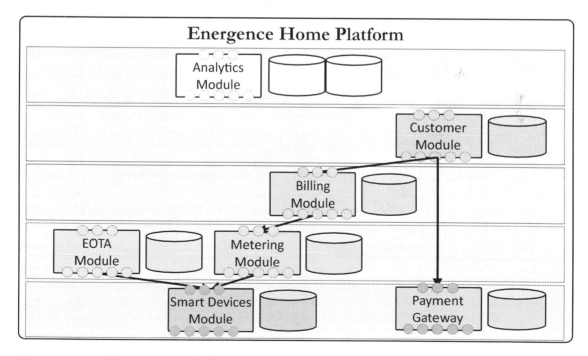

***Figure 2-2.*** *Phase 1—modules organized into a hierarchy, with segregated integration points*

The second phase in the process is to consolidate the communication endpoints of every system and standardize them into REST services (Figure 2-3). Ensure adhering to microservices guidelines—single-purpose, well-defined, loosely coupled, and discoverable—while defining them. This step is typically a series of rearchitecture, redesign, and refactoring activities. At the end of this phase, we will have turned modules into independent domains, which have well-defined service endpoints and well-managed client interactions.

Apart from services, we should also divide the domain databases into subdomains. However, we must ensure we do not lose data consistency and that subdomains are still comprehensible. For instance, we can divide the metering database into readings, rates, packaging (services/plans/tiers), and quality metrics. These are independent subdomains within the metering domain. They are not dependent on each other in storage, but we need higher-order services to collate the data required by Billing systems. Dividing any of the subdomains will break our no-smaller-than-an-aggregate rule.

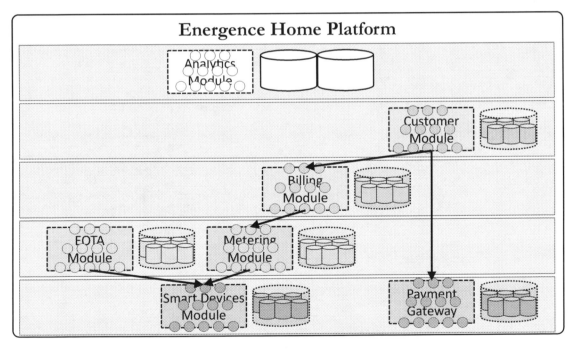

**Figure 2-3.** *Phase 2—define services and data partitions of each module*

# Establishing Microservices Architecture

After we find subdomains, we continue to segregate them further into autonomous microservices, arranged in a hierarchy of usage. To establish the microservices architecture, we need to start carving out independent systems from a monolith and monolithic modules. The most useful technique is to begin by *stabilizing the ins and outs of a component* before changing the innards of a module. We discussed how we could standardize the dependency on payment-module into a service call—stabilizing the data entering it. Similarly, it is possible to consolidate the EOTA (Energence over the air) module output into messaging or service calls—stabilizing data emitted by the module. This stability allows abstracting the module purely behind a set of service calls.

---

To establish microservices within a module, identify its entry and exit points, organize them, and standardize the format. Ensuring clear entry and exit points ease the segregation of the module.

---

We can take the example of Smart-Devices module and begin by listing its capabilities:

1. **Maintaining device metadata**: Types of devices, attributes of various types of devices

2. **Maintaining information about individual devices in the network**: Devices, their various attributes, communication channels

3. **Communicating with individual devices on the network**: Pings, reads, writes, checks, etc.

4. **Monitoring fluctuations and capturing alerts from devices**: Aids in understanding patterns. Also useful for device manufacturers, device warranty, and home insurance companies

Given this list, we can build the various services the Smart-Devices module will expose. There needs to be a *device-info* microservice that allows for maintaining metadata, a *device-listing* microservice to maintain the millions of devices in the Energence network, a *device-management* microservice responsible for managing the devices, and finally, a *device-monitoring* microservice that looks for device alerts and any events—critical or otherwise. At this juncture, it becomes apparent that individual microservices are ready to take life of their own. As evident, they can maintain different datastores—each datastore of a suitable kind, possibly of a different type.

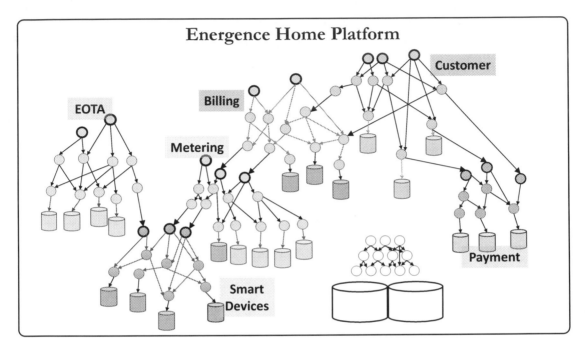

***Figure 2-4.*** *Final view of the platform, as a conglomerate of microservices*

Figure 2-4 depicts an end state of a true microservices-based architecture of Energence Home Platform. The data now exists in many small, independent databases. We arrange services hierarchically in each domain, building on top of others where required. There could be foundational services that deal with data, or with external systems. We layer in orchestration services that have business rules, which use data from foundational services. As we traverse higher in the service hierarchy, we find higher-order domain objects.

# Transition Architectures

Figure 2-4 is the final view of the Home Platform after the monolith breaks down into microservices. Each circle in the diagram represents an independently deployable microservice, exposing one or more REST endpoints. The bold ones on the periphery of every module are the top-level services, which offer the functionality of the microservice to the external world. The journey to such a result is seldom achieved by simply ripping and replacing the monolith, barely justifiable even in extreme cases. There are various implications of a wrong transition approach.

First and foremost, there are *financial implications*. Rarely do enterprises want to endeavor the transformation path without an evident and immediate return on investment. Acquiring capital to do a massive technology transformation at a single go is imprudent. A failure to transition to a new system immediately stops any changes that enable business growth, as the business is on hold for the new system. There are also *systemic implications*. A new system taking over an existing system is time-consuming. There is effort and time need to test, rectify, and stabilize. The production environment with live traffic is different from test systems. Finally, there are process implications. The new system, as is being built, needs to replicate the behavior of the old system. Rewrites, bug fixes, new features, or any other changes need to happen in both systems until the new one takes over the other. Duplication causes an additional burden on cost, effort, and processes.

We will discuss through this book the various techniques of developing microservices in the cloud, but before that, we need to master the art of change. We need a few techniques necessary to bring in change. The first technique is to ***start the changes with peripheral functionality***. Peripheral modules, which are parts of the monolith dealing with supporting capabilities, are excellent starting points. Optimization modules, data gathering modules, batch processing modules, and asynchronous execution capabilities are perfect targets for the first round of decomposition. Several advantages are immediately apparent. One, they pose a lower risk in case of failures. Peripheral applications usually do not disrupt core business capabilities, allowing us to continue regular business transactions. They can be easily segregated into standalone entities, breaking away from the whole. In our case, the EOTA module should be the first to be tackled, due to its independent nature. The payment-gateway module is the next candidate. Even though there is a dependent module—the customer-module—the dependency can be easily replaced with well-defined service calls. The second technique is to ***sever any direct data access across modules***. Once we remove cross-module data dependency, modules can start owning their data. For instance, if the customer-module is directly accessing payment information, **we need to replace it with a service call**. Single row reads, or a limited row reads, are easy to mitigate. We will discuss further ahead in the book how to handle bulk data reads.

The most important technique is remembering to *keep changes small and controlled*. The change needs to move the architecture towards the target, but has to be small enough to reduce risk and damage. A small and controlled change allows for a quick test-and-learn cycle. For instance, it might be wise to make the trigger functionality, device selection logic, and device datastore into standalone entities. We can thoroughly test the device selection logic before release. Triggers generated can be validated against the current triggers getting generated. Notice that **it is possible to compare the old monolith's output and the new independent microservice's output until we are satisfied**. Validation through comparison is a definitive way to certify the new system and reduce risk and failures when the old system is replaced.

# Microservices-Native Architecture

Energence's use case discusses the need to move from a monolithic mindset to a microservices one. This transition to microservices is a fairly common challenge. On the contrary, what if the shift is not possible at all? What if the technology used to build the solution cannot be ported over to a microservices solution? What if the solution needs a complete rip and replace because the business has completely changed? Or, consider an enterprise that is new and wants to build a software solution. In such settings, which require creation of architecture, our earlier principles and techniques still hold. We follow the domain-driven design to identify microservices and adhere to our guidelines to keep them small, single-purpose, and isolated.

## The Approach in a Nutshell

Situations for a microservices-native solution from the ground up are as common as migrating a monolith to microservices architecture. In both cases, native or migration, the architecture invariably follows the same principles and steps: apply the domain-driven design repeatedly until we arrive at small enough domains. The first step yields broad top-level bounded contexts, which constitute the overall domains that anchor the solution. These bounded contexts also make excellent candidates for *productizing* the software. In massive software projects, bounded contexts provide a way to create and organize engineering teams. As our earlier discussion, it is wise to choose choreography between bounded contexts to allow maximum independence. The process then continues to divide bounded contexts into subdomains recursively until we reach aggregates.

# Defining Top-Level Domains

*The first trillionaire there will ever be is the person who exploits the natural resources on asteroids.*

—Neil deGrasse Tyson, astrophysicist

As an exercise of creating microservices, let us pick an esoteric domain, **Asteroid Mining**. On the first scan, we realize the few significant parts of a potential solution. We will need a *catalog* of asteroids, complete with astronomic information (such as trajectory, speed, composition, etc.), classified by various difficulties of mining. We also need to manage *mining equipment*, machinery required for multiple phases of mining. Next, there is a need for maintaining elaborate *mining plans* about involved entities (asteroids, equipment, personnel, resources, etc.). Next, there is the entire act of *mining and extraction*. After extraction, we will need processors that process the extracted resources—separate, purify, palletize, and load into transportable containers. Next, we need to decide on modes of *transportation* of equipment and personnel to and from asteroids, and ore and resources from asteroids. Each of these requirements can turn into a bounded context or a top-level domain.

At this point, we have made a list of broad domain verticals for Asteroid Mining. We follow our principles and ensure the domains do not have a cyclical dependency. It is easy to notice that these broad verticals can become products themselves. Identifying products helps decide whether to build the solution or buy a packaged software that fits the needs. In case of a build choice, such products built to solve the problems of a specific business area can also provide profitable ventures for the enterprise. Figure 2-5 shows an overall view of domains, along with their interdependencies and integrations.

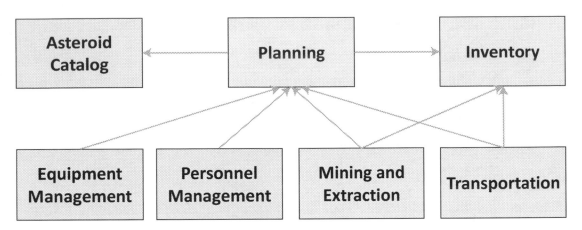

**Figure 2-5.** *Phase 1—Asteroid Mining domains*

# Deciding Interdomain Communication

Once we have identified the domains, we need to understand and define their interactions. We can start by categorizing the interactions and exchanges into classes of data based on type, volume, and frequency. For instance, the Asteroid Catalog software gathers information about asteroids, catalogs them, and triggers planning. Planning software will set up and synchronize schedule across all other domains. Equipment Management software uses data for buying or renting or manufacturing the required equipment of a specific quantity for each asteroid. Personnel Management software helps manage personnel onboarding—miners, drivers, engineers, maintenance specialists, and of any required skills. Mining and Extraction software manages mining and extraction tasks on asteroids—in terms of queuing up work to ensure maximum throughput for the duration of the asteroid visit. Transportation software sets up and manages the transportation network in terms of space shuttles, rockets, and launch pads, along with transfer schedules—on Earth, and asteroids.

The most fitting approach to integrate different domains is to allow choreography between them. As we discussed earlier, choreography allows systems with incompatible throughput to integrate. In the component view (Figure 2-5), an asynchronous data flow is opposite to the way arrows are pointing. For instance, the Asteroid Catalog domain will emit data about any newly cataloged asteroids, or changes to data collected against already listed asteroids. The planning domain will publish the plans to the execution systems. In these choreographic interactions, it is important to keep messages generic and not cater to any particular dependent domain. ***The source domain should publish only the data elements essential to itself.*** The reliant applications can obtain additional data using the source domain's microservices. For instance, the Asteroid Catalog domain should not devise messages to fit the planning domain. Instead, we should design Asteroid Catalog events that indicate any significant changes to data: for instance, detection of a new asteroid, improved data of an asteroid, and corrections to previously known asteroid data. The planning domain will base its actions on events emitted by the Asteroid Catalog domain—if the planning domain needs more data, it invokes the Asteroid Catalog domain's services.

## Toward Subdomains

In the next phase, we further subdivide each vertical. For instance, the Asteroid Catalog domain will obtain data from various sources, having a listing of asteroids, their compositions, their travel trajectories in space and time, and mining claims on those asteroids. Each of these becomes subdomains, with independent and isolated development. These subdomains can develop on the technology best suited for realizing. They can choose data sources that best manage data and technology stacks that best support processing.

Similarly, the planning domain evaluates every asteroid in terms of feasibility. Its planning engine applies historical mining patterns and future scenarios and use forecast models on data to generate a "mission plan" for any viable asteroid. Financials of the market and enterprise, various demand forecasts, and existing projects are all input data to the planning process. The generated plan is published and thus triggers equipment-management, personnel-management, and transportation-management to source and set up infrastructure, people, and material required for the mission. Each of these domains communicate failures in sourcing back to the planning domain, which triggers a reevaluation of the mining mission. Equipment-management might keep an inventory of equipment, both rental and owned by the company, and might attempt to procure more based on the need. Maintaining attributes about each machine—such as fit, usage, and operation—allows identifying the right equipment required for a mission and provides substitutions or alternate plans. It might have sourcing subsystems to maintain contracts with retailers and suppliers. The procurement-subsystem enables shopping for any gear missing in the inventory but required for a mission. The transportation domain undergoes a similar decomposition process, and we might end up with its significant subdomains. We could recognize the subdomains follow the same format. Primarily, booking the required launch-stations and shuttles, along with their trips corresponding to various transportation equipment, cargo management (in terms of factors such as tonnage, volume, speed of delivery, hazard levels). There is also a need for sophisticated navigation and trip planning to maximize the transportation network.

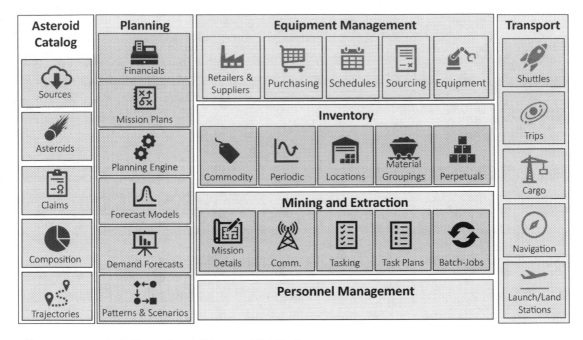

***Figure 2-6.*** *Subdomains of Asteroid Mining*

Figure 2-6 shows a subdomain view of such a system, assuming the personnel-management happens through an off-the-shelf product.

# Designing Microservices

We continue our approach to the next level of designing microservices. At this point, we start identifying the essential services of each domain. The first step in deciding the top-level services is to identify data-in and data-out paths of each subdomain of our problem space. Let us work through the subdomains to understand the approach better.

Remember how we identified transition architectures while breaking a monolith into microservices. In the same vein, it is essential to decide on ***incremental architectures*** while building microservices-native applications. The best place to start is with a tracer bullet—a complete implementation broad enough to cover the entire spectrum of functionality, but small enough to finish in a few weeks. We will start with a team assigned to every module of the system. To begin construction, each team will build the first use case required for the operation to be functional. The Asteroid Catalog team might create a simple set of microservices to provide a catalog of asteroids. The team may set up the list of asteroids manually for the first release. Next, a barebone planning engine could generate a simple need list for a given asteroid. Similarly, other systems get built as a simple set of microservices. These barebone implementations lay out the foundational system, which we can use to run simulations and validate.

The overall solution then starts to grow with every team adding more use cases, and when ripe further split into smaller subsystems, divide into smaller groups. This incremental growth allows for a natural extension of the application and expansion of engineer teams working on the various parts of the entire asteroid-mining solution. Requirements drive the growth of systems, which break into subsystems when they get larger, which are matched by engineering teams. All the while, *it is crucial to follow the concepts of domain-driven design and keep the dependency of data realized only through services.*

# Architectural Advantages and Gains

Now that we have observed the two different ways of building a microservices architecture—transitioning from a monolith or building from scratch—let us explore the rewards microservice-based architectures offer. Apart from bringing in a clean structure, simplified nature, and manageable abstraction of the solution space, microservices provide many advantages in planning, development, and managing solutions.

## Scalability

Successful businesses such as Energence that are technology and data-driven grow and take on more digital traffic on their systems as their user base and operations grow. *Scalability is the ability of systems to handle an increased workload.*

Let us take a moment to understand the ability to scale—what allows some type of systems to take on more work with increased loads, with ease, compared to others. A system's ability to scale relies on many factors:

1. The ability of the system to use all resources available in its execution environment. Does its architecture benefit from more computing (more cores), more memory, and faster communication resources, and when given, can the system use it effectively and handle larger workloads (Grama, Gupta, & Kumar, 1993)? Conversely, when moved to infrastructure with fewer resources, can it scale down efficiently?

2.  The ability of the implementation to efficiently use the resources upon increased resources. For example, does the chatter grow exponentially with more instances, as opposed to increasing linearly? If the growth is exponential, the system is not easily scalable.

3.  Whether or not the problem space itself allows the distribution of processing. If the workload is not parallelizable, scaling out onto many systems is possibly not an option (Kleppman, 2017).

A great resource that helps in understanding and helps to apply the right techniques for scaling is the scale cube (Figure 2-7).

---

## SCALING SYSTEMS

Usually, it is possible to scale systems against three different axes (Abbott, 2009).

On the x-axis, the applications are scaled by simple replication. Multiple copies of the system are spun up to meet the scaling needs. The simplest scalability option (not necessarily the cheapest) of replication offers simple deployments but demands massive coordination between users. On the y-axis, applications are scaled by splitting them by functional boundaries and allowing autonomy. The y-axis is the domain of microservices. Breaking a large solution into small, manageable microservices results allows ***asymmetrical scaling based on need***. Smaller domains also alleviate performance problems—such as row/table locks, cascading deletes—caused by attempts to maintain consistency across domains. On the z-axis, applications are scaled by partitioning data, for instance, sharding the data, and allowing an independent subsystem to work on that partitioned data. Sharding alleviates the challenges faced by applications when data sources bottleneck applications. When data exceeds ordinary computing limits, for instance, more than tens of terabytes, data must be partitioned and processed separately. Many NoSQL databases and distributed storage and processing applications allow inexpensive ways to scale with commodity servers.

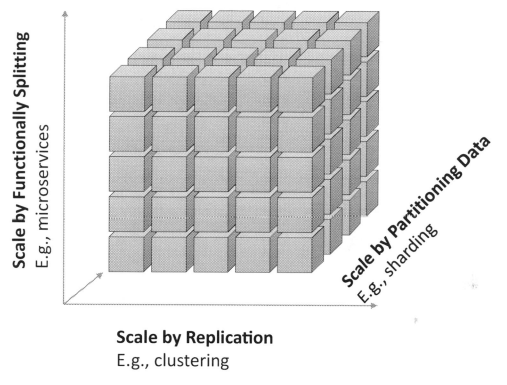

**Figure 2-7.** *Scale cube—based on Fisher's scale cube*

# Elasticity

*Elasticity is the ability to automate scaling.* The elastic nature of a solution is fundamental in cloud environments, where the cost of operations is directly proportional to usage. Along with scalability, elasticity is an innate offering of a microservices architecture. Elastic setup of microservices architecture brings in the ability to both dynamically and proactively scale to meet the demand. Elasticity indicates the capability to both expand contract) the resource usage to match the varying traffic; thus ensuring better and efficient resource usage. Efficient resource usage is huge benefit when running on the cloud, where cost of running an application is decided by usage.

What makes microservices elastic? We know that certain natural traits of microservice make them ready for elasticity. We know that microservices are lightweight—which means they can be quickly spun up or brought down. The quality of being isolated allows us to vary the instances according to the need of various parts of application busyness. They are independent of each other—running variable number of instances will not affect the overall system behavior.

Microservices give us the ability to spin up new instances on-demand and also spin down idle instances, greatly optimizing resource usage.

There is more to microservices that make them ***cloud-ready***. Most microservices are realized as REST-based (or other HTTP-based protocols such as gRPC). The usage of HTTP and standard protocols makes it easy to set up the scalable infrastructure. Traffic monitoring, shaping, mirroring, load-balancing, and many other aspects are easily achievable with HTTP-based, small, and independent services. We will discuss these topics in detail further in the book when we focus on cloud infrastructure.

# Agility

Microservices architecture lets us target updates to the smallest microservice and thereby localize changes. Changes to a monolithic system require careful analyses for side effects, which take a lot of upfront design to ensure the change does not have unintended outcomes. Long-drawn timelines thus caused also have the unintended consequence of lumping many changes into releases. The development team will naturally try to pool together requirements to reduce analysis times, which further delays the deployments. This "big ball of mud" feature of monoliths is why, inherently, changes tend to be slow and drawn out.

Compare this with microservices. In a microservices architecture, we can test small units and promote them in days (or even hours). The "speed-to-market" is not because of the simplistic and independent nature of microservices but also the reduced testing efforts. One, monoliths tend to do large, infrequent deployments, which increase the combination of tests that are needed to certify production readiness. Two, frequently, monoliths require comprehensive testing of the complete functionality. The teams will have to test not just the changes but also ensure all the previous functionality is not affected by the change.

Microservices offer speedy upgrades and feature promotions to production because of the ability to localize change and reduce testing.

# Energence's Monoliths as Microservices

Now that we have discussed the journey of Energence's applications to microservices, we realize how the goals Energence set are now achievable":

- The microservices architecture now allows systems to scale to handle the load easily. Computational load spread unevenly on various modules can now be mitigated by scaling the relevant microservice(s).

- Microservices can be hosted on the cloud, which allows elastic resource usage. There is no need to hoard hardware in anticipation of peak or traffic bursts.

- The ability to roll out small changes, by localizing modifications to a few microservices, allows great agility in development. This agility enables Energence to add new features quickly.

- With applications being split based on domains, Energence can now offer specific pieces of their application pool as services. The availability of the smallest feature as an independent microservice increases the monetizing options.

The journey of Energence does not end here. We have only peeled back a small amount of effort involved in the transformation. Many challenges lie ahead. Microservices architecture brings a significant number of problems, which need new and innovative solutions—this will be the topic of the next two chapters. Next, we will look at the process changes required to manage this modern architecture. After that, we will look at the cloud journey in detail. Finally, we will assess the changes to security, which, as we will discover, will become a crucial part of this transformation.

# Summary

Microservices architecture extends the evolved and proven concepts—of building systems as services that are small, independent, and decoupled functions, which communicate using standard web-based protocols. Smaller services are easy to understand, straightforward to debug, and cheaper to support. Autonomous services are a fantastic way of building applications that are scalable, elastic, and cloud-ready. Isolated systems allow us to compartmentalize changes, conceptualize with abstractions, and reuse without side effects. Enforcing simpler and standard HTTP-based communication will enable us to use existing infrastructure components, ideas, and resources that drive the Internet at such a massive scale.

## Points to Ponder

1. How does microservices architecture move us to a better and sustainable architecture?

2. What did we gain (or lose) by transitioning from monolith to the new system of microservices?

3. Can we split any service into smaller sub-services that adhere to the principles we discussed?

4. In this microservices journey, how could we handle legacy dependencies such as mainframes, wire protocols, and file exchanges?

5. What is the justification for teams that are either unwilling to evolve or have no ROI (return on investment) on evolution?

## Further Related Reading

*Domain-Driven Design* by Eric Evans (Evans, 2004).
   *Building Microservices* by Sam Newman (Newman, 2015).
   Fowler's article on microservices (Lewis & Fowler, 2014).

# CHAPTER 3

# Architectural Challenges

*Actioni contrariam semper et æqualem esse reactionem*

—Sir Isaac Newton, *Philosophiæ Naturalis Principia Mathematica* (1687)

*It's supposed to be hard. If it wasn't hard, everyone would do it. The hard is what makes it great.*

—Tom Hanks as Jimmy Dugan in *A League of Their Own*, Columbia Pictures (1992)

Software solutions constructed from independent and isolated microservices have clean and sustainable architecture. Apart from being flexible to quick changes and speedy delivery, they provide scalability, elasticity, and agility. Curiously, the very nature of architectural flexibility is the source of serious challenges. As we transition to a microservices architecture, problems appear on two fronts: *solution design* and *support and operations*. Solutions rely on an extensive portfolio of microservice components, thereby creating tactical problems in realizing new requirements while retaining a clean domain-based model. Monitoring and operating a system that has orchestration, synergy, and synchrony set up across numerous microservices become incredibly challenging. In this chapter, we will explore the many challenges enterprises face when they move to a microservices-based architecture. We will discuss potential solutions to these problems further ahead in the book.

© Chandra Rajasekharaiah 2021
C. Rajasekharaiah, *Cloud-Based Microservices*, https://doi.org/10.1007/978-1-4842-6564-2_3

# Identifying and Classifying Challenges

A system made up of microservices bears a daunting image. A single application transforms into a complex network of tiny interconnected systems, and such visual worries enterprises. Compare Figure 2-4, the final view of the platform with Figure 1-4, the monolithic Energence Home Platform. Where we had one deployable application with seven modules, now we have more than eighty deployable applications. *It is important not to let the optics fool us*: realize, it is the same system with the same code base but better organized. Questions arise on two fronts:

1. Are we architecturally in a better place that is sustainable?

2. In entirety, does the new system behave exactly like the earlier?

We briefly discussed the answer "yes" to the first question in the earlier chapter. We will spend a great of time detailing the various aspects of architectural progress further in the book. **Response to the second question is a "no,"** which is the topic of this chapter. Deviation from expected behavior is sometimes intentional (for instance, now the system is more scalable and agile), but is often unintentional. The aberrance and side effects need a closer examination, to identify potential concerns. Our concerns seem to fall into three groups:

- **Concerns about managing the new architecture:** In contrast to managing a few monolithic applications, the focus turns to ensuring the correct behavior of hundreds of applications and services. How do we find problem areas and overcome them?

- **Troubles in verifying the correctness of the new system:** Do more moving pieces mean greater complexity? How can QA teams ensure that hundreds of services are wired accurately and are behaving correctly?

- **Complexities in managing the infrastructure:** What used to be a single deployment pipeline that deploys to a few servers in a monolith world could become hundreds of pipelines that deploy to hundreds of machines. How can operations and support manage it?

We will explore architectural challenges in this chapter and attempt to resolve them in the next one, Overcoming Architectural Challenges. We address the other two challenges—of testing and operations—in the later chapters.

Before exploring challenges in microservices architecture, we need to understand why and how the new architecture behaves differently from the original monolith. Monoliths have many shortcomings, which we discussed earlier, but they are phenomenally good in a few aspects:

1. **Monoliths provide transactional accuracy:** A monolith, using a 2PC[1] (two-phase commit) equivalent, ensures data is consistent before responding to a request; every data element is in sync at the end of servicing any request.

2. **The complete business logic is together:** Understanding the application requires understanding a single codebase—written in a single programming language, compiled and deployed as a separate entity.

3. **All data is instantaneously accessible:** All data ever read, created, and modified by any part of the application is within reach. There are no service calls and contracts to negotiate. Cross joining large data sets is not a problem.

4. **A monolith is in a single state:** The various modules of the application share states and thus can instantly resolve the precise overall state.

5. **Debugging is limited to a specific application:** Failures are inherently localized to a single application. Walking through the application's log files (if adequately engineered and developed) allows an engineer to debug the entire flow.

The instant we transition to a microservices-based architecture, we lose all these advantages and encounter new classes of challenges.

---

[1]2PC, two-phase-commit, indicates the change-commits across multiple resources are two-phased. A central transaction manager controls all changes—it first sends a 'ready-to-commit' request to all involved entities, and upon receiving a 'yes' from all, it issues a 'now-commit' message.

# AC1: Dispersed Business Logic

Frequently, the complex business logic of a microservice involves invoking other microservices. As more features get implemented, more services are created or wired together. The new features could be brand new services with the required functionality or a set of higher-level services that join other services together. Over time, we build ourselves a system with microservice hierarchies of unmanageable depth.

We chose microservices architecture to allow rapid changes in systems, which often conflicts with simplicity. Every new service and every new variation has the potential to complicate the architecture. Architectures suffer in finding the right abstractions for overarching workflows—quickly changing microservices make it hard to keep everything in sync. As a quick fix, teams might make an exception and reimplement what they need. Implementations that are REST-based suffer the most: many times, the default "resources" for business features are unavailable. It is easy for engineers to create a new resource with similar fields. Consider a simple use case in our case study Energence Home Platform.

Assume a user has set up an automated payment request, which results in a service call chain as shown in Figure 3-1.

- POST payments: start this request from a customer management service
  - GET bills: Prepare data for billing
    - GET customer-bills: Generate customer's bill
      - GET customer-bills: get customer's bill
        - GET customer-details:    resolve billing details for customer
        - GET billing-details: Resolve address-level metering and billing account
          - GET meter-readings:  Pull metering details for a billing account
            - GET meter-readings: Get meter readings for an account
              - GET device-readings: Resolve devices and get readings
                - GET devices: Resolve devices
                - GET readings: Get readings for devices
        - POST monthly-bills: calculate and save customer's monthly bill
  - POST bill-payments: Initiate payment for account
    - GET payment-details: Get customer's bill amount and payment options
    - POST payments: Initiate payment
      - POST payments: Initiate payment of bill for account with a payment method
        - POST credit-payments: Start a payment transaction for specific amount
          - POST cc-transactions: Communicate with payment gateway
          - POST payment-records: Record payment details

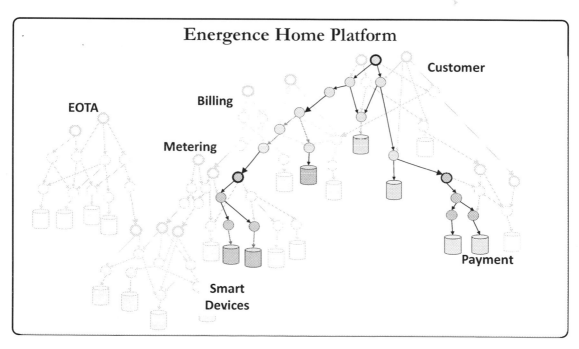

***Figure 3-1.***  *Trace of an autopay transaction*

It begs an obvious question, how do we add in new features? Roll calendar to the future, the platform team encounters new requirements that call for an additional microservice. Consider the case where a few US states begin offering discounts for electric car owners for being green. This feature should include all of the vehicle's charge events, immaterial of where the owner charged it in the distribution network—which is a departure from our earlier ideas. We can no longer tie a device to a smart meter.

To solve this disparity, and to keep the architecture clean, let us assume we decide it is prudent to track these vehicles as special-devices. These special-devices have the new attribute of ownership by a single account but could create meter readings from various outlets. A new independent system with microservices around it is born. Quickly we notice a duplication of functionality, but we live with it; in a microservices world, such duplication is acceptable (Newman, 2015, p. 59). Suddenly our accommodation for rapid changes and microservice specialization leads us down more complicated scenarios. Once enterprises have microservices architecture, they can change, replace, or retire quickly. Unfortunately, this speed mystifies the evolution of microservices and compounds problems.

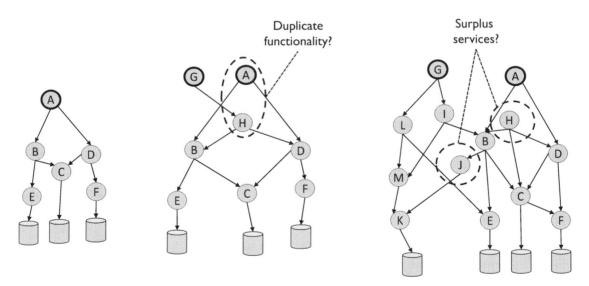

***Figure 3-2.*** *Evolution of microservices in a domain with new features*

Duplicate services and surplus services are often a side effect of the first principle we set for microservices: *single-purpose* and *straightforward*. Newer features become new services and sporadically result in duplicate implementations. Maybe engineers find it quick to build required features, rather than rework and augment the older ones. Or worse, engineers may be unaware of the comprehensive list of existing resources. In our previous example of battery-operated vehicles, special-device is a replicated resource. An engineer might find creating a new resource more natural than dealing with the device resource. It could be due to lack of awareness, or delivery deadlines, or the effort required to make the device resource extensible to handle new requirements. It is also possible that the initial functional decomposition was poor, and is simply magnified with every rework.

Whatever the reasons for duplication are, as further revisions come along, many more such business requirements materialize. At some point, we will find ourselves in a world of many surplus microservices: fragmented services with duplicate (or conflicting) business rules, produced for specific purposes. Engineers have followed the principle of single-purpose microservices, but have compromised our overall spirit of having clean architecture.

---

Splitting a monolith into many microservices creates agility in development, team structure, and deployment; however, it distributes the operating logic and execution flow of complex features among many applications.

---

# AC2: Lack of Distributed Transactions

Rearchitecting a monolith gets complicated when it involves the transition of business processes that contain distributed transactions. Such processes mandate ACID-type updates across objects from various domains to ensure data consistency. An ACID transaction guarantees all-or-none changes by ensuring all changes are atomic (all changes happen, or none does), consistent (all changes in the transaction are considered one unit), isolated (simultaneous requests to changes do not affect each other), and durable (changes last after the transaction is complete). Monolithic architectures address this by using variants of 2PC and verifying all resources are consistent before committing changes. Loosely put, the world waits for confirmation from every domain before advancing further. It is easy to realize that the same concept cannot apply to large scale distributed microservices-based architectures. First, the costs of holding locks, higher frequencies of deadlocks, and network chatter caused by transactions result in performance and reliability problems in systems (Garcia-Molina & Salem, 1987). Second, the implementation complexity (in synchronizing the vast hierarchy of services) and strict conformance (all microservices should talk precisely the same language) takes us back to the challenges we had with monoliths. The complexity does not disappear even if a very efficient 2PC is possible—with some unique language constructs (Zhang, Ren, Ahn, & Ben-Romdhane, 2019).

A distributed system is composed of autonomous computing elements attempting to act as a single coherent system. Inherently, the unreliable nature of its underlying network plagues any distributed system (Deutsch, 1994).

---

Attempting to maintain consistency among many microservices involved in a business transaction, while avoiding monolithic patterns, is extremely complicated.

---

# Orchestrated Domains

For any architecture with distributed databases or with REST-like microservices, distributed transactions are difficult to achieve. In both types of architectures, we end up in an eventually consistent world: (1) In distributed databases, either all instances must agree on truth by consensus (if data is replicated) or rely on the application layer to update the right instance (in case of sharded databases). (2) Microservices-based architectures rely on REST or equivalent protocol for uniformity, which differs from standard distributed-transaction-based protocols in monoliths. We delve deeper into how distributed databases affect architecture and design in the chapter dedicated to cloud-based datastores.

As part of such a distributed transaction, apart from inconsistent data, computational work done in each domain might also be inconsistent. In a monolith, either the change happens across all, or it does not occur in any. Consider an equivalent flow in a microservices architecture. A cross-domain microservice "POST" changes to two microservices (possibly in parallel) and records responses. If a cross-domain orchestration service encounters failure in one of the domains, it may not be capable of automatically undoing actions in others. For instance, another system could have processed the message, or dashboards might have changed to display wrong information, or end-users might have been alerted. Many times, undoing such actions is not possible without a central transaction manager that ensures atomicity—either everything happens, or nothing does.

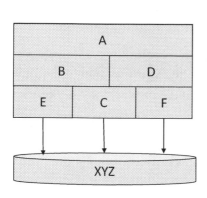

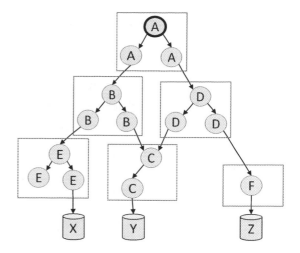

**Figure 3-3.** *Transactions in monoliths vs. microservices*

In Figure 3-3, the flow on the left depicts transaction flow in a monolithic world, and the one on the right, flow in a microservices world. On the right, arrows represent call chains between microservices A through F. Assume a partial-success scenario where E and C were successful, but F was unsuccessful. In a monolith, module A controls the states of three domains X, Y, and Z (they exist in a single database); it can simply roll back all changes and reach a consistent state. In the microservices model, X, Y, and Z reach states consistent within themselves, and not across. This flow also underlines the outcomes of eventual consistency. The only option to circumvent this is working to ensure X, Y, and Z are consistent; however, that would mean holding off other transactions until we get consensus. We already know that that approach leads us to long-running transactions, scalability issues; in no time, we would resurrect all the problems monolithic systems face. The eventual consistency brings about the definition of BASE, possibly a backronym, to define such transactions. BASE—basically-available, soft-state, and eventually-consistent—transactions dilute the ACID constraints emphasizing a system where consistency and availability are not always guaranteed.

# Choreographed Domains

Choreography is enticing for many reasons. It offers higher throughput by removing waits between service calls. By not relying on request-response, choreography can also handle larger data volumes and eases retries. However, choreography brings in a completely new set of challenges in coordination, monitoring, and error handling. Choreography has higher chances of running operations out-of-sequence, and hiding missed actions that do not have immediate consequences. The overhead of choreography is best accommodated while integrating large systems—such as high-level domains of systems.

The recurring issue in choreographed domains is keeping data in sync. Asynchronous updates through events are not time-bound—delays are bound to happen and create a disparity in data. These differences in data do not disappear until all events are processed.

Both approaches suffer from data consistency issues due to the distributed execution of transactions. Once we have signed up to allow data inconsistencies, we will have to prepare for repercussions. We will explore more challenges that originate in the next section.

---

Attempting to maintain transactional integrity of data leads to scalability issues.

---

# AC3: Inconsistent Dynamic Overall State

Related to lack of distributed transactions, lack of immediately consistent overall state is by far the most challenging problem to solve in microservices. Consistency gets more complicated with data that is geographically distributed data within the same domain because of sharding and data replication. Achieving global consistency with or without failures is a significant area in distributed systems, and many excellent papers exist on the challenges and potential solutions to solving it (Lamport, 1978) (Pease, Shostak, & Lamport, 1980). Readers are urged to understand these concepts in distributed computing. These are foundational concepts and, hence, are more critical than understanding industry trends. The foundational idea is the CAP theorem, which states that a partitioned and distributed (P) datastore cannot simultaneously be both highly available (A) and consistent (C) (Brewer, 2000). Knowledge of distributed systems become extremely important when dealing with cloud-based architecture; brief introductory treatments are further ahead in the book.

We discussed how a domain-driven approach results in a design with clean bounded contexts. It allows the many related parts of the solution to become autonomous and disconnected. Though we gain better performance, independence, and higher scalability from microservices architecture, it poses a problem for higher-level services, which need to deterministically infer the overall system state. When we connect domains through choreography, we sacrifice determinism for scalability. Domains that have a higher order of dependency may not be immediately consistent in a microservices architecture.

In the microservices world, we often partition the data and collocate it with its processing service. If smart meter readings subsystem were built on microservices, that system could be sharded and clustered, with each element in a cluster servicing a particular geographic region (time zones, US states, etc.): thus enabling scale-out, fault-tolerance, elasticity, quick feature-rollout, etc. On the flip side, domains that partition their data

1.  Pose data aggregation and data analysis challenges

2.  Have cluster rebalancing requirements

3.  Have cluster mismatch across domains

## Challenges in Data Exchange

When top-level microservices need a large amount of data from other services, performance problems appear. Consider the system depicted in Figure 3-4. Imagine that an external system that uses the service A to retrieve information from subdomains J, K, and L through microservices, possibly using REST interfaces. What if this request needs to join a hundred of its rows with a few hundred rows from J with L to execute use case?

The scenario gets more complicated if domains (and subdomains) are geographically distributed. Two common approaches exist; however, both approaches are horrendously bad, and we need to avoid both wherever possible: (1) Transporting anywhere from hundreds to millions of rows from various domains over HTTP and deriving Cartesian product in memory is monolithic in flavor, with poor performance. (2) Conversely, duplicating the required data in the orchestrating service goes against our principle of clean domain bound contexts for microservices.

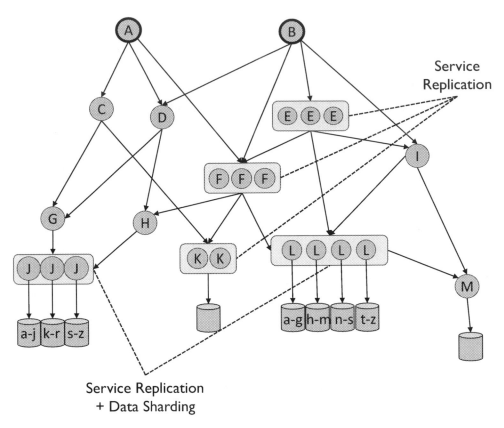

***Figure 3-4.*** *Deployment view of a domain with multiple independent systems and microservices*

Another challenge often faced is the change in response datatypes of dependent microservices. In Figure 3-4, assuming all microservices A through M are REST-based services, consider microservice A. It depends on C, D, and F, each of which returns specific "resources." Change of format in any of the resources bears a significant burden on microservice A; we might need to rework its internal logic to manage change. We will discuss more challenges in evolving microservices later in the chapter in section "AC6: The v2 Dread—Difficulty in Evolving."

# Problems with Sharding

Sharding is one of the scaling techniques that allows storing vast amounts of data efficiently for persistence and retrieval. It is an excellent practice for applications to shard data based on individual volume needs. Sharding will enable deployments to exploit the locality of data by allowing data from similar sub-contexts of a domain to be deployed locally (Neuman, 1994, p. 21). In our earlier example, we discussed regarding smart meter management system: if various domains that handle data from East Coast can coexist in a single cloud region, we achieve fast and efficient data lookup. However, this also means that if a homeowner in New York relocates to California, that homeowner's data needs relocation.

Choosing how to distribute data into shards, using ranges of shard-key, is crucial for the success of sharding. If we fail to choose the shard-key optimally, we force shards to grow out of balance. When shards are out of balance, there is a need to recreate shards of data using new ranges, or employ a completely new shard-key. For instance, in Figure 3-4, service J partitions data into three shards—[a-j],[k-r],[s-z]. If, after a year into running, we realize data in [k-r] is growing quicker than [a-j] and [s-z] partitions, we need to rebalance shards. We need to rethink our shard-ranges and redistribute data as per new sharding intervals. Shards might also need rebalancing at runtime, upon losing a node or adding a node. The remaining nodes need to pick up the ownership of data from the lost node. If a new node joins, nodes need to redistribute the data per different partition keys.

Shards growing out of balance also create difficulty in performance tuning. When sharding keys differ between services and domains, they cause cluster mismatches while extracting data across domains. Observe Figure 3-4. Notice that within a group of microservices, data gets sharded differently. Note that service J creates three shards—[a-j],[k-r],[s-z]—whereas the one on the right creates four shards—[a-g],[h-m],[n-s],[t-z]. Not only does this force the higher-level orchestration services to become query planners of how best to execute a query, but it also results in inconsistent performance. Based on the query, the required data might exist in a single shard, or across multiple shards. In our example, a query on [j-k] will hit a single shard on one microservice, but two in another, causing inconsistent performance. Such mismatches might require us to include the data-access logic of a different domain into orchestration services (Ajoux, Bronson, Kumar, Lloyd, & Veeraraghavan, 2015).

# AC4: Difficulty in Gathering Composite Data

The ability to combine data across multiple domains is a necessity in software. Enterprises need this for monitoring and summarizing the overall state through reporting and analytics. Modern applications that pursue implementing disruptive technology for more in-depth analytics, smarter insights, and automated decisioning—such as machine learning (ML), optimization, and artificial intelligence (AI) also require details combined from multiple business domains. Extracting such detailed information relies on extensive cross-referencing of data from many domains. Note that this problem exists on top of what we saw in AC3: Inconsistent Dynamic Overall State. There is no easy way of visualizing global data—even if we tolerate eventual consistency—without special constructs. Microservices architecture does not inherently address use cases that work with cross-domain data.

Consider a scenario where we want to analyze patterns in the clustering of appliances and their correlated efficiency. We want to find out if there is a group of appliances—based on the type, year of manufacture, wattage, etc.—that are more efficient than others. In the Energence Home Platform, this requires calling services to pull data from thousands of accounts, then pulling associated smart device data, correlating them, then reading data of every selected device, and so on. Such a bulk call sequence is impossible to achieve through microservices. Contrast this to a monolith: all data is collocated in the same data source. In a microservices architecture, information is fragmented and is available for access only through services: bulk operations that traditionally joined data from different domains need to find a new home.

---

Joining data for analytics of the overall system in a microservices architecture is not straightforward.

---

# AC5: Difficulty in Debugging Failures and Faults

*It is a capital mistake to theorize before one has data. Insensibly one begins to twist facts to suit theories, instead of theories to suit facts.*

—Sherlock Holmes in Sir Arthur Conan Doyle's *Scandal in Bohemia* (1891)

Finding the root cause of a problem in a microservices environment can be an arduous task. Identifying points of failure often requires analyzing logs and traces across several microservice environments. Identifying reasons for failure is another challenge: Which service failed? Why did it fail? What data set caused it to fail? What were the pre and post conditions that caused it to fail? All these questions are much harder to answer in a distributed, scaled out, fragmented architecture.

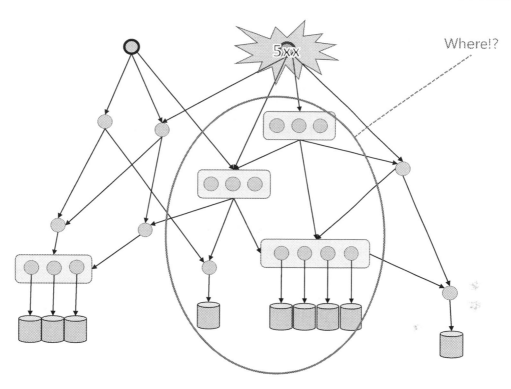

***Figure 3-5.*** *Difficulty in identifying the source of an error*

The challenges arise from the inherent qualities of microservices architecture. When a failure happens, it is oftentimes difficult to quickly identify the root cause of the problem, primarily because of deep hierarchies of microservices (AC1: Dispersed Business Logic) and the inability to determine the exact state of the system (AC3: Inconsistent Dynamic Overall State). Early adopters of microservices (and early adopters of distributed architecture) encountered this problem. In large systems running on microservices architecture, it is not possible for a single engineer (or a single team) to have the big picture of the overall wiring and working of all microservices. The absence of a holistic view makes it difficult for engineers to identify the origin of the issue (Sigelman, et al., 2010), primarily due to the continuous evolution of microservices of every domain in the system (Sampaio, et al., 2017).

On cloud platforms, the problems of infrastructure opaqueness further complicate the debugging process (Yu, et al., 2016). An option is to ignore the infrastructure and collate logs into a centralized store; however, it is not a simple task to organize, combine, and comprehend the context of the problem to a level sufficient to debug and troubleshoot issues (Yu, et al., 2016) (Sampaio, et al., 2017).

Attempting to pinpoint the source of an error might require debugging multiple applications.

# AC6: The v2 Dread—Difficulty in Evolving

Microservices architecture allows independent design, deployment, and evolution of the smallest subsystems of enterprise solutions. Engineers can rapidly add new features and promote it to production, providing quick time-to-market. It is now common for microservices to have multiple deployments weekly, even in large enterprises. Teams that own their domains publish newer versions of microservices frequently. In spite of its prevalence in the industry today, these rapid changes often suffer from a lack of sound engineering that is backed by theoretical work.

A microservice might publish a revision (minor changes to its contract, still being backward compatible), or release a new version (significant change, with little or no backward compatibility). When this happens, dependent microservices, especially in other domains, suddenly incur the overhead of upgrading their microservices without a business need. This is a massive challenge for provider/foundational microservices. If we attempt to mitigate this by allowing clients to control provider microservices changes, coordination efforts slow down releases. We have also gone against our fundamental principle of microservice independence. Forcing client microservices to keep track of provider microservices is unintelligent; so, provider services themselves must, as they evolve, ensure their solutions are sensible (Sampaio, et al., 2017).

Software evolution is a hard concept in an environment different where parts of the system evolve continuously, in parallel. If consumers are kept tightly coupled with service definitions, it makes it impossible for providers to release newer versions; if kept too loose, provider systems are burdened with being backward compatible and slowing releases (Preston-Werner, 2013). In microservices, there are a few options, such as versioning the service endpoint itself, such as adding a version to the path of the service's REST URI. However, this brings in different challenges. Maintaining many versions (or ensuring backward and forward compatibility) causes code bloat and system complexity in maintaining and testing against all definitions. Deferring these changes for long—and trying to have an overarching plan to ensure parallel versions are short-lived (Newman, 2015)—is seldom a practical plan. It sends us heading back to planned monthly deployments as we were doing for monoliths.

Though systems that are integrated with choreography have a smaller impact, the challenges do exist in a publish-subscribe model as well. When domains start publishing messages about events, many consumers might start relying on these messages for their inner workings. This will cause consumers to rework when source systems change messaging content. Worse yet, consumers may have to rework even when the change is to a part of the message that doesn't concern them. This necessity for constant alterations perpetually creates avoidable efforts across the enterprise.

---

Autonomous systems with independent life cycles force stagnant service definitions, which curtail agility.

---

# Summary

Microservices architecture's inherent nature of small, independent, and isolated components that communicate with standard web protocols provide large throughput, a high degree of scalability and elasticity, and allow rapid evolution of systems. However, each of these characteristics also brings in challenges that were naturally absent in monoliths. Creation of many small services distributes the overall business logic into many systems and teams, requiring higher coordination and oversight. The split of a system into independent parts relying on HTTP-like protocols for communication, where distributed transactions are not possible, requires us to plan and mitigate partial failures in operations. Distribution of domain data—split between subdomains, and further partitioned for scalability—makes the consistent state of the system imperceptible. It also makes the gathering of composite data, for reasons like reporting and analytics, cumbersome, requiring us to devise new techniques and solutions. The rapid evolution, though significantly superior to monoliths, is not devoid of challenges.

# Points to Ponder

1. What challenges will applications face due to a lack of ACID properties? Can enterprise systems work in BASE mode?

2. What is the right level of eventual consistency allowable?

3.  Can every system, at its smallest subdomain, be eventually consistent and still function correctly?

4.  If microservices rely on messaging for all interdomain communication, what are the advantages? What are the additional complexities?

# Further Related Reading

**Time, Clocks, and the Ordering of Events in a Distributed System** by *Leslie Lampor*t (Lamport, 1978).

> **The Part-time Parliament** by *Leslie Lamport* (Lamport, 1998).
>
> **Paxos Made Simple** by *Leslie Lamport* (Lamport, 2001).
>
> **Nested Transactions** by *John Moss* (Moss, 1981).
>
> *David Reed*'s Ph.D. dissertation on transactions (Reed, 1978).
>
> **Designing Data-intensive Applications** by *Kleppman* (Kleppman, 2017).
>
> **Semantic Versioning** by *Tom Preston-Werner* (Preston-Werner, 2013).

# CHAPTER 4

# Overcoming Architectural Challenges

The field of microservices architecture is new. There is still a great deal of learning happening, and supposed to happen, as we explore and work the paradigm. We are now aware of the benefits a microservices-based architecture brings, along with the challenges it exhibits. This chapter discusses potential ways to mitigate—if not eliminate—the problems we discussed in the previous chapter. The path to a successful implementation of microservices architecture requires *innovative thinking*, *collaborative efforts*, and *process rigor*.

When devising solutions to overcome the challenges, it is crucial not to resurrect the monolithic behavior. Solutions should adhere to the principles of microservices architecture and stay true to the spirit of the architecture.

## Service Catalog

We discussed the challenges of an evolving microservices architecture in Chapter 3. The proliferation of microservices often causes service duplication, surplus services, and business logic spread. This problem ails microservices architectures for their lifespan. A way to control the proliferation of microservices is through good governance. Good governance also avoids duplication of functionality and eliminates lingering microservices. Let us look at a potential governance model, employing a few ideas and tools.

Maintaining *a* **service catalog**, *which is an active repository of existing microservices*, is paramount. A service catalog lists essential information about all microservices: names and descriptions of resources exposed, owning domain and teams, and list of external dependencies. Adding runtime information—such as service discovery information and service level objectives—also helps in the management of microservices.

© Chandra Rajasekharaiah 2021
C. Rajasekharaiah, *Cloud-Based Microservices*, https://doi.org/10.1007/978-1-4842-6564-2_4

1. Microservices architecture can lead to thousands of microservices. The best way to manage is via a listing of each microservice, along with the various domain elements it maintains. This information is especially useful in providing the overall functionality list; the microservices teams will tend to focus on a small piece of the overall system.

2. A service catalog makes a great tool for building a common vocabulary across various parts of the enterprise. The catalog also acts as the business to technology mapping, aiding product owners in understanding existing capability, and development teams in avoiding duplicate implementations.

3. Adding discovery information eases automation efforts and support efforts. Having an equivalent of a subway map to the myriad of services piled up from the microservices architecture gives quick access to service endpoints. Automated tools can be set up to ping the endpoints, do health checks, and monitor for any failures. If severe failures are detected in the network of microservices, the catalog will aid support teams in estimating the fallout and working on containing the error.

4. Similar to discovery information, adding information SLOs (service-level objectives) regarding response-time and other metrics help monitor microservice performance. The catalog will again serve as the singular place for referencing non-functional requirements of various microservices.

---

Well-maintained service catalogs give significant advantages at both the time of development process and at production/support phase.

---

Once a service catalog is in place, architects need to ensure that it is at the center of all design discussions. Architects should ensure it is actively maintained, collaboratively updated, and widely embraced. Having a few governance rules benefit the accuracy of the service catalog:

**Every new microservice is named accurately:** In a microservices architecture built with REST services, the fundamental entities are *resources*. It becomes paramount to ensure thorough diligence before deciding the nomenclature of resources, as several benefits accompany accuracy in naming. Every resource must remain true to its name for greater clarity—using a word to exactly mean what it implies in its business domain. Accurately named resources permit us to evaluate and compare against existing resources in the catalog.

Checking against current names in the catalog helps us avoid duplication of efforts. Simultaneously, being thorough about naming ensures the concept is clear; all involved teams—business, technology, support, and operations—consistently understand the meaning of the term. An appropriately named resource assures that it belongs to the right domain and is sensible enough to be an independent entity. Placing greater emphasis on naming is a great way to avoid duplicate implementations, gain consensus on design and diction, and promote reuse.

**New features might force rearchitecture, and may not be simple patches:** Indeed, refactoring and rearchitecting microservices are often an overhead. However, not spending enough time to pause and think before implementing dirties the architecture. We have to remember to adhere to our fundamental principle of single-purpose microservices. If we need a new feature that requires a new resource that cuts across three existing resources, but is not a composite, it might be time to reevaluate the resources. Comparing the new resource against related names in the catalog, rethinking resource relations, and reorganizing them—all of these are mandatory to futureproof a solution.

**Changes to a service need examination in the context of its dependent services:** Contextual evaluation ensures any significant gaps, which cannot be caught by syntactic checks, are addressed. A composite resource that is composed of several resources might need reevaluation when any of its parts change. Again, due diligence at the earliest phase of development is required; it avoids us getting surprised by unexpected side effects of the change in its components.

Implementing and enforcing a service catalog across the enterprise has great benefits. Ideally, tooling—to enforce searchable content, standardize format, and secure accessibility—tremendously helps organize and collaborate in a microservices environment. In the absence of tooling, simple, centralized, and well-maintained documentation could be adequate. More on these techniques and their benefits are discussed in Chapter 5.

---

It is paramount to implement service registry (and hence, service discovery) with tools that are outside of the application, without embedding it in application code.

---

# Sagas (Long-Running Transactions)

The absence of distributed transactions means the elimination of lock-and-wait steps in microservices architectures, and hence better scalability and higher throughput. It is a fact that *we cannot eliminate the problem of hold-and-wait of transactions*; however, *we could alleviate problems by not holding all resources for the entire duration of transactions* (Garcia-Molina & Salem, 1987, p. 250). Avoiding hold-and-wait is the underlying compromise of microservices: parts of transactions will continue without explicitly holding resources. Unfortunately, this compromise could result in unreliable work execution and inconsistent end state of involved microservices and their domains.

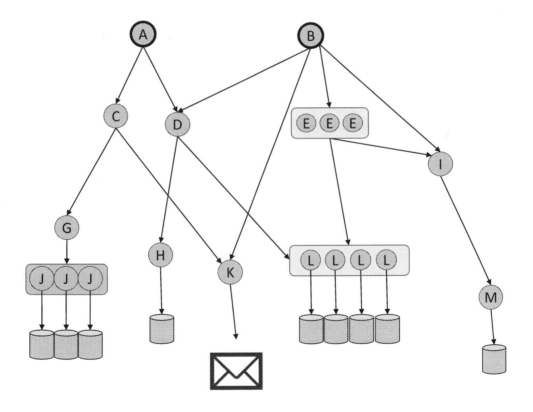

***Figure 4-1.***  *A typical nested transaction in a domain*

Overcoming unreliability and inconsistencies in a microservices architecture requires a great deal of planning and foresight. It is necessary to understand how top-level microservices orchestrate or choreograph other microservices. Let us assume a transaction is a "step" in the business flow. Our first action is to identify the sequence of sub-steps that comprise the overall step. This total transaction, which consists of many sub-transactions, is termed a ***saga***. Sagas are an extension of nested transactions, wherein a "saga"—*a story of events*—is composed of microservice calls across domains that could themselves be transactions. Sagas provide an overview of transactions as a sequence of sub-steps, and failure or partial success can happen at a more granular level. We will discuss the consistency aspects of transactions in the next section.

Figure 4-1 depicts a typical nested transaction within a single domain. For microservice $A$ to complete with success, it needs to update microdomains $J$, $H$, $K$, and $L$. Saga, in this case, is the transaction of $\{J, H, K, L\}$ updates. An error in any subset of microservices $\{C, D, G, H, K, L\}$ causes the top-level microservice to fail as a transaction. Consider the scenario of partial failure in $D$, where $K$ succeeded while $L$ did not. Now we have inconsistent actions and partial updates to state: we sent an email without correct database updates. Handling failures such as this requires careful design of involved sagas. *Handling failures in sagas is **not** a trivial task*; however, a few options exist. The rest of this section discusses potential mitigation options.

# Ignoring Errors

The most naïve implementation is to ignore errors when they happen. The solution indeed works *for non-critical services that can tolerate some amount of failures.* Failures might be acceptable for two reasons: (1) these failures are corrected in future transactions automatically, or (2) simply an error is acceptable for the current context. In Energence's example, let us say a metering service needs to persist meter reading across multiple tables: it updates the current reading of the meter, updates device information, and updates the percentage of usage across HVAC and various appliances. Failure to update a few of the tables is acceptable if meter readings arrive on periodic time slots: the data autocorrects with the next data packet. However, this does not relieve us from capturing errors—for audit and quality metrics—before ignoring them.

This approach may not work for many use cases where it is necessary to handle and resolve errors, or in situations that cause systemic actions. The result of a customer's credit-card payment not accurately reflected in their account status is a serious issue—in terms of revenue and in terms of legality. Handling such use cases requires deploying precise controls, checks, and balancing actions. If alerting consumers of their unpaid accounts via email is part of this transaction, there is no way to stop the mail.

# Compensating Errors Inline

Another standard method to handle errors is with compensating transactions, which correct the errors resulting from a failed or partially successful transaction. We can fix a failed or partially completed saga in two ways—either a *rollback of all actions* or *completion of missing actions*. To achieve a saga, *create multiple save-points in the saga* (each save-point indicates one or more steps), and *compensate starting from the last completed save-point*. To rollback saga, push transactional operations onto a stack, and upon failure, "undo" every action in the reverse sequence by popping. This way of compensating errors inline is a fantastic way of rolling back changes, especially while the changing context is still current. If implemented correctly, with this approach, microservices will leave data in a correct state when they finish. The microservice will also proactively attempt to remedy the issue before it causes additional damage to the overall system.

Compensatory transactions add another level of complexity to implementations. They require microservices to pack additional business logic to correct failed transactions. Compensations could quickly get complicated for top-level microservices, which update multiple subdomains. This approach also soon complicates testing, as it increases alternate paths and combinations that need testing. *A huge challenge here is the possibility that a compensating effort itself could fail, or worse, corrupt data further*.

# Compensating Errors Offline

Another simple approach involves spinning off a process, or another microservice, to fix the error asynchronously. The underlying idea here is, "it is possible to come back and correct the error later." This approach does handle some error cases. For instance, it is possible to trigger an update-customer-account-later process, which will retry to POST an update and correct the customer's account or bill at a later time. Backing these asynchronous tasks by a messaging queue allows for a resilient way to fix data. It also makes the pattern reusable in similar situations if we abstract the messaging and triggering process.

Unfortunately, problems still exist in this approach. *Retry attempts need to be time-bound and time-sensitive.* Consider the case from before where Energence charged the customer's credit card successfully but failed to update the customer's account. What if the asynchronous attempt is hours later, and meantime, the service that monitors defaulted accounts closed the account due to missing payments?

# Implementing Sagas

For distributed microservices built with HTTP constructs, the requirement of ACID transactions is difficult to fulfill. Apart from accepting the eventual consistency of data, an upfront design is needed to handle failures—whether partial or complete. We must sequence operations to minimize the impact of failures, create *recoverable save-points, and add resiliency to retries.*

An approach to minimizing the fallout of a doomed transaction is to execute the unrecoverable actions to the end. Moving irreparable parts to the end provides us a higher probability of a successful recovery.

*Save-points play an essential role in implementing sagas.* Skipping or skimping on proper planning of save-points leads to a design where failures corrupt the global view. We need to ensure save-points leave the data in a consistent state, which helps in recovery. When recovery attempts start from a save-point, there is a possibility that microservices between save-points are rerun. Microservices involved between save-points should allow retries without failing.

Even after we embrace eventual consistency, handling traditional transactions in microservices is an involved effort. It requires careful design and correct implementation. We should choose between the three options of handling errors—ignoring, inline compensating, and offline compensating—based on requirements and use cases.

---

Sagas are a decades-old technique that allows splitting a transaction into subtransactions and making it easy to create a consistent overall state of the system.

---

# Maintaining the Global States

Deducing consistency in states across choreographed systems—where systems independently maintain states and share them asynchronously—is a serious challenge. In orchestrated situations, an increase in invocation depths punishes the performance for deducing coarse-states. Deep call stacks result in more failure points and a longer time to reconcile states. Performance measures such as sharding further complicate the situation, as data partitions might need resolving before querying data. Let us look at the techniques to mitigate problems related to identifying coarse-states.

# The Scenario of Dynamic Overall State

Consider a scenario where Energence needs to update a million user devices with an OTA (over-the-air) fix. The solution approach involves

1.  Identifying the exact million devices that require an OTA fix

2.  Identifying the correct OTA patch for each device

3.  Downloading the appropriate fix to a million devices

4.  Scheduling an apply-and-restart on million devices

This scenario is a perfect example where all our challenges combine. There are at least two subdomains of Energence Home Platform involved: the EOTA (Energence over the air) module and the Smart-Devices module. The EOTA module identifies the devices that need patching based on the device's state. The EOTA module then determines the required right patch for each type of identified device. This information is sent to the Smart-Devices module. Smart-Devices module sends the necessary payload to all the devices—possibly creating a schedule to apply the patch and restart the device.

Figure 4-2 depicts such a microservices flow. The dotted lines indicate where asynchronous communication between microservices aptly fits. Choreography makes sense here: we can avoid bulk data merges, sequence and throttle patching, and prevent long-running transactions.

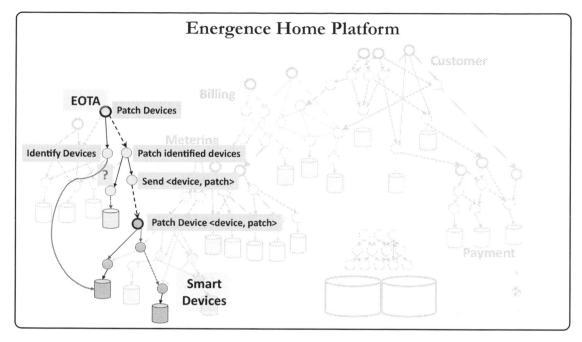

*Figure 4-2.* *Microservices interacting to apply OTA fix for a million smart devices*

Several challenges in identifying data consistently across domains surface:

1. **Smart-Devices module stores device information**: How will
   the EOTA module decide which devices to select for patching?
   Selecting the right set of devices might need complex queries
   joining data from both EOTA and Smart-Devices domains. Calling
   Smart-Devices' microservice millions of times is not performant.

2. **EOTA module sends <device, patch> tuple to Smart-Devices
   module**: What is the most efficient way to help EOTA module track
   successes, failures, postpones, device-update-freeze schedules, etc.
   if retries are required?

3. **EOTA model stores patches**: How does the Smart-Devices
   module get patches from the EOTA module? A patch-id can
   be shared in the request, but what if the module needs tuning
   based on device configuration, stored in Smart-Devices module?
   Changing the patch in Smart-Devices goes against domain
   responsibility.

Multiple techniques to solve these problems exist, each employing varied methods of caching external dependencies. The underlying theme of these techniques is to separate analytical and transactional workloads and direct analytical workloads to a cache—an eventually consistent data source. Based on how we maintain a cache, we can draw three techniques:

1. Cache is owned and maintained by every domain.

2. Cache is located centrally.

3. We leverage a messaging middleware instead.

Separation of analytical and transactional workload allows tweaking datastores to match analytical queries (which are slower by orders of magnitude) separately from transactional data sources. For instance, the cache can be a columnar database allowing retrieving states in bulk, as opposed to the database that Smart-Devices microservices use.

# Intermittent-Peek Option

A popular technique to solve this problem is to use a secondary read-only copy of data, to which data is periodically synchronized. In our earlier scenario, the Smart-Devices module could keep OTA patch binaries in a "personal copy"—a replica of the EOTA module's data. This information is synchronized often, possibly through a batched process (for instance, with a scheduled ETL (extract, transform, load) process) might adjust the offsets. This replica reduces the Smart-Devices module's dependency on EOTA to look up patch information. The copy acts as a *source-of-engagement* of the original *source-of-truth*.

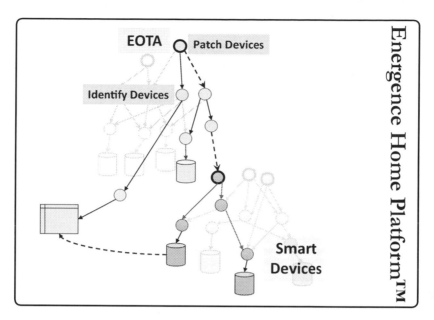

***Figure 4-3.*** *Intermittent-Peek Option: EOTA periodically syncs data required from Smart-Devices module into its cache*

**Fitting Scenarios:** This scenario works best in cases where data is either mostly static or is of a highly independent domain. The content of binary patches is a perfect example of the first case, as these patches do not change often. The binaries go through development followed by a rigorous test-and-validation phase before released for OTA fixing. For this use case, the Smart-Devices module can synchronize data as a nightly job—refreshing patch files every 24 hours.

**Shortfalls of Approach:** This approach does not work for data that changes often. For instance, states of devices in the Smart-Devices module change often. If not synchronized quickly, results from modules such as EOTA suffer by deciding against wrong data. Wrong choices could lead to missing an update or repeatedly updating the same device.

# Always-Listening Option

Every system publishes data changes as messages, and dependent systems calculate data on-demand using these data-change messages. For deducing the latest status, this technique relies on event sources that allow querying. Many stream databases and messaging middleware allow querying messages. In this example, the Smart-Devices module publishes state changes to messaging middleware. EOTA module, or any other module that needs to retrieve data in bulk, deduces the state of data by running analytical queries against the event source.

> **Fitting Scenarios:** This approach works for most scenarios if the messaging layer is robust and fast: it provides a great way of keeping domains in sync. It also minimizes communication between domains, as there are no point-to-point connections.

> **Drawbacks of the Approach:** The messaging bus takes most of the responsibility of transforming, meeting performance SLAs, etc. When it comes to architecture principles, this additional responsibility taken up by messaging infrastructure is an area of contention. Good architecture relies on using messaging infrastructure as merely a "dumb pipe"; here, we might be pushing that rule. It is important to note that this approach levies an extra burden on the dependent systems, as they must handle out-of-sequence/lost/duplicate messages. If the message store has duplicate messages or out-of-sequence messages, dependent systems must work around it.

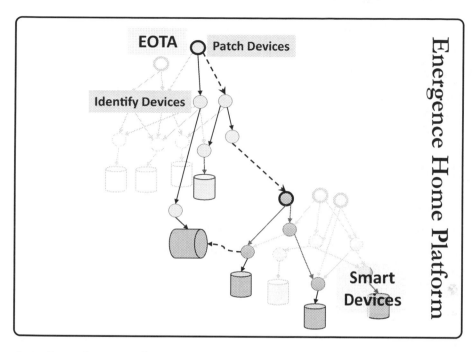

***Figure 4-4.*** *Broadcast-to-the-World option—Smart Devices maintain an event store of all changes to device state changes, and EOTA taps into it*

## Larger Questions

The third option is to have a centralized datastore instead of local caches or message stores. This option also solves AC4: Difficulty in Gathering Composite Data, which we discussed earlier. Creating a centralized store is a more daunting task, and many times beyond the scope of domains that need data: it should be an enterprise initiative. This topic is given particular attention in our next section "Centralized View."

---

Bulk information exchange between various microservice domains can be done in three ways: replicating data into a central location, or creating an event source that allows querying to get data, or allowing the client domains to replicate a local-copy synchronously or asynchronously.

---

In summary, maintaining global states is an exceedingly challenging problem as microservices evolve. Many large-scale software enterprises have created custom solutions to handle this challenge, but not without risks and failures. Enterprises such as Energence need to evaluate and choose options based on the fitness and drawbacks of each option.

# Centralized View

The earlier section offered options that required either dependent systems to maintain copies of data internally—either to cache data from external systems or to allow external systems to run analytical queries on their data. In both options, the number of replicated data sources might grow with need. Replications can quickly get out of hand, as newer use cases need more data from other domains. Soon we will end up in a *monolithic version of applications: data now resides with modules that do not own it.*

Many enterprises want to control this type of data proliferation, ensuring analytical datastores—either as caches or as event stores—do not grow like weeds across. One of the most popular techniques in this aspect is to create an oracle system. *All systems and modules will rely on a centrally stored, often denormalized, eventually consistent copy of essential data.* A central store reduces duplication of data storage/message processing/connectivity caused by other options.

Centralized view futureproofs architectures to a long-term view. *Data is centrally available to run analytical queries on, by any domain that needs it.* It suits all use cases where domains are highly dependent on mass reads of data from other systems, but accept discrepancy in values. An added advantage is cost reduction from maintaining a single copy instead of multiple copies (helpful on the cloud, as we will discuss shortly).

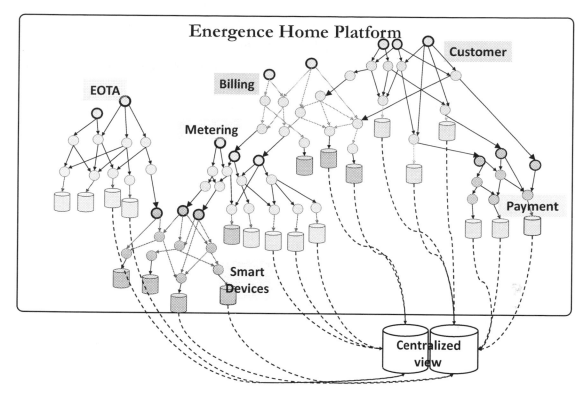

***Figure 4-5.*** *A Centralized View—wherein all databases of all domains asynchronously sync with a centralized datastore for analytical queries*

A centralized view also solves the AC4: Difficulty in Gathering Composite Data, which we discussed earlier. When an enterprise needs its reporting, analytics, machine learning, and AI teams to access enterprise data, a centralized view perfectly fits the bill. If the centralized view also retains historical snapshots of data (or an event store), these teams can leverage it.

Be warned, creating a centralized view is a huge investment, requiring firm commitment. Such *consolidation and centralization bring back challenges of the monolith*, both in processes and operation.

A single centralized datastore needs strict data governance. This setup requires dedicated teams that ensure enterprise principles govern new data. Managing multiple views that map to numerous clients becomes a requirement as source data evolves. Having multiple views create another set of governance requirements: those of data aging, translating, and retiring. The development team that owns this centralization needs to arbiter a producers' data changes with all the teams that rely on the data.

Operationally as well, failure in such a system causes havoc across all domains. Architects face a peculiar dilemma here. If all domains can use a central view, we can standardize solutions. However, too much dependency on a single system is counterintuitive to our fundamental principles. For instance, referring to our earlier problem of EOTA and Smart-Devices modules requiring view into each other's data, both modules can refer to a centralized view for data. The scenario works perfectly until the centralized view becomes unavailable.

---

Before leveraging a centralized view for cross-domain data, architects should identify the consequences of its unavailability.

---

# Observability

The challenge of AC5: Difficulty in Debugging Failures and Faults is one of the first ones we will face, but not the hardest to solve. The problem in providing an architecture with options to efficiently debug is both an architectural challenge and an operational challenge. The concept of observability originates from control theory, as a measure of a system's internal state based on its behavior. In a microservices architecture, enabling observability achieves distributed failure and fault detection by watching the overall behavior of applications. Let us discuss the architectural aspects in this section. Operational elements need special attention, which we will give in later chapters, when we discuss cloudification and security concepts. At its core, observability is defined as a triad—tracing (execution paths of every transaction in an application), logging (events recorded by applications, which could aid in diagnostics later), and metrics (the measurement of key application traits).

**Tracing** allows engineers to find the chain of actions resulting from a specific event. Tracing within a single application (or a monolith) is easy, as all log entries are collocated and mostly sequential. Gathering trace information in a microservices architecture, where services execute in isolation, requires *distributed tracing*. We need an overarching system to identify and tag service chains in its entirety, and then capture that information into a centralized store. In our example, we need to know every microservice call resulting from a top-level microservice call to autopay an account. We should be able to "trace" the call-flow we listed earlier: *untill the end of the call chain, or till an error aborts the call chain.* Many standards have appeared attempting to achieve distributed tracing, and many competing tools are built in the industry to achieve this. As of writing this book (mid 2020), an agreement between multiple standards was in the works.[1]

**Metrics** in software engineering is a generic term for assigning a numerical value to software properties. They play a vital role in assessing the quality of processes, artifacts, and runtimes, and objective comparison. Metrics cover a gamut of areas, starting from code to runtime. Code quality metrics decide the programming quality, on a standardized scale. For instance, code coverage is a metric indicating the overall percentage of a component tested from its unit tests. Engineering teams set target numbers for each metric and attempt to achieve it. Targets for metrics are to be pragmatically set, with adequate forethought and discussion. It is common knowledge that code coverage less than 50 is inadequate, more than 90 is impressive, and 100 is a lie. Similarly, *runtime metrics* measure the runtime quality of software. In a microservices architecture, runtime metrics are invaluable for observability.

Ability to capture metrics, such as *percentage of errors*, *percentage of slow responses*, and *rate of failures*, is immensely helpful in prompting action. For instance, a microservice is tested and certified to handle 1000 simultaneous requests per second, with each request not taking more than 10ms. We can set up alarms to go off if the microservice got 100 requests per second but only responded to 90, erroring out (5xx response codes from REST endpoints) on 10. We can set up dashboards to light up if 10% of the requests take longer than 10ms. These metrics indicate something is seriously wrong in the microservice, which needs our attention. We can extend these metrics to include business faults as well, for instance, 4xx response codes from REST endpoints of critical microservices. Metrics can help derive valuable information for both business and technology. Dashboards built on metrics help various business users see purposeful information and watch for notifications on important events. System metrics allow engineering teams to see systems' usage trends and state trends, helping them mitigate potential problems.

**Logging** and **log aggregation** is a routine challenge for architects and engineers. Logs are generated by applications, and if programmed correctly, at various configurable levels. Though applications configured to log at a fine-grain level will provide more insights, more logging will affect performance. Coarse-grained logging is excellent from a performance standpoint, but such applications will report only essential events.

---

[1]OpenTracing and OpenCensus merged to form OpenTelemetry.

Coarse-grained logging may not be enough to debug and root-cause a problem. Architects need to balance out based on the static and dynamic nature of each application. Newer applications might need fine-grain logging, while stable ones might run with coarse-level logging. For stabler applications, when runtime metrics alarms go off, changing logging levels might give more insight. These are not rules, but options that need judicious evaluation; for instance, detailed logging could worsen systems that are already performing poorly. Once the right level of logging is decided, *aggregating logs in a central place—where they can be contextualized—*significantly improves the observability of systems.

In our automated payment example, a single autopay request sets in motion a series of microservice calls across many domains. Consider what happens when every microservice is observable. Every service call, or an event, which triggers a chain of microservice, is tagged with a trace-packet. This trace-packet is forwarded down every service to identify the context of execution. Services have agents that aggregate this information and send it to a central store. Options for sampling traces vary; a percentage of traffic, or count per second, random trails are all popular choices. A good practice is to add this trace-packet to logs, allowing the correlation of log records to traces. Once an alarm goes off, engineers can identify the trail of a suspicious transaction to pinpoint the source of errors.

---

All microservice call chain needs visibility into its call chain for **tracing**, **metrics**, and **logging**; *these three aspects define the observability of a system.*

---

In the earlier chapter, we discussed how debugging failures and faults in a sea of microservices is hard. Often a daunting task. Building observability into every microservice is a terrific way to mitigate the challenge. Architects and engineers need to enforce discipline by forcing observability from inception.

# Contract Testing

*"Speak English!" said the Eaglet. "I don't know the meaning of half those long words, and, what's more, I don't believe you do either!"*

—Lewis Carroll, *Alice's Adventures in Wonderland* (1865)

Microservices evolve. They evolve quickly. This rapid change in microservices often spills to the edges and changes the defined contracts. A microservice might offer new functionality through a new REST resource. Or, it might add or remove a field in its REST resource. Such changes often have a significant impact on overall systems when discovered later in the development cycle. We discussed this earlier, in section "AC6: The v2 Dread—Difficulty in Evolving."

As an enterprise's microservices increase rapidly to thousands, identifying side effects to changes in microservice resources becomes difficult. An alteration that causes failures in another microservice in the ecosystem might slip through the development process. To efficiently reduce the blast radius of a breaking change, we need to enforce testing the known contracts very early in the life cycle. Let us walk through a scenario in Energence Home Platform after we have transitioned it to an entirely microservices-based architecture. Let us suppose we encounter a feature that needs a change in a resource of the Smart-Devices module. As we discussed in our earlier chapter, this means every domain and microservice relying on that resource needs to assess the impact of the change. If there is a new attribute that replaces an old one that the EOTA-domain relied on, that domain needs to change its view of the resource.

This demonstrates the need to alter the way we build software, a change that can help us eliminate this problem. We now realize that the root cause of this problem is the introduction of incompatible changes to the contract of service. What if we could stop an incoherent shift in the earliest phase of development? What if we disallow a change to a contract that breaks the dependent services? For instance, when the smart-module team decides to retire an attribute of one of their resources and unknowingly breaking an external service, can we stop the change in the first phase of development? Implementing such a technique, and somehow adding it to the software development process, mitigates the fear of change. For this technique to be truly effective, such validation needs to be automated; automation reduces the burden of repeated and aimless validations. This technique of detecting incompatibility in contracts is termed ***contract testing***.

Contract testing is the process where a microservice promises a contract with every dependent service and tests against it every time. The best approach is to embed these tests that verify adherence to contract into the microservice itself (Atkinson & Groß, 2002). If a change breaks the agreement, the microservice team will correct it by either fixing the changes to align with the contract or rolling back changes. Such testing requires dependent service teams to provide tests to describe their requirement, which validate the microservice contract at compile time. Such agreements, called consumer-driven-contracts, are a great way of solving this problem.

However, enforcing contract testing is not simple and straightforward. It cannot be either *consumer-driven-contracts-only* or *provider-driven-contracts-only*. Both approaches have their benefits and pitfalls. For contract testing to be effective, there needs to be some ground rules around when to favor one over the other. Following is a sample list that can be used, but in no way a comprehensive one.

1. The main criteria to decide between the two approaches is to base the changes on

    a. Where the system is in its life cycle—whether a system is in inception, or it is undergoing development, or if it is in production

    b. Where the system is in the hierarchy of microservices; for instance, whether it is a foundational system on which many systems rely on, or it is a customer-facing application where external entities rely on the contracts

2. A good rule of thumb is that if a new microservice is still under development, it will have to absorb changes of other systems that are in production. A new unreleased microservice cannot stop an established microservice from changing. Until the new microservice reaches a state of maturity, it will have to continue absorbing changes of stable microservices.

3. It is hard to coordinate changes to a top-level microservice that defines enterprise-level API. Foundational microservices within a domain are also hard to change due to the number of services depending on it.

In a mature and advanced software development enterprise, contract testing is set up as part of the process of building software. Contracts are created, shared, and added to the compilation and building stages of microservices. Having governance and rules around choosing the right type of contract testing brings balance; wherein we allow microservices to change their contracts when required. We also identify the affected client systems early in the development life cycle.

# Summary

In an earlier chapter, we discussed various challenges that result from microservices architecture: in processes, in execution, and operations. In this chapter, we discussed mitigation techniques for both types. We learned how maintaining a service catalog allows us to avoid proliferation, duplication, and redundancy of microservices. We understood how contract testing enables us to change microservices with confidence: any effects on dependent microservices are discovered earlier in the software life cycle. We realized that when we signed up for eventual consistency, we also signed consistency-related challenges. We saw how Sagas recommend transforming transactions into an eventually consistent setup of actions as a possible way to mitigate the lack of transactions. We discussed how maintaining caches or a centralized datastore allows decoupling parts of transactions that can work with an eventual consistency model. For operations, we discussed the absolute need for enabling observability from the inception of every microservice. Finally, we discussed how contract testing stops incoherent changes propagate throughout the system early in the development process.

# Points to Ponder

1. As an architect, how can I maintain a service catalog live? How do I ensure changes are automatically updated? How does it relate to contract testing?

2. How do I decide which parts of transactions can break away from ACID constraints? How do I choose between various levels of consistency?

3. As the architect (or as the product owner) of a centralized view, how do I manage changes in every application's data feed? What process do I put in place to monitor, detect, and arbiter changes?

4. As a developer, do I identify the right logging levels for applications? How can I create a unified view that can tie application logs, traces, and metrics?

5. As an architect, how can I enforce contract testing as part of the software engineering process?

# Further Related Reading

**Sagas** by *Garcia-Molina and Salem* (Garcia-Molina & Salem, 1987).

Conference papers on Facebook's Tao and related techniques.

**Built-in Contract Testing in Model-driven, Component-Based Development** by Colin Atkinson and Hans-gerhard Groß (Atkinson & Groß, 2002)

**Distributed Systems Observability** by Cindy Sridharan (Sridharan, 2018)

# CHAPTER 5

# Process Changes

*Progress doesn't come from early risers—progress is made by lazy men try-
ing to find easier ways to do things.*

—Robert Heinlein, *Time Enough For Love* (1973)

Modern software development requires effective techniques. For an enterprise to
incorporate the microservices paradigm, changes to development methodology are
essential. It is necessary to reorganize development teams around modern development
processes for successfully implementing any microservices architecture. This chapter
introduces a few process techniques that redefine how software is built, tested, and
delivered.

The 12 factors of applications (Wiggins A., 2012) cover some of the critical aspects of
building microservices. However, there are more elements to building microservices—in
the context of recommended software engineering practices. Any enterprise dealing
with building software will have development and operation teams following some
predefined processes. A conventional build process in any enterprise will enable
the following capabilities: managing source code, building applications, testing and
validating, prepare environments, deploy tested applications, and roll out to production.

The capabilities defined above are necessary for building and deploying applications
to production. For the process to be sound, it needs to correctly set up the steps into
various stages of a process pipeline. The recommendation of a comprehensive software
development process for a proper software engineering practice follows.

1. Managing source code via a central code repository

   a. Ensure appropriate tagging, branching, feature flags.

   b. Ensure code is committed, merged, and reviewed after every
      check-in/merge.

© Chandra Rajasekharaiah 2021
C. Rajasekharaiah, *Cloud-Based Microservices*, https://doi.org/10.1007/978-1-4842-6564-2_5

2. Tools to automatically trigger the build process. The build process should

   a. Statically check code for code smells, code metrics (complexity, maintainability indices), contract violations, and security vulnerabilities.

   b. Run unit tests, validate correctness, and gather test statistics (such as failure rates, code-coverage, etc.).

   c. Compile code into binary executable formats that can be "sealed in time."

   d. Move binaries into artifact repository, version/tag them.

3. Dynamically spin up a production-like test environment for testing environments and run integration tests.

   a. Upon successful integration testing, mark the binary as a release candidate.

   b. Tear down the test environment after running tests.

4. Prepare production deployment of the service's release candidate.

   a. Update feature flags to coordinate launches.

   b. Carve out the required resources from the pool and allocate them against the new deployment.

   c. Set up the environment for the new release by configuring resources to match service requirements.

5. Copy the binaries and launch the new service.

   a. Based on release strategy–dark launch, canary test, pilot, or rolling deploy—set up traffic shaping and forwarding.

   b. On successful testing—when new deployments are up and healthy—switch traffic.

6. Identify services that are retired as part of the new release.

   a. Monitor for errors and faults until successful cut-over to new service.

   b. Shut down retired services and recover resources.

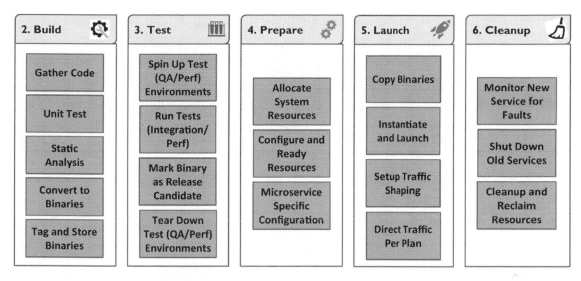

*Figure 5-1.* *Typical CI/CD pipeline for microservices architecture*

Successful deployment of any software to production requires these six steps. The good news is that most modern software enterprises have these processes in some form or fashion. The first three steps (the first step, design and development, is considered a precursor) of the six listed define CI, *continuous integration*. The last three steps outline CD, *continuous delivery*. The usage of the word "*continuous*" is to show that they run frequently; ergo, these steps can be automated. It is important to note that *continuous-deployment* is a next-level paradigm, but with meager returns. In an enterprise that has the capability of continuous-deployment, steps two through six happen at every check-in. Contrast that with a continuous-delivery ready enterprise, where steps four through six happen when the engineering team decides to.

---

In a microservices architecture, we must automate all stages and run them without any manual intervention.

---

Without automation, the microservices architecture will fail due to

1. **The overhead of manual processes**: Imagine the effort it would take to run commands for all six steps for every release of every microservice. And then there is documentation (Humble & Farley, 2010, p. 6).

2. **Delays due to coordination with the "responsible" team**: Enterprises have a separate unit that manages infrastructure. If not automated, the development team must open tickets, set up meetings, and fill out forms: for every deployment. Also, this breeds animosity (Humble & Molesky, 2011).

3. **Manual errors in executing steps**: To err is human, but to make grave mistakes is programming. Any human error that occurred in some stage of a pipeline becomes harder to debug—these errors are not reproducible or resolvable.

This need for automation requires traditional operations-engineers to develop code to automate their old job. The development team takes on more operations activities. This integration of project teams into a single group of engineers created "DevOps" (Humble & Molesky, 2011, p. 7). The intent is to enable the development team to handle operations of the application. Development teams are skilled in automating operations jobs—the same way most development teams have automated testing. Manual processes that are repeated, even as little as four or five times, are apropos for automation.

We have realized that automation makes microservices architecture development, testing, and deployment efficient. Such efficiency achieved by automation is even higher in a cloud environment, where the underlying infrastructure is invisible. The concept of "*pets vs. livestock*" compares traditional on-prem or dedicated infrastructure to cloud infrastructure. A "livestock" like *cloud infrastructure mandates us to consider it as volatile, abstract, and transparent to all engineering teams*. Automation is crucial in the cloud. *We need to consider all manual processes as primary barriers to a successful deployment of microservices on the cloud.*

---

Inflicted pains of any manual process are amplified tenfold on the cloud.

---

# Continuous Integration

*Continuous integration* (CI) is the first step to becoming an automated enterprise and readying it for cloud transformation. Traditionally, integration refers to the process of merging codebases into a single stream and vetting that the integrated system is functional and free of errors. The technique of automating this process, running them often, is the domain of continuous integration. For a successful

CI setup, enterprises need the ability to set up non-production and production environments. Typically,

1. A **development** environment that enables engineers to learn, develop, test, and prepare the application

2. **Test/QA (Quality Assurance) or integration** environments for certification of applications in an environment that connects it with other applications

3. **Performance test** environments that stress the application to its seams

4. **Production environment**, which supports the real-world business

The life cycle of each of these environments will vary; the lifetimes and capacity change. A development environment should be the shortest-lived environment, which exists only for the duration of the development team's test cycle. QA and performance will live longer based on the complexity and size of test runs. Performance environment might have higher capacity to run massive load tests.

# Non-production Environments

When completely automated, build-processes trigger compilation, code verification, unit testing, and artifact creation at any configured event. Typically build pipelines have 1) *triggers*, 2) *a sequence of stages*, 3) *configuration*, and 4) *coordinates* for repositories. A variety of activities can trigger pipelines: code merge completion/scheduled time of the day/successful completion of another one. Once activated, build pipelines run a series of steps: pulling code from repository coordinates, static checking, unit testing, packaging into an artifact, and pushing to an artifact repository.

However, setting up such an automated process for every new project itself can be drudgery. It is also apparent that various factors affect the labor and complexity involved in creating such automation:

1. It is true that based on the complexity of the system, the size of the pipeline varies. However, in the case of microservices architecture, individual applications tend to be similar. Variations are usually limited to the second step.

2.  Progress from monolithic to a microservices architecture will result in many smaller systems. When more systems exist, more pipelines are required to process them.

3.  Agile-meat-grinder techniques force engineers to work at a faster pace, resulting in increased count and execution frequency of pipelines. Though the quality and speed of software generally remain unaffected by such meat grinder techniques, the burden on infrastructure does increase.

Factors such as these underline the importance of **automating the process of creating build pipelines itself**, with an emphasis on templatizing and providing for their elasticity.

Multiple options to automate the creation of build pipelines exist. *It is possible to create a single pipeline* (the weak-hearted might choose one pipeline each for development, test, production environments), which, based on configuration and variables supplied, can build any project. This *"common build pipeline"* is the most straightforward technique to build applications. What makes practical implementation of a standard pipeline challenging is our initial goal of allowing microservices to be independent and polyglot. *Commonality requires standardization, and polyglotism offers none.* Techniques such as containerization do standardize many parts of CI and CD; however, some parts will need customization. (We will discuss containerization in the next chapter.) To achieve standardization, teams need to build the required skills and keep abreast of the tools and techniques.

Another option is *"build pipelines as a service"* offered by many providers. Many cloud platforms offer complete CI and CD processes as service. Leveraging these services still requires planning, configuration, and scripting of pipeline creation. Be advised that some enterprises might not choose these services *for fear of vendor lock-in, wanting to build it in a vendor-neutral way.*

---

Gaining the ability to automatically set up and configure build pipelines is worth the upfront effort involved.

---

# Automated Testing

A novel undertaking in the microservices world is the automation of testing. Automated testing requires enterprises to shed legacy ideas. Process changes need to be in spirit and not enforcement. Concepts such as Test-Driven-Development need to be drilled into engineers and made second nature. Enterprises define a unit as the smallest piece of the compilation and proceed to rely on unit tests to measure correctness. However, unit tests do not certify accuracy (Buxton & Randell, 1969, p. 16). Enterprise build pipelines are often non-continuous, automating minimal steps of the overall process.

Enterprises now need to place importance on unit tests, and not whether the developers write them before or after writing the main code. Enterprises should realize that "unit" refers to the smallest atomic entity of any software system in a context. In the context of microservices architecture, *a REST endpoint of a microservice is the real unit*. This realization provides us an opportunity to advance and accelerate integration testing in the build process. We can approximate correctness at a higher level, much earlier in the pipeline. **Small-sized microservices make integration testing more viable.**

It is possible to augment build-pipelines to guarantee correctness earlier in the process. Build pipelines can do Contract Testing for higher accuracy, and to ensure client compatibility. Build pipelines can run API tests, thus validating all REST endpoints of microservice as part of Step 3. They can also run integration tests, simulating the complete system.

New types of automated testing require upfront strategizing for success. Architects should chalk out a solid strategy around

1. **Test data**: dynamic vs. static vs. combination

2. **Dependencies on other microservices**: mocking vs. static vs. injection

3. **Dependencies on infrastructure**: messaging layer, cache, database, etc.

# Performance Testing

Given that microservices architecture is built for elasticity, and we will invariably engage it to that effect, performance testing plays a critical role. Performance testing should enable engineering teams to determine

1.  The behavior of systems under various types of load

2.  The resource requirement of systems against varying traffic

3.  Sustainability of handling load over time

A performance test is often a collection of various tests. For an application to be successful in a performance test, architects need to capture metrics against multiple factors of the system and confirm the ability to function correctly in the real production environment, under the maximum possible load. Table 5-1 lists the factors that are to be measured, along with the reasons for each factor.

***Table 5-1.*** *Factors and Reasons for Capturing Metrics*

| Factors | Reasons |
|---|---|
| *Response times of microservice, for various load factors per instance.* | It helps identify the breaking points of the application and ways to circumvent failures in any incorrigible parts. |
| *Resource usage percentages at extreme loads.* | Usage benchmarks help establish the apt size of the computational unit. Knowing the suitable size enables deciding multiples needed to handle expected traffic patterns. |
| *Throughput attained by a single, or multiple computational units of a specific size.* | It helps identify load factors—the points at which replication becomes necessary to handle the increased load. Contrarily, it helps identify scaling down instances to reduce running costs. |
| *Errors and response lag plotted against various load volumes.* | Identifying the breaking point of infrastructure helps size the infrastructure to support expected traffic. Entire infrastructure—microservices and its supporting resources, such as communication channels, databases, messaging middleware, etc.—are tested under various volumes. |
| *Errors and response lag plotted against surges in traffic.* | Exposing services to a sudden surge in traffic helps identify the capabilities of handling irregular variations in traffic. It is vital to capture metrics of failures and slow responses. Such metrics help redesign systems to match expected behavior under spikes. |
| *Errors and response lag plotted against sustained peak traffic.* | Subjecting services to some heavy traffic for a sustained amount of time exhibits the capability of handling traffic for a sustained duration of load. |

# Ephemerality and Equivalence of Environments

The term *ephemerality* is associated with the dynamic or temporal state of matter. This temporary existence is a mandatory requirement for environments. As we have discussed earlier, the capability of scripting environments presents us with options for creating and destroying application setups as and when needed. Such strict creation and tear-down capabilities provide some significant benefits, which are quintessential on the cloud.

1. All environments, starting from dev to production, must consistently get carved out of the same outline. Minimizing differences reduces surprises and increases testability.

2. Cloud costs are directly related to usage. Maintaining environments for the duration of necessity reduces cloud costs.

3. Development teams become habitually accustomed to deploying break-fixes or reconfiguring production environments as a quick way to continue business functionality. Ensuring automation to roll out any changes to production avoids similar problems in the future.

The final advantage is a hard requirement, and it brings us to the concept of *equivalence of environments*. All environments are equivalent—they are created with strictly the same script, set up precisely alike, and every aspect of every environment exactly matches each other. Equivalence of environments avoids surprises from the underlying infrastructure, which is vital in running microservices architecture. The key takeaway here is how all these aspects strongly emphasize the importance of automation. Achieving a complete run of finding fault, fixing in development environments, testing in QA, stress testing in the performance environment, and pushing to production should be a single, connected, automated pipeline. This automation is the topic of our next section on continuous delivery.

---

Equivalence ➤ Development = QA = Stress = Production

---

# Continuous Delivery

Achieving continuous delivery is a more demanding goal compared to continuous integration. The ability to create a production-ready application from its source code at the proverbial "push of a button"—while automatically running through build, test, and certification—requires process rigor. This section focuses on automated techniques to push newer version of applications to production with little or no downtime and business disruption.

## Infrastructure as Code

Essential characteristics of microservices—scalability, elasticity, and upgradability—increase instances of instance management. Typical scenarios include 1) creating new instances handle more load, 2) destroying inactive ones when load decreases, 3) setting up new sets to roll-out new versions, 4) and destroying and reclaiming old instance sets. The creation and destruction of instances require changes to infrastructure—networking, monitoring, load balancing, supporting services, and inter-service connectivity.

The dynamic and transient nature of the cloud requires us *to employ automation to gain control and achieve efficiency*. Every step needed to bring up a microservice and to make it functional needs to be automated. Every step required to shut a microservice down and tear down its resources needs to be scripted. It is not only needed for efficiency but also to keep the cost of running microservices down by reclaiming unused resources.

It is vital to consider the **entire infrastructure as code** (IaC): load balancers, container orchestration, databases and datastores, messaging, and anything else the microservice uses. IaC allows *standardization* of infrastructure and equivalence of production and non-production environments. It is also *cost-effective*, as ecosystems are built for use, kept running till needed, and destroyed when no longer required.

## Delivery Techniques

In the era of monoliths, there were many delivery techniques; however, all were variations of *big-bang release with a rollback plan*. A sample outline of the technique was as follows: 1) identify a "downtime" with business, when the users of the system were least affected; 2) line up maximum number of deliverables that can be forced to production in that window; 3) create a rollout and rollback plan and execute it.

## THE DEPLOYMENT STORY OF A MONOLITH

We entered a window of opportunity set aside for release, and we spent nerve wracking hours firefighting in war rooms. Oftentimes, we emerged at the other end of the downtime window bloody faced, but with a brand-new version of software running, champagne, and bouquets. On a few occasions, we rolled back to where we began, restoring business to old versions, all the efforts futile. Sometimes the gods of software would punish us by landing in purgatory hell, where we exhaust our downtime timer but still have the system in shambles. Gallantry and heroism would ensue, finally fixing the system and restoring original operations. Fortunately, these gallants would be showered with corporate medals.

With the modernization of software engineering and agile methods, we discovered new ways to deliver software. One popular technique was *blue-green deployment,* where a new environment (green) runs the next version of the application that has breaking changes. The old version (blue) continues to take traffic. At some point, we start rerouting requests from blue to green, until all traffic points to green. Once the green environment is successfully in place, the old version is retired. Variations to this technique exists, where traffic gets mirrored to both blue and green, and at some specific point, green becomes the master. Blue continues to take requests for ease of rollback. Once the green environment is certified stable, blue environment is retired. This was considered a breakthrough idea, and shower of praises ensued. However, *this was only marginally better* from our earlier approach. In blue-green technique, we had all the same problems as the original, the only thing we solved was the percentage of users affected. If our application ran on two servers, we affected half the user population by redirecting them to new servers. Failure there often resulted in requiring heroics again, in reverting the affected half.

Unfortunately, continuous delivery eliminates such heroics and cancels all gallantry awards. Microservices architecture, along with continuous software engineering, demonstrates that such heroics are unnecessary and completely avoidable. Microservices architecture fosters, enables, and encourages rapid change and deployment of systems. With the right traffic control tools, engineers *pilot new features in production*! An excellent and popular way to *test new features in production* is via a *dark launch,* wherein the new feature is running in a listen-only mode and is not affecting the outcome. A dark-launch enables test-and-learn, where we test the newer version of application without disrupting the customers. Another popular approach is roll out the new feature to a small segment of users as *canary* deployment. The canary population is selected either based on some characteristics, of user traffic, or simply based on a random percentage of traffic. Canary deployments are targeted to a very small percentage of user base (often a selected subset) as a precursor to a complete roll-out. Techniques such as dark launches and canary deployments offer a minimally invasive method of pushing changes to production. There are many tools on the cloud that enable us to do dark launches and canary deployments using techniques such as traffic mirroring, traffic shaping, etc. We will look at these techniques in detail further ahead in the book.

# DevSecOps

Akin to the Infrastructure-as-Code concept embraced by the engineering community, the idea of Security-as-Code has parallelly emerged. It was common for security to be an afterthought, possibly bolted on at the end of the development life cycle. Unfortunately, security processes in enterprises have been limited to filing some archaic security forms in "good faith." Information gathered for security improvements was restricted to data points discovered in past audits. An automated enterprise might collate scans and reports at the end of the development life cycle, and before deployment. Regrettably, *such data only surface vulnerabilities when present, and never guarantees an absence of weaknesses*. DevSecOps is a concept that attempts to address precisely this: security embedded into the engineering team that develops and manages operations. DevSecOps teams automate security controls, use security metrics to harden code, and own security of their system (Myrbakken & Colomo-Palacios, 2017).

DevSecOps is a field in infancy, with a great deal of thinking underway. Enterprises are beginning to make every team a DevSecOps team, by adding a security engineer along with an operations engineer into development teams. DevSecOps practice forces the inclusion of security into the development life cycle. The core concept is that security requirements arise at every step of development.

- **Code safety checked at compile time**: Using techniques such as *data-flow analysis* and *taint analysis* begins security checks early in the life cycle. These techniques trace data as it flows through the system, from every source to every sink, against potential vulnerabilities.

- **Unit and integration tests that verify security**: Unit tests and integration tests targeted at exploiting vulnerabilities ensure regressive testing against security-related errors.

- **Red teams/drills are needed** (Myrbakken & Colomo-Palacios, 2017): Red team drills are exercises with specific predefined goals that simulate how potential threats might attempt to exploit vulnerabilities. Automating the setup, creating a library of attack tools, and constantly updating these tools allow continuous security checks even after deployment.

- **Binaries are verified against known list threats and exploits**: There are many tools to statically check binaries engaged in the build process against known errors.

- **The attack surface is analyzed and reduced**: It is essential to continually analyze the attack surface of the application, in terms of API endpoints, external services, and classified/sensitive data (and involved code).

- **The system is subjected to random conditions**. The abstract nature of software makes it impossible to predict all possible scenarios it will face. Randomness leading to failures in systems is so common, that it might be necessary to simulate random failures. Chaos engineering[1], fuzz testing[2], exploratory testing[3] are all invaluable techniques to ensure resiliency, especially in a cloud environment.

We touched upon a small subset of aspects regarding microservices security. The engineering teams need to be aware of a large body of security principles and techniques when building microservices. The chapter Securing Microservices on Cloud addresses the various security aspects of cloud-based microservices explicitly.

---

[1]Chaos engineering is the testing of a system by simulating chaos. Netflix's Simian Army project is a perfect example of chaos engineering. Simian army has a set of tools that subject systems to random failures, such as loss of node, loss of network connection, introduction of artificial delays in communication, loss of a cluster of servers, etc.,

[2]Fuzz testing or fuzzing is a blackbox testing technique, where a system is fed random inputs and checked for failures.

[3]Exploratory testing is out-of-the-box testing technique, which relies on the tester's skills to devise test cases that will find scenarios leading to failures.

# Changes to Energence

Energence now has the overall view of process changes it needs to bring in for a successful microservices architecture. Few enterprise-wide changes are needed to the *enterprise structure, general software development process*, and the *IT setup*. The software development groups could get segregated into departments that align with the overall enterprise hierarchy. Four departments within software development organizations partner with the four verticals of Energence—Planning, Manufacturing, Distribution, and Portal.

Changes to promote a continuous software engineering process across all departments, if not already present, are the next important steps. Individual departments should invest in automating the entire process of managing environments. They should set up their team structure to enable the process, which means changing the skill set of teams. Development teams should have knowledge and skill to build software, test it, certify it, stress test it, script environments to run it, and follow the continuous software engineering process from development to production. It is important to note that these continuous processes apply to the life cycle of every individual microservice.

The IT operations, a completely independent department that maintains all infrastructure requirements, should get matrixed into individual teams. Other enterprises might have business architecture teams and QA departments, which should integrate into development teams. It is valuable to retain the departments, and only comingle engineers into team structures. Maintaining departments restricts technology proliferation, enables standardization of tools and processes, and cross-pollinates ideas and techniques between development teams.

Energence has now prepared itself for a journey to the cloud—it has broken down its monoliths, identified issues in microservices architecture, found ways to overcome those challenges, and has enabled a continuous software engineering process. The next step is cloudification—the process taking this architecture, software process, and technical solutions to the cloud.

# Summary

The underlying theme of process changes is automation, and the golden rule is any process that is manually executed more than thrice is a candidate for automation. Engineers responsible for infrastructure and QA should change their mindsets from being eager-on-the-job-to-fix-failures-immediately to being lazy-to-not-change-anything-except-correcting-an-automated-process. Every request to change a process should result in a code that implements the steps. This process of continuous software engineering, with emphasis on frequent and automated building and delivery of software, is paramount for microservices architecture. Building such processes should keep in mind standardization, reusability, and elasticity. These factors become essential with larger codebases, increased release frequency, and polyglotism. The cloud brings about an additional set of problems, due to its temporal nature and its inherent opacity of infrastructure. The importance of continuous software engineering increases when enterprises adopt modern development paradigms. For these enterprises, it is mandatory to implement DevOps and DevSecOps models.

## Points to Ponder

1. Is it possible to automate every process of operations and support? Are there any exceptions?

2. How do we balance automation effort with release urgency?

3. What are the differences between performance testing monoliths vs. performance testing microservices?

4. How can we automate the many concepts of security into code?

## Further Related Reading

**Continuous Delivery** by *Jez Humble and David Farley* (Humble & Farley, 2010).
   **The DevOps Handbook** by *Gene Kim et al.* (Kim, Humble, Debois, & Willis, 2016).

# CHAPTER 6

# Cloudification: Strategy

*"The Guide says there is an art to flying", said Ford, "or rather a knack. The knack lies in learning how to throw yourself at the ground and miss."*

—Douglas Adams, *Life, the Universe and Everything* (1982)

No conversation about transformation to a microservices-based architecture is complete without discussing cloud computing. In the previous chapters, we discussed the various advantages of moving to a microservices-based architecture. We observed the ease of change to software. We noticed the autonomy of the individual software pieces and engineers dealing with the parts. We noted the benefits of isolation—resilience, polyglot, and localization of errors—among many others. We learned about the capability to scale and shrink on demand. However, to exploit all these benefits and more, to harness the real power of microservices, we need to let microservices fly on the cloud.

Cloud computing is a revolutionary topic that has drawn an enormous amount of attention and investment. It has transformed the way enterprises plan, work, change, adapt, and mature. Cloud also opens up new avenues, in technology and business alike. *Cloud computing is an on-demand computing infrastructure service that is Internet-based, rented when required, and maintained by a third party.* The cloud is a direct descendant of server rentals, online platforms, and mainframes.

NIST defines the five essential characteristics of cloud as *on-demand self-service, broad network access, resource pooling, rapid elasticity, and measured service* (NIST, SP, 2012). All CSPs (cloud service providers) offer these fundamental capabilities. They allow acquiring resources programmatically, using a combination of shell scripts, REST calls, or a web console. CSPs run a massive communication infrastructure, with the major players setting up or renting dedicated cables.[1] The scale of operations of a CSP is enormous. Consider

---

[1] **Marea** by Microsoft & Facebook; **Havfrue**, **HK-G**, and **Curie** by Google; **Hawiki** by AWS

C. Rajasekharaiah, *Cloud-Based Microservices*, https://doi.org/10.1007/978-1-4842-6564-2_6

AWS. In 2020, it had nearly 80 data centers connected with tens of thousand miles of fiber optic and subsea cable backbone, capable of terabits of information flow. Though accurate details are not available, it is estimated that every data center is equipped with tens to hundreds of thousands of storage and compute servers—each storage server capable of storing more than 10PB of data and each compute server with 16-64 cores[2]. CSPs build capabilities to efficiently and rapidly free up unused/unsubscribed resources, return them to the pool, and reassign as demand arises. Most CSPs meter their services in various aspects, to enable accurate billing for usage.

# The Allure of the Cloud

Cloud computing is a revolutionary topic that has drawn an enormous amount of attention and investment. Gartner forecasts public cloud-based revenues of $250B in 2020 alone, growing at 15%–20% every year (Gartner, 2020). What makes the cloud so attractive? Cloud, at the most basic form of definition, is "not my server." It is the compute, connectivity, and storage that is *not permanently owned by the user*. This idea is very similar to rental services: akin to renting chairs and tables, ordering catering services, and hiring a DJ for a party. You will not own the seating equipment, not permanently employ the DJ, and not own catering service—merely for a party. This simplicity of the "pay-for-what-you-use" concept is ubiquitously appealing—from making cloud incredibly attractive to helping many countries maintain lean governments.

Many advantages attract enterprises to move their software operations to the cloud. Broadly, we can group advantages into three facets—financial gains, new business opportunities, and technological benefits. There are ***financial gains*** that result from lowering expenditure and reducing IT budgets. There are new ***business opportunities*** avenues that present themselves when enterprises move to the cloud. The IT overheads of enterprises reduce further due to many ***technological benefits*** of running in the cloud.

## Financial Gains of Moving to Cloud

**Consider the seasonal and cyclical nature of many businesses**: Many businesses go through predictable patterns, in terms of crests and troughs, in business volumes. These variations are primarily associated with seasonality—many seasonal industries make the bulk of their profits in short windows of the year. The perfect examples are vacation and

---

[2]stands for "AWS re:Invent 2016: Tuesday Night Live with James Hamilton"

retail industries, which see increased traffic on their systems during holidays. Similarly, some sectors are cyclical, having their volumes ebb and flow with business cycles. Many external factors contribute to their business volumes, almost all of the factors associated with the economy. Such industries would prefer to have a more substantial infrastructure when their volume peaks and shrink when the volumes die down. Cloud provides this very feature, by allowing businesses to expand and shrink their compute and operations footprint—immediately, and when required. The cloud is even better suited for bursty traffic patterns, as the infrastructure can be automated to scale up or down.

**Pay only for what you use**: Many upcoming businesses, primarily startups and small businesses, do not possess the capital funds to build large enough infrastructure to run their business and grow it as their business expands. These types of companies prefer to pay for what they use. Cloud offers many services where usage alone drives billing. Dependence on the cloud has proven critical for success in successful new generation companies—such as Uber, Airbnb, and Netflix—which are cloud-native companies.

**Consider the opportunity costs, TCO (total cost of ownership), and flexible spending** (Kepes, 2011): Opportunity costs are intangible: they are the costs of abandoned efforts, lost time, or any other causes of concern that taxes an enterprise. Procurement, management, and maintenance of an enterprise's infrastructure is an overhead that does not add immediate business value. Many companies consider themselves technology-first companies, but end up having to bear the burden of having large IT departments. Cloud allows these enterprises to outsource the entire IT department and focus on software development to cater to their businesses. The year 2020 in pandemic has demonstrated that enterprises that are not cash-rich easily crumble when their business shrinks and incomes dry. A model of op-ex allows these businesses to continue running in a slim-down version, instead of massive cap-ex infrastructure acquisitions. These massive infrastructures that run business solutions have a very high total cost of ownership, which is not instantly evident. There is an immense operating cost involved, ranging from utility charges such as power bills to rent/lease of floor space to a wide variety of personnel employed—IT staff, electrical and electronics engineers, and security staff. Transition to the cloud immediately unburdens the enterprise from such financial commitments.

Enterprises such as Energence benefit financially from moving to cloud: they can minimize IT expenditure, rent infrastructure as and when needed, and focus on immediate business-focused spending.

# Business Opportunities in Moving to Cloud

**Global consumer bases**: It is not uncommon for most businesses to court consumers worldwide—enterprises eye foreign clientele, which allows tapping into new opportunities. The cloud offers a great way of catering to such a user base. Most CSPs have a global presence, offering the same set of services across the globe.

**Experimentation and research**: Every business requires a significant amount of research and experimentation not only to prosper but to stay relevant. Enterprises have to become data-driven; they need deep analytics of data to discover underlying patterns in their business models, find new business models and opportunities, and make informed decisions. This requirement is evident in the rampant growth of data science, several implementations of machine learning, and the success of neural nets in the industry. Such exercises need banks of computational power, which were only available for large businesses that could afford such investments. Now, with the ability to rent such infrastructure from a CSP only when needed, every small business has access to the same potential to experiment and research.

**Mobility, connectivity, and collaboration**: Cloud offers mobility for employees and customers, thus creating better collaboration opportunities. CSPs provide better connectivity options, allowing employees to access data in a secure way using open standard tools and technology.

**Guaranteed service-level agreements (SLAs)**: SLAs are contractual agreements between providers and subscribers, which ensure a minimum level of service is maintained. All CSP services promise contractually enforceable SLAs and ways to measure the service levels. Failure to meet the guaranteed service levels results in penalties for CSPs. Service levels cover uptimes, performance/throughput, privacy, and failure rates. For instance, many of CSP's services are guaranteed 99.95% to 99.999% uptimes—which respectively translates to downtime of no more 4.5 hours/year to no more than 5 minutes/year. Such availability is far higher than enterprises that own their own data center, or even two/three data centers. The scale offered here is in dozens of data centers, distributed geographically. Also, any outage more than that results in reparations to customers for their business losses—something not applicable to owned infrastructure.

# Technological Gains of Moving to Cloud

**Access to a practically unlimited pool of resources**—storage, compute, and network. Though nothing is infinite, the CSPs provide large enough room to meet the most massive infrastructure requirement of any enterprise. Enterprises do not have to worry about planning for their infrastructure and concerning themselves about how the latest innovations in technology make their current hardware obsolete.

**Ease of upgrades**: Enterprises have large IT teams that maintain operating systems and software. These teams patch, upgrade, and reinstall software necessary for running the enterprise. Along with software, IT teams are often responsible for maintaining hardware as well. When enterprises transition to the cloud, all these responsibilities shift to the CSP. Enterprises outsource the infrastructure and focus mainly on business aspects.

**Quick development cycles because of programmable infrastructure**: All of the services offered on the cloud are built for programmatic control. The goal is that a series of programs can represent the entire infrastructure of a company! This capability of automation means the virtual machines, databases, datastores, storage, and any other requirement of an environment gets created when needed. A new development environment can be created and torn down almost instantaneously, to the required specification. Such a capability reduces the traditional process burden engineers face in on-prem setup.

**Localized servers offer better performance**: Services can be set up close to consumers' locality, in addition to a global presence. Within a specific region—Americas, Asia, Europe, and Australia—many localized data centers are available to run an enterprise's software solution. Locality reduces the time delay in using services, decreases global chatter, and restricts traffic flow to a small regional footprint.

---

It is easy for enterprises to see the benefits of moving to the cloud—pay-per-use, global reach, and access to the latest technology.

---

# Prerequisites to a Cloud Journey

The journey to the cloud requires us to implement new concepts and ideas to reach our destination. Changes are necessary for every aspect of software engineering, from inception to rollout. The software development process requires automation at every step possible. This ask brings forth the massively useful concept of CSE—continuous software engineering. CSE is the ability to programmatically control the life cycles of microservices. Without this ability, we fail in running microservices efficiently at scale in the cloud. We need this ability to

- Bundle applications and environment into a single cohesive unit

- Programmatically wire microservices together, on-demand

- Grow and shrink microservices resource usage and space

- Monitor and manage microservices for failures and performance issues

- Leverage deployment strategies such as failover, blue-green deployments, and canary deployment

Several cloud concepts require acquiring new knowledge and learning new techniques, the infrastructure being of paramount importance. Infrastructure options necessary for running infrastructure fall into four categories: *connectivity*, *compute*, *storage*, and *integration*. Connectivity is required to expose microservices to the external world (partners, consumers) and communicate with internal consumers (including cloud and on-prem). Most compute options on cloud fall into four categories: VMs (IaaS), container orchestration (iCaaS), application platforms (PaaS), and serverless computing (FaaS). The storage of microservices data varies based on need. Available options include databases, data warehouses, big datastores, temporary datastores such as caches, block storage, and long-term storage. Integration options include messaging, API gateways, and load balancers that allow communication between microservices. The offered alternatives are plenty, and cater to almost all business use cases.

# Overall Setup for Microservices in Cloud

The architecture team of Energence now needs to identify a CSP and cloud services required to run their software solutions. Figure 6-1 depicts a typical cloud solution setup and should provide a context of microservices. Usually, when an enterprise adopts a cloud, its software development organizations need to host services and run solutions on the cloud. We discussed four basic infrastructure needs to host microservices architecture successfully. We need

1. **Connectivity to the cloud** from on-prem, customers, and partners. Connectivity needs to be secure, requiring firewalls, DDOS resilience, IAM. Also, we need to ingest traffic through load balancers for synchronous services, or through some messaging middleware for asynchronous communication.

2. **Resources to build and host solutions**. Our CI/CD pipelines need a way to provision VMs or orchestration of containers on the cloud programmatically. Enterprises in specific domains (IOT/Blockchain) might need domain-specific computing solutions.

3. **Databases** (SQLDB/NoSQL DB/key-value-store/doc-store/ledger) to persist the state of business. Also, special-purpose databases and datastores of various speeds. We need cache as a service for quick access. We will need tape-based datastores for long-term cheap storage. Big data services for reporting, deep analytics, ML and other requirements.

4. **Integration technology**, or ways to integrate between various microservices and between the system of microservices and the world.

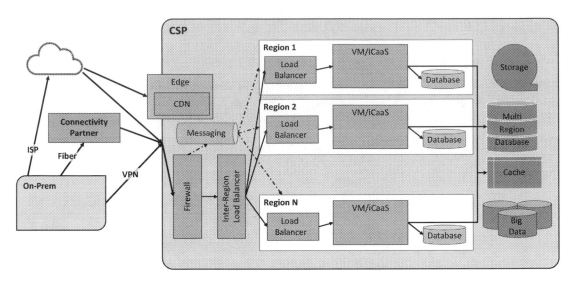

***Figure 6-1.***  *Typical overview of a cloud platform*

# Networking and Connectivity

Setting up networks and establishing connectivity are critical (and usually the first) initiatives in cloud transformation. The connectivity includes communication with consumers, business partners, and on-prem. Very often, this is the very first step in the journey to the cloud. Enterprises that have data centers need to connect with the cloud service provider securely, effectively, and efficiently. Enterprises that are born on the cloud also have some infrastructure outside of the cloud—office spaces, stores, on-site equipment, to name a few. All of these assets need to talk to the CSP's infrastructure.

For traffic ingress—the flow of traffic into the cloud from external networks—CSPs set up edge points-of-presence facilities. These facilities offer very few services, are usually used to render static content, or act as an entry point into their high-speed networking backbone. For enterprises that do not want to be on the public network— for reasons such as security and availability—CSPs offer VPN connectivity to their data centers. For enterprises that need high-bandwidth, low-latency connectivity (and have the cash to spare), the solution is a fiber-optic connection to CSP's network. Connectivity partner companies offer such a form of direct connectivity.

Once you have set up connectivity to the cloud, you would need additional services such as DNS, load balancers, and CDNs (content-delivery-networks).

**DNS Service**: Once on the cloud, you need a DNS server with the ability to resolve DNS names to VMs, containers, or other computing resources' IP addresses.

**CDN**: Also important is the ability to deliver content such as videos, static data, API from edge locations.

**DDOS Protection and Firewalls**: All providers have products in the space of firewalls and security against threats such as DDOS attacks.

**Load Balancers**: When enterprises move to cloud, there is a need for balancing traffic loads on horizontally scalable and potentially geographically distributed solution infrastructure. Here, it is essential to know that CSPs offer products in two flavors: a global/multi-region load balancer that can route traffic across all regions and a regional load balancer. Global load balancers tend to be more expensive than the regional load balancers. Most CSPs provide this option as a variation as DNS based traffic balancer. In the chapter, more discussions on load balancers are further ahead in the book, in the "Securing Microservices on Cloud" chapter.

# Regions and Zones

CSPs manage their global networks as an aggregate of many *regions*, each region serving a geographical area. Regions are collections of multiple closely located *zones—physically autonomous data centers*. A data center is considered an availability zone when it is completely isolated from others; for instance, it has independent power, network connectivity, and cooling. Complete isolation ensures high availability, reducing the chance of multiple zones failing simultaneously. Zones belonging to a single region reside within the same county or city, sometimes on different floors of the same physical building. Due to the proximity of zones, CSPs can provide a high level of consistency across zones in the same region. When hosting solutions on the cloud, it is crucial to make clear choices on the services based on need.

*Zonal cloud services are available in a single zone*, which are the least expensive option. However, loss of a zone results in a total loss of availability. Regional services are resources that get replicated across many/all zones of the region. *Regional cloud services offer a higher level of availability*, often to three-and-a-half to four nines.

It is essential to understand the concept of an availability zone, region, and multi-region classification of resources. This classification allows development teams to make the right choice to balance availability and cost.

A complete failure of a region is rare; however, it might not be a tolerable option for services that require incredibly high uptime. Ecommerce web fronts are an excellent example, as loss of a region means loss of revenue and customer dissatisfaction. For best results, such applications should utilize global or multi-region resources, but be warned—applications with multi-region or global resources are tough to architect and manage, especially when the applications need to maintain state.

Architects should thoroughly evaluate CSP services before choosing between regional and global resources. One of the prominent challenges is that *not all CSP services are global resources*. When an architecture involves regional resources with global resources, systems should manage this disparity intelligently. CSPs might have several restrictions on resources as well. Based on the CSP, resources need a closer inspection from the perspective of virtual private networks spans, load balancer setups, regional replicas of global resources. We will explore some of these further in the book, in the chapter "Securing Microservices on Cloud."

As of writing this book (mid 2020), AWS had a total of 24 regions—7 regions in North America, 8 regions in Europe/the Middle East/Africa, 6 regions in the Asia Pacific, and 1 region in South America. GCP had a total of 24 regions as well—8 in North America, 6 in Europe, 9 in the Asia Pacific, and 1 in South America. Azure has the most extensive footprint with 50+ regions—15 regions in North America, 14 in Europe, 20 in the Asia Pacific, 2 in Africa, and 1 in South America. These statistics make the seriousness of the cloud computing future evident.

# Compute

Microservices need computational infrastructure to run. Most enterprises might have already graduated away from physical hardware running their systems to either virtual machines (VMs) or containers. CSPs provide services to *create and run VMs on cloud (IaaS)*, or *a way to manage containers (iCaaS)*.

VMs are synthetic machines simulated on an underlying system (host system) by a software, firmware, or hardware called *the hypervisor*. Comparatively, containers can be loosely termed as emulations of a machine on a host system. We discuss these topics in detail in the next chapter.

**VMs and other compute options**: Most CSPs offer VMs as a core service. Users can create, start, stop, or destroy VMs programmatically. These VMs can be created from templates or created by code. CSPs also allow VMs to get stored as images on storage. For managing containers, CSPs tend to differ in how they offer the capability. Usually, we can expect three flavors: *a proprietary implementation of iCaaS*, or a *standard container management software* (usually Kubernetes) as a service, or *PaaS-like elastic container management*. CSPs also offer bare-metals, servers that directly map to physical servers.

**Application servers as PaaS**: Apart from developing applications in open source frameworks, it is also possible to run applications on CSPs' custom application servers. This PaaS approach, though potentially locks an enterprise to a vendor, frees architects from planning for non-functional aspects such as scalability and HA. This is a cost-effective (even free for basic and limited use) way to build and run applications on the cloud.

**FaaS/Serverless**: CSPs provide FaaS (function as a service, or more commonly known as serverless computing), where service calls or temporal events trigger programs. The code is deployed and run only upon request and is usually mandated to be time-bound. This option gains popularity because of the "micro-billing" advantage: application incurs cost only when used—no continuous billing.

# Integration

Apart from setting up servers to run the software and leverage other services of CSP, there are a few integration software required to allow communication and connectivity between microservices. For choreography-based integrations, we would need messaging services. For orchestration types of integrations, and to enable APIs and REST endpoints of microservices to become accessible to the external systems, we need a gateway for managing clients.

> **For Messaging**: Orchestrated systems require asynchronous communication between applications. On the cloud, there are two options: (1) using open source queuing products or (2) provider-native messaging middleware options. Option 1 is preferable; however, choices for the first option tend to be in the form of service by third-party vendors. Option 2 potentially creates vendor lock-in, along with feature limitations.

> **API Gateways**: Apart from asynchronous communication, microservices need to manage API contracts of various services. Usually, CSPs offer assorted options ranging from web proxy to a true API gateway. Most offerings support standard specifications such as OpenAPI.

# Databases and Traditional Datastores

All applications need to maintain state, either with or without transactional capabilities. Traditionally, on-prem, architects have resorted to either commercial RDBMSs or open source RDBMSs for dense, relational datastores. Also popular are NoSQL databases: columnar, or document stores, or key-value stores.

CSPs offer traditional open source databases as service; however, most of these database options tend to be region-bound. Some CSPs provide closed source transactional databases that are capable of having multiple masters across regions. Few CSPs offer commercial databases as a service, with a BYOL (bring-your-own-license) model. Closed source databases are tricky to choose from, as every CSP has its "secret sauce" of a solution. For instance, there are distributed-and-partially-SQL-compliant multi-region transactional database options available from CSPs. Apart from closed source solutions, a few vendors provide managed open source options; these open-source databases are distributed, transactional, and real RDBMSs.

For applications using NoSQL stores, CSPs offer many variations of distributed NoSQL stores, with high throughput and global distribution of data. Most CSP solutions are variants of document databases, applicable for use cases involving semi-structured data, but needing all the features of a traditional RDBMS.

# Special-Purpose Datastores

Apart from the regular run-of-the-mill databases, enterprises have requirements to store particular types of data. Enterprises might also deal with blockchains, where they need specialized datastores to handle relevant data. Apart from the special types of data, there is a need for storing temporary data for fast access. Various cache solutions have already made their way to many architectures. Similarly, there is a need to store large amounts of data, possibly historical copies of transactional data, for reporting, machine learning, and other analytical needs. When microservices of a domain need to access a copy of another domain's data, they need caches for fast access and large datastores for analytics. Apart from these types of datastores needed for transactions and analytics, there is the need for traditional disk-based storage needs—file-stores, mapped network drives, and equivalent of traditional tape backups.

> **Special-purpose databases**: Apart from regular general-purpose databases, applications catering to various business domains have needs for specific types of databases. Top on this list is the class of *time-series databases*. Microservices might deal with time-series data, where *data is simply snapshots of data taken at regular time intervals*. Time-series databases, used to store large volumes of data indexed by time, are offered as a service by a few CSPs, though not all. Another specific datastore available as PaaS is the *blockchain ledger*. A blockchain ledger is a centralized cryptographical database for immutably storing transactions. Even fewer CSPs offer a centralized ledger. Though not entirely accepted by the blockchain community, it is an option for those who are considering blockchain and are looking for options other than Hyperledger or Ethereum.

**Caching solutions**: Traditionally, solutions that require fast data access have multiple levels of cache. For all caching needs private to an application or shared/distributed, in-memory key-value stores such as Redis are used on-prem. Most CSPs have PaaS offerings of Redis. Caching solutions are a key ingredient in microservices architecture, enabling services to access data quickly—thereby improving performance.

**Data warehousing and big datastores**: Typically, enterprises warehouse historical data for many reasons—legal compliance, reporting, insights, analytics, and machine learning, to name a few. Enterprises on-prem employ Hadoop or any of the data warehouse systems for data warehouses or lakes. CSPs offer data warehousing PaaS, columnar datastores that offer parallel query execution with the ability to directly query data in bulk storage. The only difference across CSPs is whether charges are based on pre-allocated compute power, or on-demand compute credits (costs-per-query).

**Bulk storage**: Bulk-storage services enable enterprises to store bulk data cheaply. CSPs offer storage options that are available in various classes, based on retrieval times and frequencies.

We comprehensively examine datastores further ahead in the book, in the 'Core Cloud Concepts – Storage' chapter.

# Cost Analysis

Cost is an important factor when moving microservices to the cloud. A careful analysis of the various cost factors before mapping a virtual architecture to services available on CSPs is essential. Apart from pricing, we need to understand how billing can be set up and managed—this is especially useful for enterprises like Energence where its different organizations have various levels and cycles of funding and need to maintain it separately.

# Billing

Most CSPs allow customers to separate the billing into *accounts*. This type of segregation enables enterprises to compartmentalize their expenditure. Attaching accounts to the organizations or departments enables them to be self-managed. CSPs also make it possible to connect security controls and connectivity separation. Where CSPs cannot provide a logical equivalent to accounts, enterprises need to organize their billing differently. Various techniques are possible, such as tagging every resource to separate billing. Such tags have to get applied *programmatically* through scripts that build the environment to ensure accuracy. Billing can get very complicated based on the complexity of the enterprises' internals.

---

It is also important to note that a hierarchical setup of accounts within an enterprise, with each account representing an organization within the enterprise, provides a greater drive of conformance and standards. For instance, certain assets—such as VM images, libraries, static content—can be shared across the enterprise, promoting reuse and instituting standardization.

---

An important aspect is the necessity to set usage limits, commonly termed *quotas*. Quotas play a vital role in capping usages, hence protecting enterprises from runaway spending in instances such as breaches, malintent, or even programming errors. Most CSPs allow enterprises to place restrictions on the amount of compute instances, subscription counts, and service usage.

---

GCP and Azure provide controls to segregate billing at department levels. On Azure, an enterprise can hierarchically divide their billing into multiple levels—*departments*, *accounts*, *subscriptions*, and *resource groups*. Resource groups of Azure are simply a group of CSP's resources, and a *resource* is a generic name for any of Azure's IaaS, PaaS, or FaaS offerings. In GCP, enterprises can compartmentalize their billing into *folders* and further subdivide them into *projects*. Projects can be group services in different regions and can have separate access controls. In AWS, resources can get grouped into a three-level hierarchy. The top-level is an 'organization,' which can have 'organizational units'; organization units, in turn, can have 'accounts.'

---

# Cost Factors

Though the price tag of running in the cloud depends on various aspects, they can be classified broadly as "*hard*" and "*soft*" factors. Hard factors are fundamental differentiators, and soft ones are negotiable aspects. For instance, *service dependability is a hard factor that affects prices*. Services offering higher reliability, availability, and performance cost more than lower ones. Same with *service usage*—higher usage means bigger bills.

Similarly, reserved and dedicated resources cost more than shared or on-demand resources. Soft factors are flexible aspects of billing. They vary based on *aspects such as an enterprise's partnership with a CSP, its buying power, and opportunity factors*. CSPs tend to offer lower rates to strategic partners, and for enterprises that they see a potential of growth in usage. There are opportunities when services are available at a lower price for a limited amount of time or availability, such as auctions and promotions. CSPs frequently auction their services at lower prices; CSPs gain in auctions by limiting the time required in negotiations and sales conversations, and users get lower prices. CSPs could also run promotions on services for varying reasons—minimizing stock levels, sales-boost efforts, or even some of CSP's internal financial plans.

Architects of enterprises migrating to the cloud need to choose between various options *based on hard factors*. Overrides or changes based on soft factors—based on the enterprise's vision, guidelines, and partnerships—should be added later. However, there are acceptable overrides and unacceptable ones. For instance, if Energence chooses not to have vendor lock-ins, the choices available from CSP's service options change from if Energence wants to be native to a single CSP. Such a compromise might be acceptable override from an enterprise guideline. An example of an unacceptable override is choosing a CSP's service because of short-term incentives, discounts, or sales pitches.

---

## STAYING CLOUD-NEUTRAL

When on the cloud, it is sensible to choose cloud-neutral options over a CSP's proprietary service where possible. Here is a quote from Richard Stallman speaking to The Guardian on how CSPs make PaaS and SaaS solutions appear enticing with the promise of speed-to-market, simplified-infrastructure, low total-cost-of-ownership. This quote is more than 12 years old in 2020, but still rings true.

*It's stupidity. It's worse than stupidity: it's a marketing hype campaign. Somebody is saying this is inevitable — and whenever you hear somebody saying that, it's very likely to be a set of businesses campaigning to make it true.*

Engineering teams should plan for multi-cloud architectures, however infeasible it may appear. Even if a development team stays with CSP, CSPs routinely discontinue services creating efforts and deadlines they do not need. Staying cloud-neutral does not mean that the enterprise's footprint on the cloud is only IaaS. Instead, it means that as we progress from considering IaaS to iCaaS to FaaS to PaaS, the diligence needed to adopt increases.

Architects need to be thorough in validating options early in the migration. Table 6-1 shows a few questions that are essential in choosing CSP's services and sample questions to be asked.

***Table 6-1.*** *Factors and Reasons for Capturing Metrics*

| Factors | Questions about CSP's Service Offering |
| --- | --- |
| *Performance levels needed* | Does my service really need 99.99% availability? Does it have bursty traffic or is the traffic pattern predictable? |
| *Cost of running* | Can my service run on a temporary resource? How long in a day/month/year does my service run? |
| *Future-proofing* | Is the cloud service (PaaS/SaaS) viable in the long term? At what point—usage or performance requirement or SLA—does an option become expensive or inapplicable? |
| *Industry trends* | Is the cloud service offering used widely in the industry? Are there skilled engineers available? Is a service offered compatible with my technical stack? |

# Energence on Cloud

Now that we have walked through the cloud setup, we can attempt to picture Energence's business setup on the cloud. The key takeaways

1.  We have to separate the various departments into their accounts. The Manufacturing department needs separate billing account, and so will the Distribution department, Forecasting department, and Portals (Figure 6-2).

2.  Energence has most of its users in the East and West coast. So, Energence can start with two regions of the CSP—East and West regions.

3.  As Energence expands its business and becomes a global company with a presence in Europe, Asia, and Australia, it can host applications in those regions. Presence in a region close to customers improves response speeds and avoids long haul of data (Figure 6-3).

4.  Applications not tied to a locality can run in the East (or West) region only, others in two regions. Forecasting applications can run in only one, whereas others in two (Figure 6-4).

5.  The selection of datastore depends on the domain. Forecasting applications might have a severe need for big data to do deep analytics. Portals might need multi-region databases.

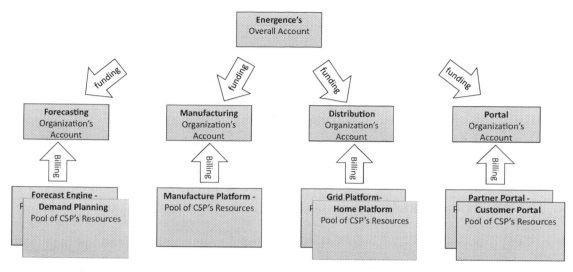

***Figure 6-2.*** *Depiction of a sample view of funding and CSP's billing model for Energence*

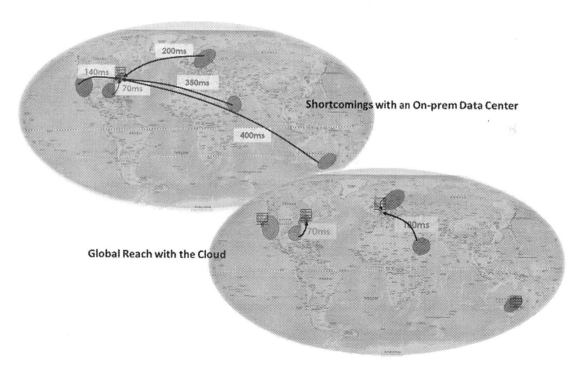

***Figure 6-3.*** *Diagram showing the advantages of hosting on a CSP, where multiple data centers decrease overall service latency*

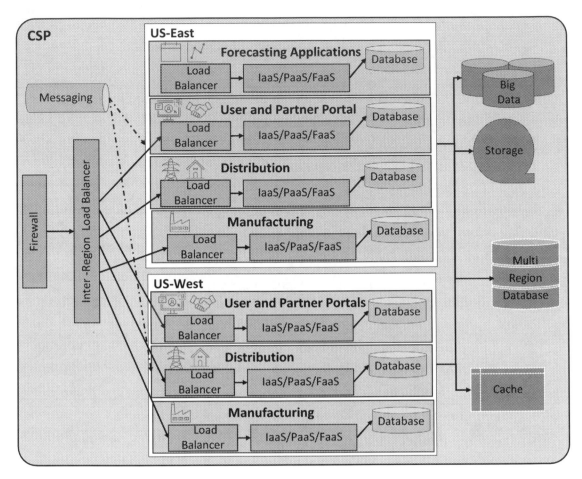

***Figure 6-4.*** *Energence's potential cloud footprint*

Now that we have visualized how Energence will set up their cloud presence, the next step is to dive into the details of implementation. In the next chapter, we discuss the compute framework needed in detail. We look at various ways to run the microservices architecture, with detailed analysis on how to leverage CSPs IaaS, iCaaS, and FaaS services to run these applications. We will also discuss the available messaging options.

Following the chapter on computation options, we will spend a chapter on various datastores. We discuss DBaaS, cache stores, big datastores, and file stores needed to run microservices architecture. Finally, we wrap up with how to secure this infrastructure on the cloud. The discussion focuses on setting up for global availability, securing all communication, enabling business continuity, and ensuring data security.

# Summary

Distributed architectures are at the forefront of these transformations for two reasons: global economies and the advent of the cloud. Enterprises are no longer limited to local customer bases: they can reach a global audience to offer services and goods. Cloud realized the idea of enterprises renting out infrastructure when they need and paying only for what they use. Instead of maintaining massive data centers, they can rent from a catalog of services a cloud service provider offers.

Once an enterprise finalizes on a CSP, to ready the enterprise for cloud, architects have to work through setting up a long list of services. There are a few enterprise-level decisions that happen before anything else. The first enterprise decision is on deciding networking and connectivity between CSP and all involved parties: on-prem/existing data centers, partners, customers, and Internet-based customers. The next decision is around the appropriate regions and zones of CSPs the various organizations in the enterprise will use, based on geographic impacts and geopolitical mandates.

Apart from enterprise decisions, architects need to decide on application-level infrastructure. Decisions on how microservices architecture run—VMs, dedicated machines, and CSP-native options—are needed. Decisions on how to integrate services with other entities—other services, web endpoints, and asynchronous communications—are required. Selecting the right datastore on the cloud, based on specific needs, is another important architectural decision.

All these decisions—both enterprise-level decisions and application-level decisions—need to be made while being mindful of billing. Architects need to thoroughly research and determine factors such as best possible billing options, potential vendor lock-in scenarios, optimizing cloud costs, etc., at every step.

# Points to Ponder

1.  How can an enterprise select a CSP from the many available ones? What are the factors that sway this decision?

2.  How do we choose between a service offering of a CSP and an open source alternative?

3. Should enterprise limit the technology options? Or should the enterprise allow its organizations to choose their technology and only review costs?

4. What complexities are involved in using multiple CSPs? Is the effort involved worth the returns?

# Further Reading

**Cloud computing — The business perspective** by *Marston et al.* (Marston, Li, Bandyopadhyay, Zhang, & Ghalsasi, 2011).

**Cloudonomics: The Economics of Cloud Computing** by *Kepes* (Kepes, 2011).

# CHAPTER 7

# Core Cloud Concepts: Compute

The breadth of cloud computing is evident from the legion of services that CSPs (cloud service providers) make available, the massive infrastructure deployed globally to support it, and the billions of dollars getting invested into the field. As more enterprises adopt the cloud and start investing in it, architects and development teams face a tough job. They need to make many choices toward the setup of an enterprise's cloud footprint. *Many of these are infrequent and lasting decisions*; they seldom change after the initial setup. For instance, the choice of connectivity from an enterprise's existing data center to a CSP is a one-time setup. However, for rolling out the microservices architecture on the cloud, *some of the platform choices will need more variations*. We walked through the various facets of cloud computing—compute, storage, and connectivity.

Enterprises need to make sound decisions on all these fronts for a successful on-prem monolith to cloud-based microservices. The primary emphasis needs to be on **selecting the right computational option**—along with a deep understanding of the *reasons for selection* and a thorough analysis of the *implications of every decision*. To aid this, we discuss concepts of *virtualization*, *containerization*, and *container orchestration, and* briefly discuss *FaaS/serverless* options. Next, we focus on **integration services**. We look at cloud-neutral way of integration, via *service meshes*. The final section of the chapter presents a few more *integration options*, specifically focusing on *MaaS—* messaging as a service. The next chapter discusses the various storage options, their applicability to microservices architecture, and inherent complexities in cloud-storage services.

© Chandra Rajasekharaiah 2021
C. Rajasekharaiah, *Cloud-Based Microservices*, https://doi.org/10.1007/978-1-4842-6564-2_7

# Containerization over Virtualization

Microservices and cloud discussions are incomplete without considering containers. For decades, ***virtualization*** had allowed engineers *to craft virtual environments of various sizes and shapes (i.e., different guest OS) on any machine.* They allowed carving large bare metals into many smaller VMs (virtual machines) of different operating systems. A hypervisor commissioned each of the VMs with an entire footprint of a real computer, including the whole operating system. The late 2010s saw significant adoption of containers over traditional VMs. The IaC (infrastructure-as-code) movement in the late 2000s triggered the beginning of this transition—engineers wanted to *build the environments programmatically.* Programmatically constructed environments allow testability, better troubleshooting, and precision at scale. These efforts led to tools such as Chef and Puppet that allow crafting virtual machines to spec.

Virtualization continues to be a powerful concept in the cloud. Virtual machines provide the flexibility of selecting the number of cores, GPU (graphics processing unit) addons, memory size, and attached storage (equivalent to HDD or SSD on a laptop). In general, it is best to avoid running microservices architectures on virtualized infrastructure. However, there are reasons development teams might need to use virtual machines. The adjustability in creating VMs is useful when running special software or running an open source software unavailable on a CSP. For instance, it is typical for enterprises to use products and software that expect the underlying machine with specific attributes—a particular number of cores, fixed IP, etc.—to satisfy licensing agreements. It is also common that enterprises use older versions of open source software, but not available as a service from CSP. Apart from the reasons mentioned, the best option to run most enterprise software is using *containerization.*

## IAAS ON TOP CSPS

Amazon's raw computing option, which include VMs, is called *EC2.*[1] Azure's offering is *Azure VMs,*[2] and *Cloud Compute*[3] from Google Cloud Platform (GCP). All service providers provide many pre-created templates available to create a VM. All CSPs have the provision of attaching GPUs to VMs. The image format from which a VM gets built is not standardized— AMI (Amazon Machine Image) is the format for AWS, and VHD (Virtual Hard Disk) is the standard for Azure. However, all CSPs provide the ability to import standard VM formats such as OVA, VMDK, VHD, or RAW. Autoscaling of a group of VMs—the ability to clone new instances and destroying existing ones—is available on all CSPs. Similarly, resizing of a VM instance is offered by all CSPs.

Virtualization continues to be the barebone of a lot of infrastructure on the cloud. However, in the early 2010s, concepts of ***containerization*** gained momentum. It was born from the same idea of virtualization—simulating a machine on top of another. Containers, in the purest form, ***are an isolated set of processes running on a host machine***. Imagine that the microservice application's process is solitary and is made to believe that it is running in its familiar environment. In containerization, unlike virtualization, the *target machine gets created with merely the differential.* Containers use the host OS in entirety, without installing the entire guest OS. The absence of the guest OS gives them quicker bootups and smaller size. Apart from lean size and shorter startup times, they are easier to create and distribute (Strauss, 2013) (Seo, Hwang, Moon, Kwon, & Kim, 2014).

When the containerization movement started, entities and enterprises began competing in the container space. This competition resulted in multiple platforms and divergent thoughts. To ensure cooperation between container projects, and consolidate efforts in the field, the *Open Container Initiative, or the OCI project,* was born in 2015.

---

[1] https://aws.amazon.com/ec2/

[2] https://azure.microsoft.com/en-us/services/virtual-machines/

[3] https://cloud.google.com/compute/

OCI's responsibility is to define the container standards for the industry. This self-governing body, comprising of the most significant players in the field at that time, drafted two sets of specifications as standards for containerization:

1) *image-spec* for how images get created, transported, and initialized

2) *runtime-spec* defining running and managing the container images[4]

OCI has a development community as well, which maintains an open source project with a reference implementation.[5] Subsequently, there was more attempt in this direction as the Cloud Native Computing Foundation (CNCF) started standardizing the infrastructure needs for running OCI compliant containers.

A **container image** is often an *immutable image* of a machine that can be loaded into memory and started instantaneously. Immutability addressed an essential set of problems that engineers traditionally faced when they built VMs. Normally, a script was responsible for defining and creating a VM. Scripted creation meant that every instance could be different, as there was no guarantee that these snippets ran entirely and correctly. Differences manifested while constructing VMs of the same microservice increased the complexity of debugging and troubleshooting. From this challenge, the concept of *VM images* was born. Development teams started building a VM image in dev and started moving the VM image through all development environments, and finally to production. The natural extension of the idea of VM images was of container images: *make the VM image smaller and faster by removing the kernel from the image*. The concept of a container image is that once it gets created, it will never change—thus guaranteeing absolute equivalence of every environment from the application's perspective.

Another added advantage of containers was the quick launch times. The containers are thin enough images that can run without a hypervisor, making them easier to use and faster to deploy (Raho, Spyridakis, Paolino, & Raho, 2015). Even though hypervisors continue to get better, containers offer superior performance—even comparable to the physical machine, as proven by multiple benchmarks. (Felter, Ferreira, Rajamony, & Rubio, 2015) (Li, Kihl, Lu, & Andersson, 2017).

---

[4]https://github.com/opencontainers/image-spec and https://github.com/opencontainers/runtime-spec

[5]https://www.opencontainers.org/

Immutability and instancy are the key reasons to prefer containers over VMs while building microservices-based architectures.

# Containerizing Microservices

A *containerized application* is a container image embedded with the application and everything the application needs—operating system, libraries, and configuration—to allow independent, immediate, and on-demand instantiation. The images are composed of layers; for instance, the layers could be as follows:

1. **Layer 1**: The base OS layer

2. **Layer 2**: The base OS layer + enterprise tools

3. **Layer 3**: The base OS layer + enterprise tools + application binaries

4. **Layer 4**: The base OS layer + enterprise tools + application binaries + application

Having layers *allows quick build times*; for instance, if only the application is new, it is slapped onto Layer 3. The containerization concepts are more than a decade old, made mainstream by Docker in the mid-2010s. Docker—both the container technology and the company behind the technology—created the concept of containerized applications. The Docker container runtimes are stateless, immutable instances running on a volatile space. Docker container fits perfectly with the principles of microservices: of being lean, fast, and stateless. These principles encouraged most enterprises to choose to run their microservices as Docker containers.

Typically, engineering teams that develop microservices set up their build pipeline to convert from source code to container. A typical build pipeline, as depicted in Figure 7-1, consists of

- Checking out code from code repository, compiling code, static checking, converting to a binary—application in a runnable format

- Versioning the binary and storing it in an artifact repository

- Downloading the binary, transforming into a container image by adding environment information, and creating a container

- Checking the container images for security flaws, versioning them, and storing them into a container registry

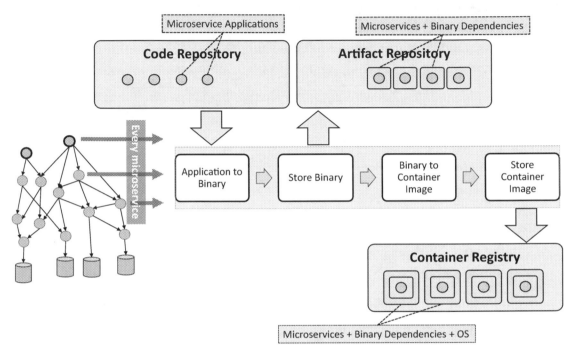

***Figure 7-1.***  *Typical process of creating containers*

---

Docker, a container company, is the force behind making containerization popular. Note that container ≠ Docker; many other options, such as rkt, lxc, and containerd, exist. However, in this book we focus our attention on Docker's general capabilities and principles, since it is the de facto standard for containerization.

---

It is especially important to get this automated process in place *before the cloud journey.* In the container world, the release candidate chosen can—and should be—locked from editing. Locking ensures the microservice, which is bundled along with its environment in a binary form, is frozen and tagged. It also ensures that application images are

- **Portable**: The image can be downloaded and run anywhere from developer's machine to production server on-prem or on the cloud.

- **Predictable**: The behavior of not only the application but also its environment is known and is traceable.

- **Performant**: The deploy, un-deploy, rollback, and many other processes are quick.

Containerization has undergone a great deal of research, evolution, standardization, and refining in the past decade. Consider containerization as a *mandatory requirement* for running microservices, with *two critical observations in mind*. One, *applications are **not always faster** on containers as compared to VMs* for any computational case. There are situations where computation is bound to storage interaction—such as heavy I/O bound operations—where VMs fare better (Li, Kihl, Lu, & Andersson, 2017). Two, *damage caused by insecure containerized applications (or containers themselves) can be much severe than in VMs*, as containers share a lot more with the host operating system kernel (Gao, Gu, Kayaalp, Pendarakis, & Wang, 2017). These two cautions are not to discourage use of containers but, on the contrary, to show the research in the field and what engineering teams should consider when containerizing their applications. As these problems get addressed and more work gets done in the field, containerization continues to grow. Engineers are working to improve containers and operating system kernels to achieve tighter security and better performance. More details on these topics are the focus of the chapter on securing microservices.

# Container Orchestration

Containers run as processes on a host operating system, while emulating an entire machine. Though they are a significant step toward resource efficiency, by themselves, they are not a complete solution. *Many complexities arise when we attempt to run container-based applications at scale.* Imagine the Energence Home Platform with more than 40 microservices, resulting in more than a hundred containers. *It is impossible to manage provisioning, monitoring, availability, scalability, load balancing, etc., at this scale with manual scripting.* There is still a need for processes (manual or automated) to manage the life cycle of containers—as they are created, replicated, monitored, retired, and destroyed. To efficiently use the power of the cloud, we need the ability to leverage the on-demand capability of the cloud. So, for efficient usage of containers in the cloud, we need *a programmable infrastructure that takes care of*

- **Create**: Configuring, preparing, scheduling, and starting containers on the underlying compute engines

- **Setup and monitor**: Connecting containers to network, setting up traffic flow, and monitoring their health

- **Recreate**: Destroying failing containers, removing them from network, and creating new instances to replace

We also need *controls to scale up* (or scale down) the container instances and *to set up connectivity and route traffic* between container instances as they come up. Wiring traffic is a continuous activity—as new ones get created, or the old ones are retired.

Mature architectures contain hundreds of microservices. Each microservice runs anywhere from one to a few tens of replicas. With that many instances, we end up in an enormous expanse of running systems. *Managing the life cycle of the immense number of containers without automation is a Herculean task.* This necessity of automatic management of containers created platforms such as Kubernetes, Mesos, and Docker Swarm, among others. These platforms provide capabilities of managing container lifecycles, *at scale*.

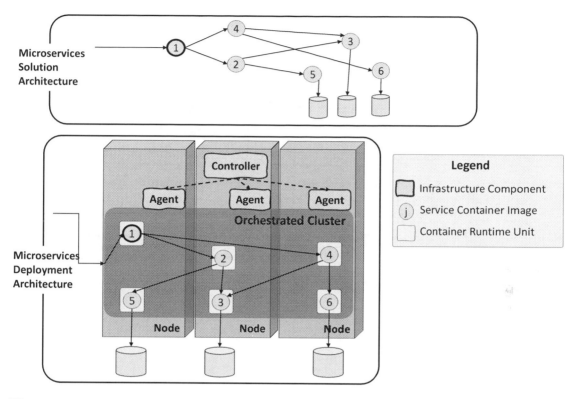

***Figure 7-2.*** *A runtime view of microservices on an orchestration platform*

Figure 7-2 shows a typical runtime view of a microservices orchestration platform. Usually, container orchestration platforms differ in their architecture; however, foundationally, they are made up of the same components:

- They realize an artificial *cluster*, set up on many virtual or physical machines—the machines are called *nodes*.

- They all have a set of *controllers*, which centrally control the life cycle of various containers. Typically, these controllers allow a command-line or API type of endpoint for submitting configurations, topologies, and other specifications of how users want to run containerized applications.

- Potentially, there are *agents* on every node to locally manage node and allow the centralized set of controllers to manage processes and container instances on nodes.

- They also define a *virtual network*, which is overlaid on top of the basic networking present between nodes. This overlay ensures addresses and other physical network characteristics needed by running container instances are abstracted. The containers do not need to know which physical machine other container instances are running in.

A typical process of container orchestration is outlined in Figure 7-3. A build process submits a request to container orchestration platform specifying *topological details of the deployment* such as

- Coordinates of the container image in the container registry (name, version, etc.)

- The number of replicas that need to run, service endpoints to be exposed and consumed

- Environment configuration

The container orchestration platform follows the steps outlined in the diagram. Upon receiving this request, the container orchestration platform will execute the following actions:

1. *Pulls* the appropriate container image from a container registry.

2. *Plans* how much computing power is needed to run a specified number of container instances.

3. Attempt to find and allocate resources based on performance and availability guarantees.

4. *Schedules* and *starts* container images as running processes.

5. *Periodically probes running containers* until they are ready to receive traffic.

6. Once ready, it *diverts traffic* and has effectively commissioned the container image as specified, and attempts self-healing.

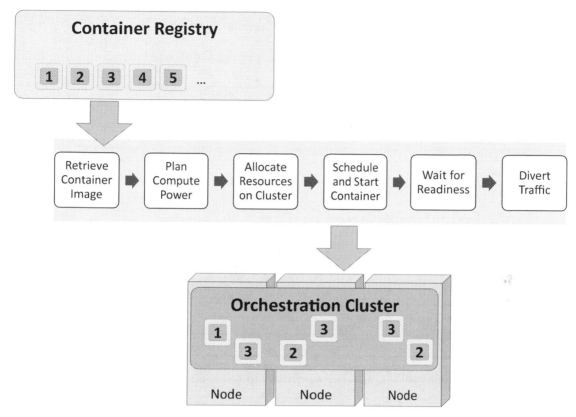

***Figure 7-3.*** *Typical process of container orchestration*

Figure 7-3 depicts the outcome of a request, which had specified one instance of container-image-1, two instances of container-image-2, and three instances of container-image-3 to be started. The platform found space on the three nodes and distributed them across.

Apart from the initial configuration, the orchestration platform can also be set up to handle the *increase or decrease in the number of container instances, based on traffic and workload.* The ability to scale container instances is extremely helpful in managing the footprint of applications as their traffic ebbs and flows through various periods. For example, consider the Energence application that monitors device states at home. Suppose one of the application monitors garage doors. Most of the messages to these systems will usually be centered around two peaks a day, once in the morning when people leave home for work and again in the evening when they return from work. Such applications in the ecosystem might take on traffic during specific times of the day and might need to scale to meet traffic.

It is important to note that the container orchestration's roles and responsibilities continue after setting up and starting a container as per specification in the request. Failures could be due to failure in the underlying hardware, connectivity issues, or any other unforeseen issue in the infrastructure. Additionally, containers are entities programmed by humans, which means they might fail. In reality, they often fail, and in various spectacular ways. They become unresponsive to traffic, or they start consuming system resources uncontrollably, or they continuously crash or stay unhealthy, or end up in an undecidable state. If any such scenarios arise, *container orchestration platforms should provide tools to detect, root-cause, and resolve such failures.*

The importance of using container orchestration in any microservices architecture is paramount. A container-based deployment of microservices architecture necessitates an orchestration infrastructure. Container orchestration is a growing field with many features regularly added, revised, and modified for efficiency, performance, and portability across cloud platforms. However, this technology has reached a reasonable level of maturity to make it an essential component of microservices' cloud journey.

## CONTAINER MANAGEMENT SERVICES ON TOP CSPS

All three CSPs offer various options for container management. For managing containers, AWS has three offerings. First is Elastic Container Service,[6] which is an Amazon proprietary container management solution, commonly known as "Docker as a Service." ECS allows docker images to be built, deployed, and managed from your app + Dockerfile. Second is AWS Elastic Container Service for Kubernetes,[7] which is an AWS's version of Kubernetes. Third, AWS Fargate,[8] which is a PaaS for running Docker containers (managed by ECS). Fargate is a real PaaS, and unlike k8s, with ECS+Fargate, the underlying VMs need not be set up and maintained.

Azure similarly has three products. Azure Container Service[9] is an open container management platform to run Docker containers. ACS also allows open source container management services such as Docker Swarm and Mesos. Azure Kubernetes Service[10] is their Kubernetes

---

[6]https://aws.amazon.com/ecs/

[7]https://aws.amazon.com/eks/

[8]https://aws.amazon.com/fargate/

[9]https://docs.microsoft.com/en-us/azure/container-service/

[10]https://azure.microsoft.com/en-us/services/kubernetes-service/

offering. Azure Server Fabric[11] is a very opinionated platform to build and run applications as containers using ASF SDKs; however, it allows guest Docker containers to be run. Finally, Azure offers Azure Batch,[12] a service targeted at running big data workloads as containers.

Google's offering in this space is GKE, Google Kubernetes Engine.[13] Kubernetes is based on Google's internal Borg project,[14] and hence GKE is possibly the best Kubernetes offering.

# Service Meshes

Service meshes are a concept that gained popularity alongside orchestration; as a concept, service meshes serve a different purpose than container orchestration. Analogous to the way container orchestration came about to solve management problems of microservice containers, *service meshes were built to manage communication between microservices.* We discussed earlier how a microservice-based system might end up with thousands of running containers and how managing it would be difficult. There are other important factors that need to be discussed; let us start with inter-service communication. It is important to note that *inter-container communication is different from inter-service communication.* The difference between the two is the same as the difference between syntax and semantics of operational complexity.

Anyone who was involved with the original SOA movement should quickly associate this with the hype created by normalized-message-routers (NMRs) and enterprise-service-buses (ESBs). When enterprises adopted SOA and attempted to create services, they realized there is a considerable penalty incurred—the overhead of application-integration. This overhead excavated the need for abstracting communicating between services so that they can evolve independently. The abstraction of communication had led to the conceptualization of SOA brokers, such as ESBs and NMRs. These brokers routed communication *intelligently*—they not only *managed communication between services, but also translated messages as services need.* This intelligence meant brokers

---

[11]https://azure.microsoft.com/en-us/services/service-fabric/
[12]https://azure.microsoft.com/en-us/services/batch/
[13]https://cloud.google.com/kubernetes-engine/
[14]https://kubernetes.io/blog/2015/04/borg-predecessor-to-kubernetes/

took up the job of transforming content between services as they evolved, creating the very monolithic omniscient that SOA attempted to solve. SOA presented us with breakthrough ideas before its 'overload of verbiage' and 'tool hype' killed it. Luckily, enterprises which adopted SOA did learn some important lessons.

Microservices architectures have the precisely same need for brokers. *As microservices architecture becomes unbearably complicated, abstracting communication between microservices becomes compulsory.* Like ESBs and NMRs, service meshes are brokers. However, they only manage communication between services, *no translation*. A typical service mesh is comprised of three foundational components: *proxies, a central traffic manager,* and *a central security manager.*

A *proxy or a sidecar* is an application that coexists with every running microservice instance. The instance could be running on a VM or a container. The sidecar intercepts every incoming and outgoing traffic of the microservice application. With sidecars, ensuring applications' non-functional requirements is drastically simplified—sidecars integrate easily and allow greater control over the traffic entering and exiting the microservice. In most REST-based microservices, they are layer-7 proxies, which coexist with for every instance of every microservice. In a virtualized environment, a sidecar could be running as another application on the same VM. In a container orchestration environment, most sidecar implementations coexist in the container runtime unit, along with the container, but some sidecar implementations run at the node level.

A *central traffic manager* to establish and enforce communication rules between microservices running on VMs or containers. The features include discovery of sidecars, intelligent routing of traffic, and gracefully handling various failures in traffic. It is also assigned the job of telemetry, such as gathering information about traffic flow in the service mesh.

A *security manager* to secure connections between microservices, securing connections as they come into service mesh, and any authentication/authorization required for users of the services in the service mesh.

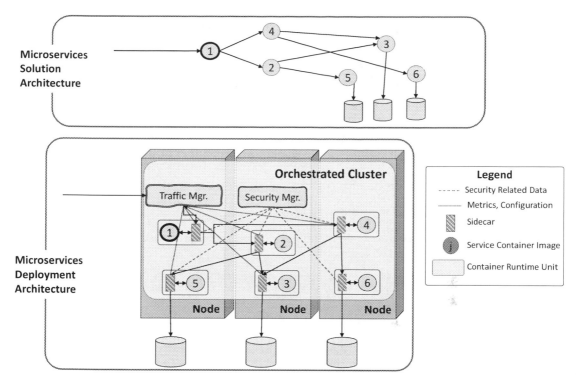

*Figure 7-4.* *A runtime view of a microservices architecture on a service mesh*

Service meshes solve some key issues that appear in large-scaled microservices-based architectures. Enormous designs run thousands of microservices, and whether they run as containers on an orchestrated platform or not, three key challenges emerge:

1. Traffic control, traffic management, and traffic shaping

2. Establishing and securing inter-microservice communication

3. Overall observability

Though many standardization efforts are underway, as of writing this book, two competing service meshes were prevalent.[15]

---

[15]Istio https://www.istio.io and ContainerD https://www.containerd.io

# Traffic Control, Traffic Management, and Traffic Shaping

Challenges in traffic management, traffic control, and traffic shaping are some of the best substantiations of service mesh necessity. Building capabilities to control traffic as it flows across the entire microservice ecosystem is a big challenge. The daunting problems in a massive microservices setup are usually

- Enabling circuit breaking upon detecting service failures

- Handling deployment strategies (e.g., blue-green, canary, dark launches)

- Rate-limiting on services through traffic shedding or prioritization of clients

- Load-balancing across service endpoints, with highly complex rules

*Circuit breaking* is a critical concept to handle failures. Let us assume we have a service A that relies on service B for some part of its functionality. In production, service B suddenly starts failing requests from A: service B might be encountering failures or might be choking under load. Service A needs to handle failures gracefully. Circuit breakers allow service A to take a different route (for instance, use some default preconfigured data as an alternate). Circuit breakers can continue to check periodically (by "closing" the circuit and resume calling service B) until service B stabilizes. Once stabilized, the circuit is closed, and service A relies on service B and not the default data.

Another fundamental concept in microservices architectures is *rate-limiting*. Microservices, though scalable quickly, have limitations on workloads we can route. Apart from having a hard ceiling somewhere for performance, we might want prioritization—the ability to limit traffic from various clients based on some variation of priority. A typical example is where we want to allow 100 calls per second from tier-2-high-priority clients, but not more than 10 requests per second from tier-3-low-priority clients.

Traditionally, engineers have gotten around these challenges *using disparate pieces of infrastructure*, or worse, *sometimes embedding solutions in code*. For instance, circuit breakers were implemented via specialized HTTP proxies, or embedding and leveraging special libraries[16, 17] in code. Using disparate infrastructure fragments is a non-standard

---

[16]Hystrix - https://github.com/Netflix/Hystrix
[17]Polly - https://github.com/App-vNext/Polly

way—various requirements of traffic control require different techniques/software setup. Such variations lead to technology proliferation, causing maintenance headaches, quicker aging to become legacy, and difficulties in find engineering talent. The option of embedding in code is "plain dirty." Including infrastructure code into an application's code is never a good practice.

*Service meshes offer a clean and standard way of achieving all the requirements of traffic control* we discussed earlier. The ability to redirect traffic between various instances supports many deployment strategies, many of which we discussed in the earlier chapter on processes. The standardized and clean solution is by using the combination of sidecar and traffic manager. Refer to Figure 7-4. Sidecars that are the gateways of traffic in and out of the application instance: they can observe failures and perform circuit breaking. Consider a dark launch, where the service mesh mirrors the traffic to the new version, for testing only. Consider canary, where the service mesh directs a small portion of traffic to validate against a tiny portion of real users. Traffic managers can shape traffic to need: it can split and redirect traffic to two different sets of application instances based on a configuration. For example, the setting could be 0%:100% split for dark launch, or 10%:90% split for canaries and pilots, or 50%:50% split for A/B, or a gradual switch of 100%:0% split to 0%:100% for blue/green. It is also possible to have complex load balancing rules—direct traffic to services in multiple regions based on weights, for instance, which is harder to achieve otherwise.

# Establishing and Securing Communication

Once microservices start up, they need ways to discover other services that are temporary and transient. Required services could be replaced with a newer instance, scaled out to multiple instances, relocated to another data center, or some other unknown network change. The discovery problem needs to be solved in a manner that is transparent to the consuming microservice. Even though a container orchestration platform provides such features, there are a few additional features, such as URL-to-service mapping, that are not offered by container orchestration platforms. If microservices are running on VMs, then we have a whole lot of discovery and wiring to do.

Apart from establishing inter-microservice communication, there is also a need for securing connections. We need to build the capability to enforce TLS between all microservices. An excellent secure implementation also requires mutual TLS, with all certificates periodically recycled with newer certs issued from a cert authority. The certificate management adds more overhead and needs more capabilities built. The requirement is not only to secure communication between microservices within a system but also to handle authentication at the periphery. Again, we end up resorting to different solutions to solve each challenge.

Service meshes solve this problem with their security manager component, which handles security across the board. In most service meshes, the security manager sets up sidecars with certificates. It also contains certification issuing and certificate distribution entities to create new certs and distribute them to sidecars. All microservices are talking to each other through sidecars, and not directly, allowing a service mesh to secure all internal communication with certificates. Most service meshes also have capabilities of peripheral authentication: they can authenticate requests coming in. This feature is usually offered either passively by validating security tokens and claims, or actively communicating with IdP (Identity Provider). In passive validations, incoming service calls are expected to present authentication and authorization tokens (JWT, for instance, embedded in REST HTTP requests) that are validated. Validation can be either implicit (by checking the content) or explicit (by verifying the token with the issuer). When validation is active, the client credentials are checked with a central IdP for access rights or claims.

# Building Overall Observability

We walked through the challenges of observability in Chapter 4. We discussed how in a microservices world, where the call depths can be tens of services deep, it is easy to lose sight of the performance and precision of individual microservices involved in a top-level service call. Having a distributed trace, wherein we can see calls across microservices—from every source to every sink—on a single pane of glass is a necessity. Next, the ability to tie application logs to traces, and triggering them on P9x performance indicators, is a great way to gain complete real-time visibility into any microservices-based architecture. Finally, monitoring the performance and collecting metrics from every running microservice instance allows engineers to understand the runtime characteristics of microservices better.

Service meshes offer many of these functionalities by tapping into the power of sidecars, security managers, and traffic managers. They leverage distributed tracing solutions by feeding data from sidecars about the traffic flow by adding "tracing data" to requests as they flow through the service mesh. This tracing data allows sidecars to report information about service calls to the distributed tracing application, which connects various service calls into a hierarchy for analysis.

Consider Figure 7-5 for an illustration. Notice that all service calls pass through the sidecars of microservices A through F. Note that a trace-id is added to the original call out from microservice A. This trace-id is passed along every call to every sidecar. The trace information from all sidecars allows the service "call-flow" based on the trace-id and sidecar data.

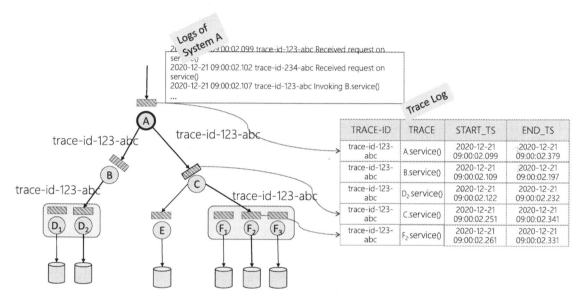

***Figure 7-5.*** *Example trace flow in a microservices setup*

Sidecars often offload logging from the main application. They can record the ins and outs of microservices or collect application logs from the container/VM. It is easy for the sidecars to collate and present logs and then to match service calls to logs. This capability of correlation is an excellent feature, which aids tremendously in observability. Sidecars can also maintain metrics such as service call counts, response times, failure rates, as they proxy traffic requests and responses for the microservices. This data can be scraped, collated, and dashboarded to understand the overall health, performance, and state of the systems.

---

Up until 2020, there were competing standards on achieving observability on the cloud—OpenTracing and OpenCensus. As of writing this book (mid-2020), there was a consensus in the industry, and the standards merged to form OpenTelemetry under CNCF.

---

## Challenges and State of the Art of Service Meshes

A brief observation of the architecture shows the presence of a sidecar, which grabs our attention. The sidecars proxy every bit of traffic into and out of a microservice. It immediately raises *concerns on performance*: what used to be a single hop between two microservices is now three hops. Without sidecars, service A directly accesses service B. With a sidecar, service A talks to its sidecar (first hop), which in turn talks to the sidecar of service B (second hop), and microservice B and its sidecar (third hop). Unless the sidecars are highly performant, they add a severe overhead to the overall performance of the system. The second challenge is *the increased complexity* of adding a service mesh to the architecture. Various new components get added, and many of which add to support and maintenance costs. Added to this is the *lack of tooling* when it comes to automated generation of service mesh configuration. Popular service meshes like Istio need a lot of configuration. Tools to templatize, populate, and maintain the configuration for every microservice do not exist.

The service mesh field is heading toward standardization, thanks to enthusiastic contributions from bright minds and active interest from industry. When we survey the service mesh options, it is evident that only a few options for sidecars are popular in the industry—indicating that we are close to standardization. Apart from progress in standardization, the performance of sidecars continues to improve. Several tests have been done on implementation with the latest sidecar setup, and the tests have found sidecars to be efficient enough to have a minimal performance penalty of using them (Dattatreya Nadig, 2019). Tests also indicate that under heavy loads, systems based on service mesh offer better performance than the ones that do not use it—due to factors such as higher scalability (Amiri, Krieger, Zdun, & Leymann, 2019) and increased throughput with fewer failures (Larsson, Tärneberg, Klein, Elmroth, & Kihl, 2020). The complexity of maintenance of service mesh continues to decrease with time, with the advent of newer tools and standardization.

# FaaS aka Serverless

We discussed two patterns of deploying and running microservices: IaaS, the model for building and controlling virtual machines in the cloud, and iCaaS, the pattern of creating container images and relying on CSP's container orchestration options. IaaS offers a higher degree of control but includes maintenance overhead. Container-based iCaaS provides a lower degree of regulation but significantly reducing maintenance efforts. This comparison brings us to the third option, FaaS (function as a service, or popularly known as serverless computing), where the underlying compute is invisible to engineers. Serverless is a pattern where an application is built as code snippets and gets submitted to a platform that runs them. The application has no control over the underlying infrastructure (Baldini, et al., 2017, p. 2), apart from specifying compute and memory requirements. The serverless architecture of microservices mirrors the event-driven architecture style, where stateless services get called to action on some event.

---

Many authors and technologists classify serverless cloud computing into FaaS and BaaS. BaaS is an entire platform with specific use cases in mind. Popular types of Backend-as-a-Service offered by CSPs focus on particular domains, such as mobile development and website development. For the discussion at hand, we will restrict our focus to FaaS.

---

There are some compelling reasons for the increasing popularity of serverless computing:

1. The overhead of maintaining infrastructure, scaling, and tuning is removed.

2. Under lower loads, they could potentially share infrastructure, which means they run cheaper than dedicated servers.

3. Pay-per-use with finer metering (micro-billing); if service runs for ten minutes a day, pay for ten minutes a day.

Serverless also fits well with the goals of microservices. Functions, the units of serverless computing, are forced to be stateless by default. Functions are entirely independent of each other, to the extent of being unaware of their location. FaaS *is highly elastic, able to scale to as much as needed quickly*—also readily shrink to nothing in a shorter window of time. Functions are an excellent programming model for use cases where *bursty traffic gets computation-intensive sporadically for short periods.* However, the resulting challenge is that *cost of running functions is not readily deducible.* Many factors—invocation frequency, the duration of execution, and memory used—play into the monthly bills (Wu, Buyya, & Ramamohanarao, 2019). This complexity *demands new techniques for development, testing, and monitoring.*

Using a serverless computing framework also creates a *higher scope of vendor lock-ins*. There is very little standardization across CSPs on the nature of FaaS implementations. Porting a FaaS application across clouds is a potential rewrite. Functions also suffer from *cold-start penalties*—when a cloud function gets triggered after a long period of idle, the overhead of instantiating the function could cause loss of performance and throughput.

Serverless is an entirely new and exciting technique for building systems and microservices. However, being a nascent and upcoming field, there are challenges and scope for evolution. First, serverless computing lacks standardization. Though the underlying theme is the same—compute capacity is provisioned on-demand— every CSP's implementation is vastly different. The framework of building code, programming language choices, options and methods of triggering code, and infrastructure setup vary by CSP.

---

**FAAS ON PROMINENT CSPS**

---

AWS is the earliest[18] to offer FaaS, in AWS Lambda,[19] which allows running node.js, python 2.7/3.6, .NET (C#), Go 1.x, and Java 8 language code in a serverless fashion. Azure's offering is called Azure Functions,[20] which allows almost all languages supported by AWS Lambda (barring Java code) to be run in a serverless fashion. Azure functions allow individual functions to be grouped together as a program, as opposed to in Lambda where each function is independent. GCP's offering Cloud Functions[21] is similar, and languages allowed are Python 3.7, node.js, and Java. GCP also offers kNative, which is more an iCaaS than a FaaS.

---

[18]AWS re:Invent 2014 | Announcing AWS Lambda - https://www.youtube.com/watch?v=9eHoyUVo-yg
[19]https://aws.amazon.com/lambda/
[20]https://azure.microsoft.com/en-us/services/functions/
[21]https://cloud.google.com/functions/

# PaaS

Apart from FaaS, most CSPs provide PaaS solutions for running applications. PaaS solutions tend to vary across various CSPs, but a few fundamental features remain common.

1. **An opinionated view on applications:** Most compute-PaaS expect a specific way of application build, layout, and communication. These expectations vary between CSPs, so there are no standard definitions.

2. **Completely transparent application management**: Once a PaaS-based application is submitted, the life cycle and scalability become CSP's responsibility. Autoscaling to match traffic and recreating failed instances are some of the inherent features.

3. **A vendor lock-in**: Due to the lack of standardization, PaaS-based solutions are rarely portable. In most cases, porting—to iCaaS, or to another cloud—requires extensive rework on the application.

However, CSPs provide PaaS options for solving unique problems. Some typical examples are 1) running node.js applications, 2) hosting SAP solutions, 3) packaging and running legacy applications as-is. PaaS solutions ease the problem for such use cases. *Typically, PaaS solutions are not suited for running microservices architecture.*

# Integration Services

We limit our discussion to various integration options on the cloud. The focus is on exploring the CSP's multiple services that provide connectivity to microservices. The connectivity that allows microservices to talk to the external world or with other microservices. Microservices running on the cloud need ways to manage traffic from many resources—internet users, dedicated networks, and hosted websites—to name a few. Traffic management requires ways to shape and route traffic to microservice instances strewn across the globe and provide secure ways of doing so. We did discuss using a service mesh to achieve intra-organizational synchronous microservices communication. However, when there is a need for inter-organizational communication, service meshes need closer observation.

Enterprises compartmentalize their cloud footprint into organizational chunks—for ease of billing, control, and security. These organizational compartments break visibility across enterprise systems. In Energence's scenario, the planning department, manufacturing wing, and distribution branch could sever direct connections between each other. Where the setups spread across different clusters, we might have to rely on solutions other than service meshes. We had identified that inter-organizational communication is best achieved by choreography when possible. Choreography leads to the usage of messaging services, which allow asynchronous communication. Where services need to talk to services from other organizations synchronously, we will need HTTP-based mediators to abstract interfaces.

We will discuss in detail many of the synchronous entities thus employed—global load balancers, API gateways, and regional load balancers—in the chapter under Securing Microservices on Cloud.

# MaaS: Messaging Services

In this section, we focus our discussion on asynchronous communication techniques. *Asynchronous communication is the backbone of choreography-based integration.* Such integrations vary from massive data-chunk exchange to trickle-feed of small data packets. For instance, in Energence, forecasting engines could publish large forecast plans as a message, which manufacturing platforms use for planning production. In contrast, the EOTA module would queue up individual device information for the Smart-Devices module to patch. Asynchronous communications through messages fall into two categories: *point-to-point* and *publish-subscribe*. A point-to-point connection is a queuing technique. The originator of data—called the *publisher*—has a single *consumer* of data. The messages get piled up from the publisher as it generates more events and notifications. A publish-subscribe setup is a broadcast-of-data model. Here, the producer of messages, termed *publisher*, announces the new content on a messaging board, termed *topic*—the interested consumers, called *subscribers*, who watch the messaging-board and receive the messages.

In both types of messaging alternatives, the key terminology remains the same.

- **Producers** create the messages and send them to the **messaging service**.

- **Consumers** listen to the messaging service, grab the messages from the messaging service, and process them.

- Producers and consumers are bound to one **messaging channel** for a particular type of communication.

- Messaging channels can be **partitioned**, with some sort of partition-key. This helps in **load leveling** and **load balancing** messages across many copies of the same channel.

- Consumers need to **ACK** or **NACK** the message from the messaging service. ACKing removes the message from the channel. NACKing puts the message back to the channel and sets up another delivery attempt. Messages can also have a **TTL** and expire after the set timestamp.

- *Poison messages*, payloads which cause the consumers to NACK them constantly, create the possibility of infinite redeliveries causing a catastrophic failure. CSP's messaging services offer **dead-lettering** services that pull such messages out of messaging channels.

- Channels can **route, filter, and batch messages**. They could also have the capability to participate in **transactions**.

## Point-to-Point Messaging

Point-to-point messaging is an essential technique when two microservices want a guaranteed communication channel. The publisher sends a message to the consumer and expects the consumer to process it. Apart from reliability, many applications look for ordering in point-to-point communication channels. In Figure 7-6, Service A, the producer of messages, expects Service X, the consumer, to process messages in the exact sequence it was generated. The events that cause the payload generation in the sequence {A1, A2, A3} require the consumption of those messages in the very same order.

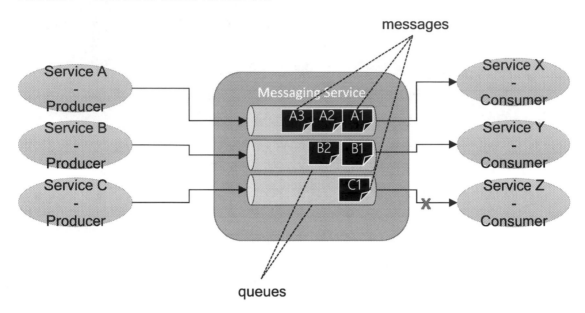

***Figure 7-6.*** *Point-to-point messaging—three pairs of consumers and producers exchanging messages*

Perfect examples for this type of communication are *the high-value business transaction messages.* Energy signals created by storage engines of the grid cannot go to distributing systems out of order—it could result in overconsumption. Outside of our use cases, there are a plethora of such scenarios in every industry.

CSPs strive to have a high availability of point-to-point service offering. Every CSP provides a service that is point-to-point at a regional availability. However, it is easy to notice that achieving a global availability of such services is impossible. CAP theorem, speed of light, and all such wonderous limitations and challenges are difficult to overcome.

For P2P channels, there are some essential features CSPs offer. The engineering teams and architects should thoroughly understand these features before setting up a messaging channel for choreography between two microservices. Note that the features' importance varies based on the use case.

- **Reliability**: The property of guaranteed at-least-once delivery.

- **FIFO**: The messages generated first are always delivered first. It is important to note that FIFO does not mean ordering.

- **Ordering**: The promise of delivering the messages and maintaining the sequence.

144

- **Transactions**: The ability for messaging service to participate in transactions, where an exception in processing the message NACKs the message.

- **Competing consumers**: If more than one consumer listens to the same channel, consumers split the messages between them. There are no copies to share.

Messaging on the cloud is sophisticated but straightforward, as CSPs provide excellent messaging options with guaranteed SLAs. However, engineering teams must consider various limitations and boundaries of cloud-based messaging while designing their applications. Limitless as the cloud is, there are some hard ceilings—either because of CSP's technology limits or cost constraints.

*Many limiting factors affect the architecture of asynchronous communication* in a microservices architecture. For instance, several designs need reprocessing of messages—correspondingly, the requirement for a replay of messages from a point-in-time or a save-point. To enable this, CSPs allow you to configure *depth*—the size of dedicated storage for storing old messages—for the queues and subscriptions. As we learned, depth is directly related to the size of individual payloads and duration of the storage, and also *depth corresponds to the cost incurred*. Some messaging channels have *limits on the maximum message size*. Such factors need thorough investigation and mitigation early in the architecture's life cycle.

# Publish-Subscribe Messaging

Unlike point-to-point messaging, wherein a subscriber listens to a specific queue and acts on every message, in publish-subscribe messaging, multiple listeners get a copy of the message only when they are listening. Every subscriber receives a copy of the message, and if messages are published when no consumers are listening, the messages are lost. If point-to-point messaging is like a-la-carte service, where one dish gets prepared for one order, publish-subscribe is akin to a buffet. The food gets prepared and set up on tables, and guests eat what they like. The cook has no connection with any consumer in particular. Publish-subscribe is the model where the publisher broadcasts the events, and subscribers get these messages for the duration of their subscription.

This type of messaging is prevalent in exchanging non-critical messages in an architecture. The widespread usage of these channels on the cloud is for event broadcasts, mobile push notifications, and email push notifications. This technique has enormous applicability to use cases where a domain has critical updates to more than one domain. For instance, in our Energence software solutions, when Energence Grid Platform intends to publish an error, alerting both the Manufacture Platform, Home Platform, and User Portal. A failure in a grid needs to alert manufacturing systems to offset lost consumers. Similarly, home platforms need to be alerted of potential load diversion. Finally, the user portal should be capable of notifying the affected users. For this, the Grid Platform should raise an alert with necessary details of the failure—type of loss, begin time, and grids affected. The other domains will listen to this message, retrieve the required information, and process it accordingly. A publish-subscribe of setup will allow the three applications to subscribe to the Grid Platform's channels.

*Publish-subscribe is an excellent way of enabling one-to-many communication between publishers and consumers.* Unlike point-to-point channels, in traditional publish-subscribe models, messages are lost if no consumers exist. To circumvent this problem, CSPs allow setting up a *subscription—a point-to-point queue from the topic to the consumer.* This queue backed subscription turns the consumers into durable consumers. Even if consumers are not listening, they will not miss the messages.

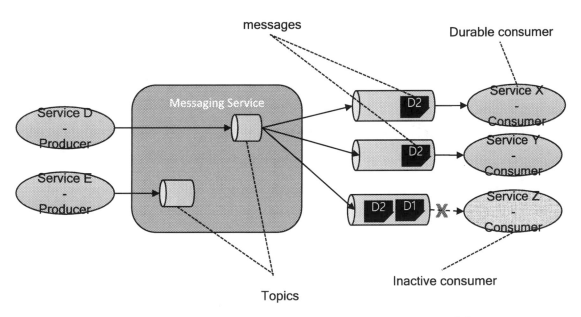

***Figure 7-7.*** *Publish-subscribe based communication—scenario of three consumers, listening to a producer*

Figure 7-7 depicts a sample setup of publish-subscribe service usage. Two publishers—D and E—are publishing messages to their topics. D publishes two messages D1 and D2, while E publishes a single message E1. Services X, Y, and Z are consumers. Service X and Y are durable consumers, which has a backing queue connecting it to D's topic. CSPs usually term this as "subscription." As Service Z is not listening, the messages start piling up in the subscription. Note that the payloads generated from E are lost, as there are no subscriptions. The MaaS infrastructure manages the forwarding of messages from the topic to its subscriptions. It is also possible to set up filtering for subscriptions and selectively post messages to subscriptions.

Various cost factors affect the pricing of publish-subscribe—number of consumers, message queue depth (total size occupied by persisted messages), and replication factors. The more consumers there are, the more processing and storage to manage. Similarly, the longer the history of events and the higher is the queue depth, it costs more to store these messages. If more copies of the messaging topic need to exist— spread across availability zones or regions—the costlier it gets.

## Streaming and Distributed Commit Logs

Other variants of publish-subscribe are *streaming* and *distributed commit logs.* In its most authentic form, streaming involves transporting *large volumes of data with no guarantee of delivery.* Streaming is standard in use cases such as event broadcasts and streaming services. Distributed commit logs are the most common way CSPs provide for streaming data transport. At their core, distributed commit logs are similar to publish-subscribe, with the main difference being the durability of messaging. *All messages get persisted by default, and consumers can browse the topic as needed.* Figure 7-8 depicts a typical distributed-commit-log setup.

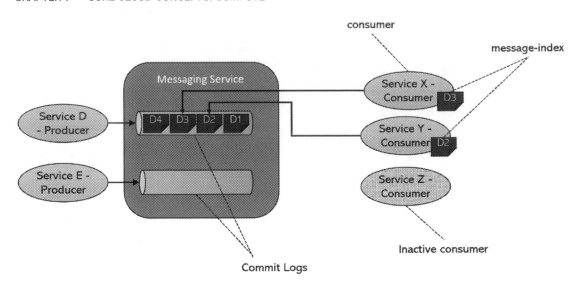

***Figure 7-8.*** *Distributed-commit-log: Consumers maintain read pointers to the log*

Streaming has gained extreme popularity in enterprises due to the potential in *analyzing every bit of data they encounter*. From mouse-clicks to page hovers on the user interfaces, from data snapshots to data changes in datastores—*all data is precious*. Processing such data with deep analytics provides valuable business insights, while processing the data in real-time opens opportunities to react instantaneously. *Lambda* and *Kappa* architectures introduced concepts to handle large streams of data efficiently. For deep analytics, streams are emptied into big-data datastores. Simultaneously, streaming data gets processed in real-time for real-time insights and immediate decisions.

A perfect example is Energence's device data. This data can be used for predictive analytics, prescriptive recommendations, long-term forecasting, etc. The devices' states and statuses can be analyzed over a period of few years to gather immense amount of details about device behavior, such as failure rates of various types of equipment, the relation of failure to manufacturing fluctuations, list of most affected geographic areas. Processing this data in real-time provides the ability to respond quickly—alerting consumers about failed devices, alerting operators of fluctuations in the electric grid, and similar alerts. The most efficient way to do this is to *simultaneously run both real-time processing and batch processing*. Batch processing will continue to gather coarse-grained analytics, while stream processing will fill in the finer details.

Consider the use case of identifying the optimal setting of HVAC systems. For this to be successful, it needs analytics over historical data such as temperature of the house, temperature outside, weather, and thermostat settings collected multiple times a day. Analytics need to consider all the data ever collected from each house, and identify relations between various factors that affect HVAC usage—factors such as weather models, characteristics of the house, customer usage patterns—and draw business intelligence. Then, as HVAC streams data, decision systems process it in real-time to find the right setting to manage each house.

Distributed commit logs decouple publishers and consumers similar to the way publish-subscribe topics do. Some implementations of this technique can also act as *event stores*. Distributed commit logs are very similar to distributed datastores—they partition and store messages on multiple nodes for high availability and horizontal scalability. We will discuss distributed datastores in detail in the next chapter, which is dedicated to discussing various cloud datastores.

## MESSAGING ON PROMINENT CSPS

CSPs might contain services that offer all variations, or different services per variations. It is essential to choose the right type based on use cases. For architects who still want to rely on open source messaging, but need it as a service, AWS offers Amazon MQ,[22] which is a managed ActiveMQ solution. Azure and GCP do not have equivalent offers but provide homegrown solutions as services for messaging. For point-to-point messaging queues, AWS offers SQS,[23] while GCP does not have such an offering. Azure's offering Service Bus[24] provides both point-to-point and publish-subscribe models with reliability. For publish-subscribe models, AWS offers SNS.[25] GCP's Cloud Pub/Sub[26] caters to both publish-subscribe and streaming models. For streaming, Azure Event Grid[27] and Azure Event Hub[28] are available, and AWS offers Kinesis.[29] One of the critical notes is the cross-region availability of a few messaging middleware. A topic on Cloud Pub/Sub is a global resource, while subscriptions are regional resources. In Azure Service Bus, the topics are regionally replicated with different namespaces.

---

[22]https://aws.amazon.com/amazon-mq/

[23]https://aws.amazon.com/sqs/

[24]https://docs.microsoft.com/en-us/azure/service-bus/

[25]https://aws.amazon.com/sns/

[26]https://cloud.google.com/pubsub/

[27]https://azure.microsoft.com/en-us/services/event-grid/

[28]https://azure.microsoft.com/en-us/services/event-hubs/

[29]https://aws.amazon.com/kinesis/

---

**OPEN SOURCE OPTIONS**

Architects could consider leveraging open source messaging middleware offered as a service (or run as a supported service) on the cloud, usually provided by vendors other than CSPs. Using a CSP neutral messaging middleware is an excellent option for enterprises. Not relying on CSP's service is especially beneficial where many enterprise applications are still running on-prem. Such open source messaging middleware also removes the vendor lock-in solution of the CSP. Cost becomes a factor to consider again, and factors such as volume, continuous usage, connectivity, and production support, among others, decide which of the two options are better. Sometimes CSPs offer open source options, AWS's MSK[30] and AlibabaMQ[31] are good examples. Azure allows Kafka tooling to work with their Event Bus, which is another variation. In the absence of such options, using Kafka as a Service provided by vendors (Confluent Kafka[32], for instance) could be an option.

---

# Energence's Cloud Setup for Compute

In Chapter 6, we established an abstract view of cloud setup for Energence. Energence will host in at least two regions with different compute requirements for each organization. Let us try to ascertain the various choices, based on the needs of each domain within an organization.

Within a single domain, the compute option and communication methods can vary greatly. Let us consider the Energence Home Platform. The metering domain requires ingestion and stream processing data on a large scale. The options are

- To use a FaaS type of infrastructure, where each meter reading triggers a function call. Though simple and inviting, they could potentially become expensive due to unbound elasticity.

- To use a PaaS solution that does stream processing. A PaaS solution will be the quickest way to set up. We can cap PaaS instances to control billing.

---

[30]AWS Amazon Managed Streaming for Apache Kafka - https://aws.amazon.com/msk/

[31]AlibabaMQ for Apache Rocket MQ - https://www.alibabacloud.com/product/mq

[32]Confluent's Apache Kafka as a fully managed cloud service - https://www.confluent.io/confluent-cloud

Once the metering domain ingests data, it needs microservices to serve the domain objects. Microservices will provide the basic functionality required for billing, device management, etc. The best compute option for these microservices is on iCaaS solutions, deployed as containers on a container management platform. Attaching a service mesh to the container management platform provides all the goodies we saw earlier in the chapter.

Let us look at other potential scenarios of an enterprise. Imagine that the planning department buys a standalone product, which is capable of doing linear programming to solve their optimization problems. The product is released as an installable, requiring a particular type and version of an operating system. There are two options here:

- Using IaaS, creating dedicated virtual machines, and installing this product. It is then possible to create an image of the virtual machine and to spin-off instances when scaling is necessary. VMs are perfect if the application has peculiar requirements, such as a unique operating system, massive machine sizes, specific rules for licensing, etc.

- Using iCaaS, creating a container image of the product, and deploying onto CSP's container management platform. Containerizing and deploying is the best option if the software is not bound to the underlying OS or hardware for running.

The previous examples demonstrate the type of evaluation needed to determine the right compute option. ***Such due diligence is mandatory for designing every microservice of every domain***. Choosing the right compute-service option is based on three aspects—*matching traffic patterns, reducing costs, and the desired level of control*. We looked at examples such as *legacy applications or third party applications* with specific hardware dependency; they run best on IaaS or iCaaS platforms. *Computationally intense microservices*, such as most business transactions, need iCaaS services. Microservices with infrequent but bursty traffic patterns require options that are *dormant when not used but scale up quickly when needed*. For such use cases, it is best to choose from the CSP's PaaS and FaaS—these options also lower running costs. For applications that *always take traffic and infrequently scale* (such as seasonal traffic spurts), iCaas options are the most suitable. *High-velocity data,* ingested at internet scale, is best processed with specifically designed PaaS solutions. Typical data streams such as clickstream data or Twitter firehose are examples where stream processing compute is needed.

# Summary

Successful microservices architecture on the cloud requires computational power. The most advisable method is to create a runtime image of the microservice, and complete it with all the necessary hardware and software configuration. For ease of maintenance, assurance of environmental equivalence, and facilitating automation, we need to create a runnable image of a microservice from our build pipelines. For running on the cloud, this runnable image can be either a VM image or a container image. It is also possible to leverage CSP's custom options or go completely serverless. This decision is usually based on many factors—security, long-term vision, applicability, and cost-effectiveness. It is possible to integrate microservices with CSP's custom services, or by selecting open source options as needed, or using a service mesh that provides most of the required functionality. Apart from compute, we need methods to enable communication between running instance and to the external world. Messaging and HTTP-based service invocations are the de facto standards to achieve communication.

# Points to Ponder

1. What are the security implications of using containers vs. virtual machines? What are the elasticity factors?

2. Will using service meshes prepare us for the future? Or, will it bind us to the overheads service meshes inherently possess?

3. What other factors, apart from micro-billing, validate the use of serverless? How does microservices architecture alter in a FaaS world?

4. After knowing that PaaS usage creates a vendor lock-in, what type of use cases justifies using a CSP's PaaS options?

5. Do we need point-to-point asynchronous integration? Can all message interactions be modeled as publish-subscribe?

# Further Related Reading

**The Docker Book** by *James Turnbull* (Turnbull, 2014).

**Kubernetes: Up and Running** by *Brendan Burns et al.* (Hightower, Burns, & Beda, 2017).

**Getting Started with Istio Service Mesh** by Rahul Sharma *et al.* (Sharma & Singh, 2019).

Paper on service meshes by *Amine El Malki and Uwe Zdun* (El Malki & Zdun, 2019).

*Philipp Muens'* **GitHub** project, `pmuens/awesome-serverless`.

# CHAPTER 8

# Core Cloud Concepts: Storage

Any system, whether a microservices-based one or not, has three needs: 1) a place to run, 2) ways to communicate internally and with the external world and, 3) a way to persist resources. We discussed the first two necessities of microservices in the earlier chapter. Let us discuss the storage options on the cloud. CSPs (cloud service providers) are equipped with a multitude of storage options to meet our needs. For every aggregate, we will need to examine databases for handling *transactional* domain data, and for *internet-scale domains*. We will touch *upon big datastores* necessary for analytics and reporting. Microservices employ *temporary datastores* such as caches that provide very low-latency data access, useful for boosting the performance of microservices. Finally, a brief look at *long-term storage options* such as file stores and blob stores needed for storing static data.

## DBaaS

CSPs offer a variety of services for storing application data. Enterprises need a wide variety of data storage options. However, in this book, we focus our attention on the ones related to microservices architecture. The primary requirement is to store domain data for transactional needs, and databases are the most suitable way to persist such information. Databases come in many flavors—relational, document stores, wide-column stores, key-value stores, to name a few. Each type has a specific purpose and applicability. However, the right way to look at relevance is from two angles—CAP requirements and data formats. We have briefly examined CAP earlier; this chapter delves deeper into the topic.

© Chandra Rajasekharaiah 2021
C. Rajasekharaiah, *Cloud-Based Microservices*, https://doi.org/10.1007/978-1-4842-6564-2_8

# Classifying DBaaS by Data Type

A useful way to categorize databases is by the formats of data they store. We discussed broad classifications in this space—*NoSQL refers to most types of databases that are not RDBMS*. However, NoSQL has multiple variations, depending on the kind of data they can efficiently store. There are variants of databases that rely on the data types, use cases, and business domains they satisfy. In this section, we will discuss document stores, wide-column databases, graph databases, key-value stores, and in-memory data management.

## Relational Databases

The software industry still relies heavily on relational databases, primarily due to the historical success and available talent pool. Enterprises own monoliths, which hold all data in a single monolithic relational database. In monoliths, it was easy to maintain high levels of consistency. However, inherently, the microservices model requires rethinking the traditional setup of relational databases. In a microservices world, we would need many small databases, potentially distributed across regions. As in the case of Energence Home Platform, where one monstrous relational database was sufficient for the monolith, we will need more than 20 databases (at least one for each domain) in a microservices architecture. When deployed on the cloud, we could end up with many smaller databases if we consider partitioning and global distribution.

---

Maintaining many smaller databases allows us to scale domains individually, reduce catastrophic system failure, and evolve them independently. Consider the overhead and risk of maintaining a single database with 10TB or data over 200 databases each storing 50GB. Taking backups, restoring from failures, cleanup and maintenance, overall system availability—are all easier to achieve in the latter setup.

---

Running more database instances is not a problem. CSPs offer traditional relational databases (both open source and closed source) as services. However, a thorough analysis of options to identify applicability, cost, and performance factors is required. On the outset, running more database instances does sound expensive, but often it is not. CSPs charge an exact fraction of cost for running smaller databases as of large databases. A two-core database instance might cost half of a four-core database and an eighth of a sixteen-core database. *It is easier to scale smaller databases*, both in terms of scaling up and scaling out. However, running several smaller databases incurs *operational overhead*, thus *underlining the importance of automation*.

The best scenario to select an RDBMS type of datastore is when the data is *highly relational* and *dense* and has an *ACID requirement for transactions*. Highly relational data consist of tight relationships between various data elements. Also, in a relational scheme, data validity depends on accurate data in related entities. The relational databases have dense data, where entities have fixed attributes—all instances of a particular entity exhibit minimal variation from each other. Finally, OLTP (online transactional processing) applications require strict transactional guarantees, where changes to data need to be ACID compliant.

It is important to note that relational databases cannot easily be scaled out; the scalability aspects are discussed in the next section. As fully managed relational DBaaS tends to be single-instance based, there are some essential requirements CSPs have to offer. First, there must be *frequent backups* helping recovery from catastrophic failures, such as a lost node or data corruption—automatic by default, with a manual option to force a backup. Backups can be a global store or a different region to aid in disastrous situations. Apart from a backup option, there must be an option to run a *standby replica* for quick failover. A standby replica is especially useful in case of loss of an availability zone. Some CSPs might allow *read*-replicas to handle read-only queries, thus reducing the load on the primary instance. Next, any *patching, security fixes, or minor version upgrades* should be handled *transparently and without an outage*, along with an option to turn off automatic updates. Another essential feature is the *security of data*, both at rest and in motion. The right level of encryption and access controls are mandatory to keep the data safe from breaches and losses. Finally, a *dashboard to view database metrics* is essential for the development team to analyze the performance and usage patterns. Though the level of detail in these dashboards varies with CSPs, they are crucial tools for development teams; dashboards help them fix their database access patterns, troubleshooting applications, and scale-up or scale-down instances.

---

## RELATIONAL DBAAS IN TOP CLOUD PROVIDERS

Cloud providers offer traditional **open source databases** as service. MySQL, PostgreSQL, and MariaDB are all offered as managed databases as part of AWS's Amazon RDS.[1] AWS also offers AuroraDB,[2] which is fully compliant with MySQL and PostgresQL, but is a closed source transactional database capable of multiple masters. RDS has an advantage over its counterparts in other CSPs that it allows users to tune many of the configurations. GCP's CloudSQL[3] offers MySQL and PostgresQL variants, no MariaDB. Interesting here to note is that AWS also offers Oracle and SQLServer databases as a service with BYOL. Azure Database[4] is also available in MySQL, Postgres, and MariaDB variations. Azure, as SQL Server is a Microsoft product, also offers SQL Server as a managed service. Special note on GCP's CloudSpanner,[5] which is a closed source and a pseudo-RDBMS. Largely built-off of BigTable[6] ideas, CloudSpanner is a distributed, partially-SQL-compliant, multi-region, transactional database.

---

# NoSQL Databases

NoSQL databases originated from the necessity of handling "Internet-scale" data in a database. Traditional relational databases had tremendous overhead because of many reasons. *ACID requirements* require data to be consistent across, slowing down writes. *High normalization* requires data to be joined across multiple tables, slowing down performance. *Lack of scale-out options* means the databases cannot grow beyond a particular size without tradeoffs. We examine these aspects in detail in our next section, while discussing how CAP affects databases. Apart from performance, relational databases can *only handle a few types of data* well—data such as documents, graphs, and any other complex categories are unsuitable. All these challenges gave rise to a special breed of databases, called ***NoSQL databases***. This class of databases negotiated on some aspects of traditional relational databases but solved most of the drawbacks.

---

[1] https://aws.amazon.com/rds/

[2] https://aws.amazon.com/rds/aurora/

[3] https://cloud.google.com/sql/docs/

[4] https://azure.microsoft.com/en-us/product-categories/databases/

[5] https://cloud.google.com/spanner/

[6] https://cloud.google.com/bigtable/

There is an abundance of NoSQL databases; let us look at the varieties that most CSPs offer and are useful for building microservices. Fundamentally, most NoSQL databases have similar characteristics: allowing sharding to enable easier scaling out, permitting entities of various definitions to coexist in a single collection, and offering blazing fast response times with excellent performance. Further in the chapter, we discuss the NoSQL datastores variations, which partition data and replicate it onto multiple clusters to achieve reliability.

However, monitoring the throughput, the performance of indexes, request counts, and other metrics of these datastores is vital. Performance penalties not only cause slower response times but also increased billing due to increased compute usage. To ensure optimal performance, avoiding normalization of data is essential in NoSQL datastores; however, keeping related data together positively impacts speed and performance.

## Document Stores

Document databases store all data in a document format.0 A document is an entry in the database that describes an entity completely, in terms of all its attributes. The attributes themselves can be documents, resulting in nested structures. The most popular technique is to store in JSON format, but a few other variations exist: XML, BSON (binary version of JSON), and YAML being the popular ones. The underlying definition is always the same, *a recursive list of key-value pairs*, where a value itself can be a key-value pair. Documents of similar type belong to a *collection*, akin to tables in a relational database. The versatility of documents in storing subdocuments, lists, and links to other documents is beneficial in modeling data that exhibits both structured and unstructured behavior. A schema can enforce the structured part of the document, and the unstructured part left free to change.

When used correctly, document stores can have significant performance improvements over relational databases. Nesting structure often creates duplicate data, which is one of the reasons document stores have *higher performance*. Parallel updates to multiple entries with the same attribute are permitted, due to the *reduced contention in updates*. Unlike relational forms, the documents in a single collection do not need a fully predefined structure. A loosely defined form means data of various definitions and types can exist, encouraging a *more straightforward evolution*. Document databases still retain the grouping of documents in collections and allow defining a schema. They also provide capabilities of indexing documents with multiple keys allowing faster searches.

## Key-Value Stores and Wide-Column Databases

*Key-value stores are massive associative arrays*, which are the core data structures for many classes of computing problems. Consider *maps* and *dictionaries*, which are the lifeblood of most programs that employ dynamic programming techniques. Such techniques rely on the concept of *memoization*. As problems get split into tree-like recursive subproblems, the memoization technique enumerates subproblems and remembers solutions by associating with the subproblem number. Memoization retains the answers for the short-term and ensures quick solve up the problem-tree. Similarly, in large systems, key-value stores are useful in storing data *where a portion of the data uniquely distinguishes every instance*. The unique part is the *key* (aka *row-key*), and the rest of the entry is the *value*. *Wide-column databases are key-value stores where the values fit a structure*, and a schema possibly backs the format.

Though the key-value stores are simplistic, specific, and constrained, there is a wide range of suitable scenarios. Many modern-day applications have data that fit the bill: generic use cases such as caches to specific use cases such as shopping-carts and user-preferences. Energence can use key-value stores for device information,

CSPs routinely offer key-value stores that can work with Internet-scale data. Development teams can easily store data as tuples, where one or more elements are combined to form a key. The nature of the key-value format *permits tremendous flexibility in scaling out but creates severe limitations in access*.

Extreme scaling out is possible on account of *minimal relation between entries*. The absence of dependency with other entries makes each entry independent and portable. Thus, partitioning the data by key-ranges is ridiculously simple. Even rebalancing partitions after a change to the key-ranges is easily manageable. The most critical limiting aspects of key-value datastores are the *access challenges*. Every entry is only identifiable through its key, which signifies the limited set of possible key-based operations. The data access is limited to the elementary operations: *get* (finding a tuple), *put* (adding a new entry), and *update* (changing a tuple), all based on the key.

Some generic rules help in obtaining the best performance from key-value stores. First, defining keys properly: the datastore's reliance on row-keys for all operations underlines the importance of their correct definition. Not all key-value stores allow secondary-indices on the key-value store; row-key is the only way to index entries. Most key-value databases encourage row-keys to contain enough information to help them distribute data, and thus distribute processing; this ensures that the keys can double up as *partition-keys*. Next, designing the tuples to follow the right data structure is paramount for safeguarding against poor performance. Many key-value stores maintain historical snapshots of data. In these cases, creating different partitions for various time periods is a good option; when the next period starts, data goes to the next shard. This technique also concentrates read/write on a small section of data. Finally, *it is crucial to avoid certain types of data as row-keys*: 1) using sequences as row-keys creates *hotspotting*; pooling data together reduces the chances of distributing reads and writes; 2) using values such as hashes and random-numbers for row-keys creates an inability to look up data based on partial key-values, making debugging difficult. For instance, in Energence's case, storing a device reading with row-key of is better than using. Similarly, readings and timestamps are linearly increasing, causing a single partition to be busy while the rest are idle.

# Classifying DBaaS by CAP

In the earlier sections, we classified DBaaS from the types of data they stored. We realized how most databases offer some advantages and disadvantages based on their architecture. Some databases get constrained in their performance by factors such as the type of data, ability to scale out, maintaining consistency, to name a few. In these scenarios, the most important method of classifying databases is not only by the type of data but also by observing what effects CAP theorem has on them.

## Applying CAP Theorem to Databases

CAP theorem is evidence of limits in the universe. No distributed system, partitioned into smaller pieces, can be simultaneously consistent and highly available across its parts. We discussed CAP constraints to distributed systems in Chapter 3. Databases are particularly vulnerable to these CAP constraints, as databases have the primary job of maintaining data for reads and writes. It is possible to allow availability by allowing a leader/follower setup—a standby follower instance takes ownership if the leader dies. Well-tuned monolithic databases can solve **CA** of **CAP**. While we broke the monolith, we realized that microservices might still allow us to employ smaller databases. We chunk the database into smaller partitions at the domain level and remove any direct cross-domain data access. However, this puts the burden on growth, where we cannot scale this database horizontally. The only way to get better performance is by increasing the size of the database.

So, do we have other options that attempt to achieve different combinations of CAP triad? We discussed sharding the database and allocating ranges of data to smaller instances of databases. Such setups offer high consistency within the data range and allow partitioning and growing databases horizontally. They do not solve availability—as loss of shard results in loss of accessibility to that data partition—thus providing **CP** of **CAP**.

Many scenarios do not need immediate consistency, especially the use cases that deal with either large quantities of data or large bounds on response times. Such use cases can compromise on consistency and choose high availability with partitions. The metering-component is a perfect example, which stores a large volume of data and has more leeway on being off by a small amount. The class of NoSQL databases is primarily rooted in this concept of providing **AP** of **CAP**. NoSQL databases run on multiple nodes, each holding parts of data. They replicate data across multiple nodes and synchronize them quickly, thereby providing high availability of data. Consistency is still not instantaneous; it takes time to copy data. It is possible to get stale data by reading partitions that are not yet synchronized. There are a few classes of databases that provide "tunable consistency" on top of AP. These are the **C\*AP** class of NoSQL databases, which *attempt* to provide all three aspects of CAP by simulating consistency. Figure 8-1 depicts three subset combinations of CAP, as achieved by various database types.

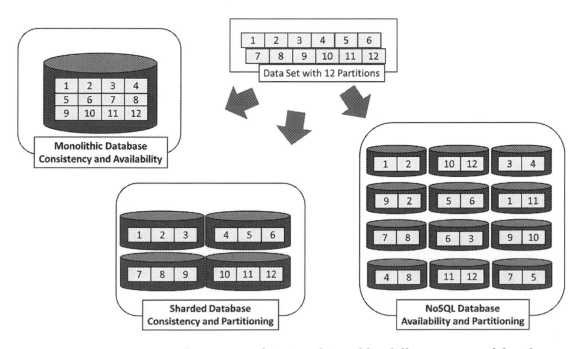

***Figure 8-1.*** *Various combinations of CAP, achieved by different types of databases*

# Relational Databases: CA

An enterprise attempting to use any database on the cloud has two options: rent VMs and install their favorite licensed/open source database, or employ the relation DBaaS (database as a service) provided by CSPs. The best course of action is to select the DBaaS available unless the enterprise uses a particular type of database offered by the CSP. When it comes to relational databases, all cloud providers avail of the most commonly used open source ones. CSPs offer up a few of the popular licensed databases through DBaaS, where enterprises can *bring their licenses to the cloud*. DBaaS frees development teams the burden of maintaining and managing the databases, and all the goodies of cloud—completely managed, available-on-demand, and ease-of-vertical-scaling—become available. There is a flip side to this: developers might have less control over the database. Not all CSPs allow users to tune the base configuration of the database, which the development teams routinely do on-prem for better performance. Development teams will have to adapt to the as-a-service model and get ready to relinquish control.

A significant advantage of microservices is the isolation of parts, which allows for a quick rebuild of the application. Quick teardown and rebuild of instances is not only widespread but is also encouraged. Contrary to this, database instances are relatively fixed. When an application requests a relational database, the CSP will create a DBaaS instance on their private network and peer it for connectivity. Maintenance of the database is transparent to the application domain. It is advisable to enable high availability on the database, which triggers a standby copy in another availability zone. The standby copy gets continuously synchronized with the primary instance. Loss of an availability zone will cause the standby to take over and resume operation immediately. It is best to check the SLAs, (service level agreements) on RTO and RPOs. RTO (recovery time objective) is the measure of how long it takes for the failover to happen. RPO (recovery point objective) is the measure of how much data could potentially get lost. For instance, a delay in synchronizing the standby could cause data altered in that period to become unavailable after the failover. It is also vital to enable periodic snapshots of databases, which will allow domains to recover to a particular instance in time.

It is important to note that relational databases cannot allow partitioning, which is why they are regional resources. Losing a region brings down your application, even if you have deployed it across regions or globally. Additional efforts are needed to make a relational database ready for failing over to another region. We will discuss this in detail further ahead in the book.

CSPs provide relational DBaaS for users, which is the best option—it is often wise to focus on speeding up application and leave database tuning to the provider.

## Sharded and Distributed: CA*P

A common technique to achieve horizontal scaling of databases is to employ *sharding*. In this technique, data gets partitioned into shards, which contain only specific parts of the overall data. This data model based on sharding is commonly known as the share-nothing model. CSPs provide sharding on top of existing relational DBaaS or offer alternate DBaaS that maintains data in shard. Also applicable are key-value stores, where the information is always tied to a key. These databases are best suited for domains with 'dense-data'—domains whose data has a great deal of relation between different entities, but individual entities are independent.

Sharding immediately opens up many possibilities in scaling databases. The primary advantage is that a sizeable monolithic database can now reside on *many smaller databases* partitioned by a shard-key. Partitioning the data every time data grows beyond a manageable size allows for easier maintenance. Many techniques will enable applications to be *global*. Data shards can contain only local data, thereby enabling horizontal scalability when the enterprise expands business in other areas. Shards also *improve performanc*e due to the independence of data entities, which creates minimal contentions in data access. Finally, a significant advantage that is a side effect of sharding is the localization of failure. Loss of a shard will only affect data in that partition; services for users whose data is in other sections are unaffected.

A perfect example is the Energence Home Platform's metering domain. The metering domain always stores data, device-specific data against the same device identifier. Seldom will access to one device's data depend on any other device's data. Once the platform has consumers internationally, metering domain needs to run globally. In this scenario, data can be sharded per region, thus providing better performance. Metering domain can shard the database further as the size grows, for example, using the meter number.

Attempting to shard and distribute a database manually has a few severe drawbacks. We discussed this in our chapter on challenges faced in a microservices architecture. The first and the most obvious challenge—accessing data across shards. Access across shards requires special techniques such as centralized views, which we discussed in Chapter 4.

The challenge of repartitioning data when partitions grow, in size or in retrieval times, could cause massive downtimes to rebuild the shards. The final challenge is the query engineering required to ensure data access is accurate. Cross-domain queries need to make sure the correct partitions are accessed to get the data, which might add extra complexity to applications' data access.

---

Sharded and distributed database choices of a CSP are great for storing share-nothing data models; here structures have almost no interdependency (such as imposed foreign-keys). This type of database provides horizontal scalability, consistency within the shard, and localization of failures.

---

## NoSQL Databases: C*AP

*By persisting in your path, though you forfeit the little, you gain the great.*

—Ralph Waldo Emerson

In earlier sections, we realized that the concept of sharding onto multiple nodes does not guarantee availability. Even though the loss of a node does not bring the entire database down, there are parts of data missing. To solve this, we tried replicating the data across nodes to ensure availability, but we ended up with the challenge of consistency. The CAP theorem indeed seems to be the evidence of limits in the universe. However, humans do not believe there are limits. We have designed a few variations to the AP class of solutions that artificially achieve consistency, C*AP. These variations are characteristics of most NoSQL databases and a handful of relational databases. In this concept, the data gets replicated to an odd **quorum** of nodes, and updates need to happen to more than 50% of copies to be successful. The variations of this concept have an extremely flexible type of consistency and allow several variations of quorum. Note that this model exhibits *tunable consistency*—achieving the right level of consistency requiring tuning the desired level of "strength." Let us explore how picking quorum-based operations allows for balancing performance with precision. This section deals with various techniques that attempt to achieve tunable consistency and their effects on microservices design.

---

## REAL-WORLD EXAMPLE OF A QUORUM

---

Understanding quorum helps us comprehend the importance of quorum to mitigate CAP limitations. To understand the concept of the quorum, consider a real-world example. Before the advent of modern-day banks, three friends Alice, Bob, and Carol, lived in NY, Los Angeles, and Atlanta, respectively, wanted to run an institution to transfer money long-distance. The idea was people could pay any one of the three friends and receive from any of the three friends. The business idea was that Alice, Bob, and Carol would talk to each other about any transaction—whether they receive money from clients or give money to clients. They all maintained a ledger, which was an exact copy across three. It contained all transactions and kept in sync with others. If anyone of the three did a transaction, they would call the other two and update their personal copies. Alice, Bob, and Carol are about to have a rude awakening about their simple business setup. They are about to learn how the CAP theorem will ruin their business if they are not careful.

Erin, a friend of Alice, is excited to learn about these services and decides to use it. She would have planned a trip to LA, so instead of carrying cash, she deposits a thousand dollars with Alice and tells her that she will collect her money in LA from Bob. Alice accepts the money, but the trunk line between LA and NY breaks down due to maintenance. Unfortunately, Alice was unable to tell Bob about this transaction; when Erin reaches LA, Bob refuses to give the money. It was only after a few days—when trunk services were finally restored, and Alice was able to reach out to Bob—Erin got her money back. Erin was distraught and gave Alice and Bob an earful. Now, Alice, Bob, and Carol are afraid of this happening again—cases like this could ruin their business. They start thinking of paying out a small fraction, 10%, of money to people who register with them, even if they are unable to get confirmation from other partners. Alice, Bob, and Carol realize this should solve some of the issues.

Eve finds out about this mishap and tells her friend Heidi and Mallory, who lives in Atlanta. Heidi sees the problem in this setup. She devises an ingenious plan to break this business. She registers with Carol and asks her friend Chuck to enroll with Bob. Their names get exchanged, and now Heidi and Chuck are part of this registration. Next, she waits for a failure in the trunk that connects Atlanta with NY. She then proceeds to ask Carol for ten thousand dollars that her friend Chuck has supposedly deposited with Bob. Carol has no way of knowing whether Bob received the money or not. Simultaneously, Chuck approaches Bob requesting ten thousand dollars, which he claims his friend Heidi has deposited with Carol. Bob again has no way of knowing this for sure. Heidi and Chuck get paid thousand dollars each with their ingenious plan. Meantime Mallory secretly disconnects Carol's phone and demands for twenty thousand dollars, which supposedly her friend has deposited with Alice. This situation is worse because Carol can reach no one else and has to pay up.

These scenarios show how availability breaks down in a partitioned system, leading to severe failures. After these fiascos, Alice, Bob, and Carol devise a strategy. They decide that for any deposit to be successful with one of them, they have to communicate the credit to at least one more. For instance, Bob can accept money only if he can update Alice's or Carol's books, if not both. The same rules apply for withdrawal. This simple technique, where two out of three of them have their books in sync, tremendously reduces failure. Next time Erin wants to deposit money with Alice, she will update Carol of this transaction. When Erin asks Bob for money, even though he cannot reach Alice, he can check with Carol of this deposit and can definitively disposition the request.

Similarly, when Heidi and Chuck approach for money, Carol and Bob can check with Alice for such a deposit. The requirement of checking with at least one more of the triad helps them know that the transactions did not happen, thus evading false payouts. However, this cannot solve complete unavailability scenarios. However, when Mallory disconnects Carol's phone line, they avoid paying out falsely to Mallory. However, if Carol receives a legitimate customer, she would upset the customer. Similarly, if Frank wants to deposit ten thousand dollars with Carol for his trip to NY, Carol cannot accept his payment as she cannot reach either Alice or Bob.

This example demonstrates the use of quorum to achieve consistency in a partitioned system. Distributed systems, which wish to achieve consistency, use this concept heavily—we will explore the applicability of this principle in this section.

# Quorum-Based Transactions

Most NoSQL databases run on multi-node clusters. We discussed two ideas that help us understand the concept of tunable consistency. First, we discussed the idea of sharding the data onto multiple nodes. Next, we discussed the notion of quorum using the business plan of Alice, Bob, and Carol. Now let us apply those principles to C*AP type databases. NoSQL databases allow partitioning of their data, and hence horizontal scalability. As many of the variations partition the data based on shard-keys but also copy it onto multiple instances in the cluster. The number of copies, termed replicas, is less than or equal to the number of nodes. *The number of replicas that accept updates for a successful transaction decides the degree of consistency.* Request for a read/write is redirected to a fixed leader or any of the nodes (depends on the database and its configuration), and this node triggers the read/write across all nodes. For a highly consistent read, more than half of the nodes should agree on the result. For instance, a successful *quorum read* on a cluster of five nodes requires that at least three of the five nodes return the same value.

Let us apply this to a microservices domain. Consider the domain model for Energence's customer-module represented in the diagram. Assume that we decided to split the domain model of customer-module into eight shards: {A, B, C, D, E, Q, R, T}. Two shards hold account information about commercial users, and the rest six hold residential accounts. For high availability, we replicate these eight shards onto multiple nodes that are across different availability zones. Let us ensure the two partitions containing commercial users, say A and B, need to be globally available, so they are made available across both regions. Figure 8-2 shows the spread of such data. The database is spread across two regions, US-East and US-West, thereby ensuring a very high level of availability. Both regions are running four nodes each, and each shard of data is replicated thrice in both regions. Data is continuously synchronized between all copies. In this scenario, we have achieved high availability (through replication and redundancy), consistency (constant synchronization of data), and partitioning (due to multiple nodes). The catch, however, is that *consumers have the option of choosing the type of consistency they need.*

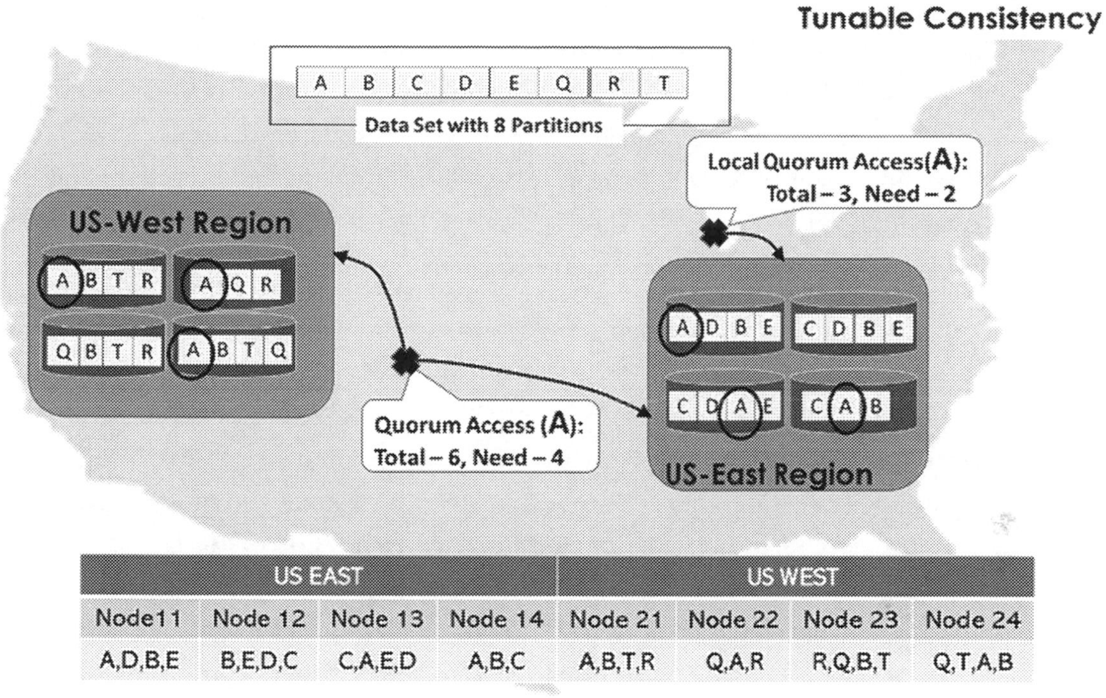

**Figure 8-2.** *Tunable consistency, demonstrated by local and global quorum reads*

Consider a commercial customer in Chicago, who is accessing data in shard A and wants consistent data. Chicago knows that their spread is only limited to the East, so she decides that a read that is consistent within US-East is enough. She issues a *local-quorum read*. A local-quorum read implies that as long as most nodes from the current region have consistent data, the response is considered accurate. When the database receives the command, it waits for most nodes to agree—in this case, two out of three nodes to agree on a value—before returning.

Let us suppose there is another commercial consumer in Denver, whose transaction requires a very high consistency. Denver is sure that updates to her data could happen on both coasts, which means the last update could have occurred in either region. To ensure she gets the most accurate data, she issues a *quorum read*. A quorum read needs the majority of nodes, across both the regions, to agree on the final value. In this case, the database has to wait until the majority of nodes across both regions agree on the data—four out of six total copies. Such a read operation might have to wait a long time before gaining consensus on the state. An update to data in partition A of US-East might take hundreds of milliseconds to synchronize with US-West. The response is available as soon as the quorum agrees on a value.

169

The ability to select read types demonstrates that we have achieved all three aspects of CAP, but have allowed the reader to choose the elements of CAP they need. For high availability, users could issue reads from a single node—a very high performance at the cost of accuracy, achieved by choosing availability over consistency. A quorum read opts for consistency over availability. This way of determining the value, similar to all decisions ever made by a committee, is never quick; it sacrifices throughput, and hence, availability.

# Distributed Consensus

In our earlier discussion on quorum, we discovered why it is an excellent concept. We realized how it helps us approximate consistency in a distributed system. We briefly mentioned that these distributed databases replicate data elements on multiple nodes for availability. At the heart of the exciting domain of **consensus theory** are two questions about distributed systems: first, what constitutes a successful replication, and second, how to define the success of a read or write. Though the origins of consensus theory are from the 1970s, it continues to be one of the topics at the forefront of computing science innovation. Readers are strongly urged to immerse themselves in the rich technical literature on the subject, as the concepts are technology agnostic and intellectually invigorating.

One of the primary challenges in achieving consensus in a distributed system is the inherent communication delay between various nodes. Preserving an overall consistent state and the consistency of data in each node is the goal of a successful distributed operation. The real challenges appear when updates happen to the same data element across two nodes. *When changes to a data element happen at more than one place simultaneously, the overall consistency of data is necessary.* There are two competing schools of thought for achieving consensus in a distributed system: **leader-follower** and **leaderless** techniques. In a leader-follower scenario, one or more nodes act as leaders—*leaders are responsible for coordinating with the rest of the nodes and gaining confirmation of changes.* In a leaderless setup, either there are no fixed leaders, or there are simply no leaders.

In a *leader-follower* scenario, two variations exist; the cluster could have a single leader or have multiple leaders. Leaders are determined through an election, a fair election. When a database-cluster with multiple nodes comes online, all the comprising nodes vote to select one or more leader-node. The elections continue to happen regularly to account for lost nodes or change in topology. Once leaders are elected, they frequently send heartbeat signals to all followers to indicate their presence. Reelection is required when a leader is lost. Leaders are responsible for communicating with the other nodes and confirming all copies are in sync.

In this setup, clients request their updates to a leader. The leader sends this to update to the other nodes and waits for confirmation. In a quorum-update scenario, the leader waits for confirmation from more than half the nodes before responding with success. In our example with Alice, Bob, and Carol, the leader is the person who receives the money. If Alice accepts the funds, she has to gain consensus with at least $\left\lfloor \frac{3}{2}+1 \right\rfloor$ members,

which is at least two out of three. If Alice is unable to reach Carol, Carol's transaction log gets updated after Alice or Bob contacts Carol. To generalize, a quorum of n copies should contain gain consensus from at least \lfloor\frac{n}{2}+1\rfloor copies.

When building microservices against NoSQL databases at a highly distributed scale, knowledge of distributed consensus is hugely beneficial. When we began refactoring to microservices, we relied on domains to eliminate interdependency. We also tried to eradicate shared states in microservices by forcing the parts to be small enough to avoid the need for consensus. However, as we attempt to scale the microservices architecture across regions, the distributed nature of data source reappears and lands us right back in the consensus space. However, we are further ahead in the journey and are more informed. We now know the techniques of setting the database and its data elements correctly. We know the various quorum access patterns to allow for consensus of data to the appropriate level. *This knowledge of implications of CAP and distributed-consensus enables us to use the right type of datastore without resorting to a single relational type database.*

# DataStores for OLAP

Analytical jobs and transactional operations are inherently different. They differ in purpose, speed, and performance parameters. *Transactional applications depend on a massive scale of record-level mutations.* Consequently, the databases that support transactional applications excel in reading and writing individual records—stored as rows or tuples or documents. Over the decades, databases have worked in several elegant features for performance, keys and indices for fast searches, caching frequently accessed elements, block reads and writes, and read/write locks, to name a few. Contrarily, *analytical jobs focus on running complex queries that read and process enormous amounts of data.* These jobs require collating, comparing, and aggregating features across millions of data records. The focus often is reading a few columns of a massive amount of rows. This class of datastores traditionally constitute *online analytics processing* (*OLAP*) datastores.

Enterprises have routinely run business intelligence divisions and have maintained extensive data warehouses to support analytics. *The field of analytics and data warehousing transformed into an even more incredible asset with the advent of big data.* Big data provided the capability to store various types of information, including data such as multimedia content. Simultaneously, the reemergence of machine learning intensified the efforts to collect and retain as much data as possible. Businesses now hope to learn from the past and make more informed decisions, systemically.

Outside the role of analytics, *big datastores provide immense support to microservices architectures as well*. In Chapters 3 and 4, we discussed the challenges of microservices architecture and some of the solutions. One of the biggest technical challenges is joining data across domains in bulk for use cases such as reporting and analytics. The difficulty in gathering, combining, and analyzing data across various microservice domains needs a different type of datastore.

In this chapter, we look at popular cloud solutions relating to data warehousing in the next section. Big data is an entirely new and exciting field and needs serious focus. However, we limit our discussions to data warehouses' capabilities—they are more relevant to microservices architecture. We need to discuss the criticality of loading data into these datastores, an associated aspect. Infrastructure to push data into these datastores in a timely and efficient manner is of utmost importance. Traditionally, ETL (extract, transform, load) jobs achieved data movement from various datastores into data warehouses or big datastores. In a cloud setup, ingesting data into big datastores has its own set of tools and techniques. We discussed some aspects of data ingestion earlier in this chapter while examining the concepts of streaming; next, we look at related strategies for data warehouses in the same space later in this chapter.

# Data Warehouses on Cloud

Data warehouses are employed to pool together schematic data from various data sources and provide analytical capabilities. In our microservices architectures, data warehouses are perfect candidates for *centralized views*. Chapter 4 describes the underlying reasons for employing a centralized view. We wished to create an event store (or point-in-time snapshots of data) in the microservices domains and use it for all our analytical and reporting needs. Data warehouses are a perfect fit for these needs.

A familiar concern of data warehousing, the ability to handle increasing data volumes, arises. Traditionally, data warehouses lacked the scalability aspects of big data. However, data warehouses on the cloud are much more scalable, primarily due to the inherent elastic nature of cloud and scale-out options of CSP's data warehousing solutions.

For the Energence Home Platform, the data from the various databases of EOTA (Energence over the air), billing, metering, smart-devices, customer, and payment domains, should flow to the data warehouse near-real-time. Reports that span across the multiple parts of the home platform are rendered from the data warehouse. Consider the reports such as the following that originated from the monolith's database itself:

- **The number of customers who have smart-device updates pending**: It requires combining data from the customer, billing, metering, and smart-devices domains.

- **The number of customers who have more than some specified number of smart devices**: It requires combining data from billing, customer, metering, and smart-devices domain.

As data warehouses are born to provide business intelligence, they also prove immensely useful for making analytical decisions.

- **The list of meters that have to be turned off due to non-payment**: This report requires combining data from the customer, billing, metering, and smart-devices domains. Metering-system can pull this information from the data warehouse and automatically switch off those meters.

- **The users whose smart-device patching attempts have repeatedly failed**: This report requires combining data from the customer, billing, metering, smart-devices, and EOTA domains. The customer microservices can retrieve information from the data warehouse, alert users of this, and apply a discount to their next bill.

To be effective, especially *when working with microservices on the cloud, the concept of data warehousing being for after-the-fact analytics has to die.* Data warehouses have to bear the burden of regular reporting and analytics, which many enterprises offloaded to the monolithic applications. In a microservices architecture, the various domains that make up the solution need to keep the data warehouse in sync, making it the centralized view of the solution. *It is paramount that the data warehouse is updated near-real-time*, to create precise reports and support correct analytical decisions.

# Data Movement on Cloud

Unlike big data, data warehouses need highly curated and clean data. Data ingestion needs to be accurate, timely, and clean. Traditional nightly ETL batch jobs moved data through multiple levels of filtering and enrichment. They pulled data from various data sources and staged them into a "raw data" layer. Another set of jobs cleansed the data and created a "clean data" layer. This clean data layer is then further massaged and prepared for ingestion into the data warehouse. The same patterns apply in a cloud data warehouse. Most CSPs allow for batch and real-time data ingestion.

For our use case, let us consider *the data warehouse is updated near-real-time* and look at the required tools and techniques. Every transaction in a domain updates multiple tables and changes the overall state of the system. Capturing these changes into a data warehouse—the snapshot of new data every time it changes—provides a great event source. If we can cleanse and land the data into the data warehouse, we have created a running snapshot of data changes. The series of recorded data changes are the ideal technique to relate various microservice domains and use for reporting and analytics.

The primary requirement from each microservice is to broadcast the state changes as they process through their transactions. The underlying idea here is to use the trace-id associated with the transactions and emit the changes committed by each domain. Alternatively, any of the tools that monitor data changes and create events on data changes can also be employed. Next, the ability to sink this data into a data warehouse is required. CSPs provide tools to stream data into their data warehouses and big datastores. These tools allow modifications and customizations to enable mapping, transformation, and cleansing of data as it passes through them. At this point, we have successfully created an event store, akin to the CQRS (command query responsibility segregation) pattern. The final step is to create a clean-data layer, which stays current and in sync with transactional datastores.

Reporting from these datastores will rely on both data snapshots and the clean-data layer. Reports and analytics that require current states will collate the latest versions of data from the clean-data layer. Historical reports for business intelligence and deep-analytical queries will sift through the event snapshots and clean-data layer to gather the required data.

In this section, we attempted to solve the problem of transitioning reporting and analytics from a monolithic data model to a microservices architecture. We realized that the challenges of moving from a monolith, which has a highly relational data source, requires an external data repository. This technique also helps us accommodate the polyglot nature of datastores of a microservices architecture.

## DATA WAREHOUSES BY THE TOP CSPS

AWS's Amazon Redshift[7] is the data warehousing PaaS, a columnar datastore that offers parallel query execution. Another feature of Redshift is the ability to directly query data in bulk storage like S3. Azure's SQL Data Warehouse[8] is very similar to Redshift, offering parallel query execution and the ability to run against Hot Blob Storage. GCP's BigQuery[9] is an automatically scaled SQL data warehousing PaaS. BigQuery can also query bulk stores and even data stored in spreadsheets. Unlike Redshift or Azure, wherein a compute size needs to be specified, BigQuery is provided as compute credits that are on-demand: charges are per query.

## CLOUD STORAGE ON TOP CSPS

Apart from databases, data warehouses, and big datastores, enterprises need infrastructure to store their software resources. These resources refer to all data and applications traditionally stored in network drives and backed up to tape stores by the enterprise. CSPs classify the storage options based on need: 1) object stores, aka blob stores, are for generic data, anything that can be written to a file and accessed from anywhere and anyhow; 2) file storage, a folder-like structure of files similar to an enterprise's network drive; and 3) block storage, storage blocks that can get attached to VMs, identical to SANs in an on-prem scenario. Object stores

---

[7]https://aws.amazon.com/redshift/
[8]https://azure.microsoft.com/en-us/services/sql-data-warehouse/
[9]https://cloud.google.com/bigquery

are of particular interest for applications dealing with binary data, such as images, videos, audio. For Energence, storing binary patches is a perfect use case of using object stores.

All of cloud providers' costs can indirectly be mapped to compute and storage. The cheapest storage options on cloud providers are a way to store bulk data. Amazon's famous S3 is the bulk object-store option, offered in various classes based on retrieval times. S3 Standard is for frequently accessed data, akin an on-prem shared drive. S3 I/A and S3 Z-I/A are for infrequently accessed but rapidly read data. S3 Glacier is for secure and low-cost storage where retrieval could take minutes to hours.[10]

Azure's offerings in the same tiers are Hot Blob Storage, Cool Blob Storage, and Blob Archive Storage.[11] GCP's offering are Cloud Storage Standard, Cloud Storage Nearline, and Cloud Storage Coldline.[12]

# Summary

CSPs offer an assorted platter of storage options to choose from, and architects need to select based on factors such as need and cost. We can group storage options into three classes: *datastores*, *big data*, and *blob storage*.

Datastores are traditional databases and NoSQL datastores. Microservices-based architecture promotes polyglot development. Similarly, the architecture encourages using the right type of datastore for each microservice. Choosing the right kind of datastore is based on two parameters: data type and access type. Data type refers to the way information of the domain exists—dense, key-based, document-type, etc. Access type refers to the amount of distribution it needs for better accessibility—limited to a single data center, partitioned across the globe, or data that is (literally) globally consistent.

Knowledge of how to work with distributed datastores is quintessential for microservices architecture. The way we deploy and allocate microservices footprint across regions heavily relies on the datastores they use. Different microservices have

---

[10]https://aws.amazon.com/s3/storage-classes/
[11]https://docs.microsoft.com/en-us/azure/storage/blobs/storage-blob-storage-tiers
[12]https://cloud.google.com/storage/docs/storage-classes

different requirements: some can handle data in a single region without needing data from other regions; some microservices need data from across the globe for functioning. Understanding the details behind the datastores helps make the right decision.

The big datastores include both data lakes that collect a variety of data and data warehouses that collect clean and curated data. Various data movement tools are available to ETL data into the data warehouse and data lakes. Finally, CSPs also offer storage for objects, files, and block storage for VMs and other IaaS products.

# Points to Ponder

1.  How do various consistency factors affect our datastore selection? When do we choose CA vs CP vs C*AP

2.  Consider the various schema in your organization. How many of them are best stored in NoSQL?

3.  How will multi-model databases—databases that can store documents, relational data, and graph—affect our solutions? What will they simplify? What will they complicate?

4.  Can NoSQL databases double up as analytical datastores, along with transactional stores? Why or why not?

# Further Related Reading

**NoSQL Distilled** by *Sadalge et al.* (Sadalage & Fowler, 2012).
    **Distributed Algorithms** by *Nancy A. Lynch* (Lynch, 1996).
    *The Modern Data Warehouse in Azure* by *How* (How, 2020).

# CHAPTER 9

# Securing Microservices on Cloud

*Safety brings first aid to the uninjured.*

—F.S. Hughes

The perceived importance of security in an enterprise is directly proportional to the devastation caused by the previous attack. It does not have to be, but it often is. A genuinely secure enterprise discusses the security of software right at inception. We discussed the importance of securing the application right from its beginning in an earlier chapter, under the "DevSecOps" section. We briefly discussed what it takes to safeguard microservices (or any application) on the cloud. In this chapter, we discuss some of the most critical aspects of cybersecurity.

Security is traditionally considered a triad: *confidentiality*, *integrity*, and *availability*. A system must maintain the confidentiality of data and information by restricting to authorized entities. It is crucial to ensure that data integrity is maintained: data is not corrupted, not compromised, and not lost. It is essential to guarantee the availability of both services and data to the predetermined service level objectives (SLOs).

Given these, let us discuss Figure 9-1, which depicts a typical microservices cloud deployment setup. It also represents essential aspects that need our attention and shows how security is best achieved in layers. There are five different aspects shown in the diagram:

1. Defensive ingress of data into the cloud infrastructure

2. Securing data flow into public microservices endpoints on the cloud

© Chandra Rajasekharaiah 2021
C. Rajasekharaiah, *Cloud-Based Microservices*, https://doi.org/10.1007/978-1-4842-6564-2_9

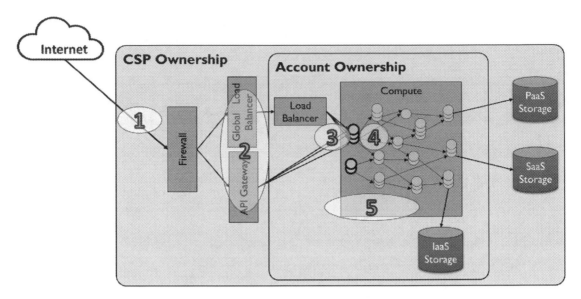

***Figure 9-1.*** *Security hotspots in microservices cloud deployment*

3.  Guarding communication into microservices instance endpoints

4.  Protecting data exchange between microservices

5.  Shielding compute infrastructure leveraged on cloud

In this chapter, our focus is on each one of these five aspects. First, we discuss the general, cloud-agnostic guidelines around securing microservices, immaterial of their deployment destination. Next, we discuss safeguarding data flow in a microservices architecture on the cloud. After that, we need to look at the integrity of computation itself—how do we ensure computing infrastructure is shielded against malicious intent? Finally, we will look at the various availability challenges—how to set up against failures and how to prepare for disasters.

# Securing Microservices

A microservices architecture, especially an API-enabled one, moves businesses to an information-boundaryless[1] and connected state. Such boundaryless information exchange results in magnifying vulnerabilities and exacerbating breaches. Exploit in one

---

[1]In most enterprises, accessing information across organizations is difficult. With APIs, all organizations expose their data for other organizations of the enterprise to access.

organization could quickly cascade to an enterprise-level breach. Regrettably, a perfectly secure infrastructure cannot be created—the only guaranteed way to protect a computer from online attacks is to take it offline. These orthogonal needs, of being simultaneously secure and open, are the bane of a microservices architecture.

In this section, we focus our discussion on mitigation strategies for risks.

# Reducing the Attack Surface

In a microservices architecture, independent domains contain top-level orchestration services. These high-level services are used across the enterprise, on a larger scale. They can be leveraged by client services, web-clients, and enterprise partners. These endpoints, usually situated at the extremities of the infrastructure, are the most vulnerable points of attacks.

The first step is to *isolate and expose only the top-level services* and completely *restrict access to other services*. We thus reduce the attack surface, thereby focusing on securing the few top-level services. For instance, only the top-level services are wired to an external load balancer or API gateway, while others are unreachable from outside the domain.

The second step is to *restrict the communication options* of these top-level services. We need to *limit the communication protocols* to a minimal set; for instance, we only allow HTTPS and disallow all other techniques such as RPCs[2], socket communication, custom connections, etc. Such a restriction allows standardizing the tools used for securing, monitoring, and controlling communication channels. Next, we also need to *enforce verifiable client identification at entry points*; for instance, mandate every request to contain a client-ID. Once we identify the client, we can apply rules on service—denying or allowing usage by individual clients, or a class of clients.

The last step is *to create and enforce policies*. Enforced policies can limit usage (maximum number of requests per time unit, the largest number of simultaneous requests allowed, etc.) and stop intentional or unintentional DOS attacks. Policies can also restrict clients to a subset of available services based on identification.

---

[2]RPCs (remote procedure calls, such as CORBA, COM, Java RMI, etc.,) are legacy techniques of application integration, wherein systems exchange binary information over TCP sockets.

# Securing Services

In practice, the majority of microservices are realized as web services. This reliance on web protocols means that *the problem space of securing microservices is identical to securing any web service*. The trick is to ensure that the client has the authority to invoke a microservice. The services that face the client need defending against malicious usage, which means we need to shrink the attack surface. First, we start by exposing only the top-level services that the clients need. Next, the top-level services need to follow security policies to safeguard content and delivery. However, enforcing policies requires standardized IAA (identification, authentication, and authorization). Several standards exist for IAA, which are broadly grouped as *implicit-trust based* and *explicit-trust based*. Both standards require clients to submit an identity (aka principal), an equivalent of a token, to prove their identity. Once authenticated, the service controls the authorization of what content the client can access through security policies.

Standard techniques such as SAML, OAuth2, and OIDC allow authentication and authorization between clients and services. These techniques enable clients to obtain a token that encapsulates identification and authentication information. The underlying concept is of a *central trusted entity* that can verify the identity of the client and issuing a token. For instance, upon verifying identity, SAML issues SAML assertions, OAuth2 issues Access Tokens, and OIDC issues JWT tokens.

Figure 9-2. Securing services via API Gateway with tokens and applying policies. Figure 9-2 depicts a secure interaction between client and services via an API gateway. In the absence of API gateway or service endpoints (for instance, service mesh), the services bears the responsibilities of both entities. In this flow, a trusted entity confirms the client's identity and issues an *access token*. Temporary access tokens, which expire after a duration, are preferable: they fare better against brute force attacks. The clients attach this access token to the payload of every service call they make. When the gateway receives the request, it validates the embedded token, extracts the *claims*, and uses them to enforce security policies.

For these tokens to be implicitly trusted, an issuing authority should digitally sign them[3], confirming their genuineness. When explicit trust is in place, gateways will check the token's validity with the trusted entity every time.

---

[3]For readers familiar with PKI (public key infrastructure), a digital signature is an attachment to the message that the provider encrypts the hash of the key with its private key. The recipient can decrypt the hash with the provider's public key and validate the payload. This enables detecting any tampering of payload and also guarantees non-repudiation.

We have now secured the service and prepared it to accept requests over a secure channel. The gateway will extract tokens from the client requests and validates their digital signature. Using token's validity and contained claims, policies are applied and requests are accepted or denied.

## Securing Outgoing Communication

Services use external resources such as datastores and other services to complete their task. Connecting to datastores follows a definite pattern. A service will authenticate with the datastore upon startup and will maintain an active connection (or pool of connections) with the datastore.

When a top-level service is a client to a service, the top-level service will **attach the token it received from the original client, unchanged,** to its outgoing request. This concept, termed *principal propagation*, ensures the rest of the service tree enforces policies applicable to the originating client. It is a smart idea to propagate the original principal into every change to persistent datastores. Transmitting the principal down the microservices tree also ensures traceability and audit of every data change.

## Securing Microservices on Cloud

To ensure the security of microservices running on the cloud, we need to focus on parts of the cloud marked in Figure 9-1. Unlike on an infrastructure entirely owned and managed by enterprises, **cloud infrastructure tends to be opaque and disparate**. We encounter challenges in 1) *securing Internet-facing service endpoints*, 2) *federating access management from enterprise to cloud*, and 3) *securing inter-service communication on an opaque infrastructure*.

The most critical aspect of a cloud security setup is the network setup. CSPs (cloud service providers) allow you to carve out *Virtual Private Clouds* (VPCs, aka *Virtual Private Networks*)—private networks virtually overlaid on CSP's network. At least one VPC is available for every account, and each VPC can further have subnets inside it. A successful setting up VPCs needs a good knowledge of networking theory and security knowledge. We will spend a bulk of this section discussing VPCs.

The *service endpoints are open to the Internet*, requiring enterprises to plan against Internet speed attacks—for instance, denial of service attacks, brute force attacks, SSL attacks. These attacks could result in resource exhaustion, which could curtail the ability to acquire additional resources by applications that need them.

Another aspect architects need to deal with are the challenges in *federating secret, identity, and access controls* on the cloud. CSPs seldom integrate transparently with an enterprise's password vaults, LDAP servers[4], or IdP[5] infrastructure. An option is to use the CSP's IAM (identity and access management), thus avoiding enterprise IAA calls altogether.

Microservices architecture creates a substantial number of service endpoints: both between and within domains. On the cloud, the *communication between microservices is on a shared infrastructure.* Unauthorized access gained to any microservice could result in a ripple effect of security exploits.

---

### OPTIONS TO SECURE THE PERIPHERY IN A CSP

All providers have products in the space of firewalls and security against threats such as DDOS attacks. AWS's product WAF (Web Application Firewall)[6] is equivalent to Azure Firewall[7] and GCP's CloudArmor.[8]

---

# Virtual Private Clouds

Figure 9-2 shows a typical view of a typical VPC configured on the cloud. VPCs are not a concept that originated in the cloud—they are similar to VPNs. Enterprises had their virtual private networks overlaid on multiple physical networks, both public and private. Similarly, VPCs are logically isolated networks for CSP's resources.

---

[4]LDAP (lightweight directory access protocol), a centralized repository of directory information services—with information such as employees, users, groups, group memberships, roles—is common in enterprises.

[5]IdP, or identity provider services, are similar to central trusted entity that provides authentication services.

[6]https://aws.amazon.com/waf/

[7]https://azure.microsoft.com/en-us/services/azure-firewall/

[8]https://cloud.google.com/armor/

VPCs are an excellent way to isolate connectivity between cloud resources. Figure 9-2 shows the concept involved in understanding VPCs. Let us assume Energence's Enterprise Home Platform team owns VPC-1234, and hence it needs a few capabilities: it has to expose web services to the Internet, for users to check their accounts, make payments, etc. The metering-system needs to receive readings from devices to calculate usage. It needs to interface with the Manufacturing Platform, which resides on VPC-4567.

Each of the connections in VPC-1234 needs a different type of control defined. To solve this, let us assume we define each application to reside in its subsection of the network, termed a *subnet*. Subnets are segregations within a VPC, each with its IP ranges and closed off for external communication unless explicitly stated. IaaS and iCaaS resources reside on the subnet, and their access is dependent on access controls of the subnet.

All communication between cloud elements needs setting up *routes* in the VPC, enabling communications between entities within a subnet and with external entities. Usually, by default, routing rules allow communication between subnets in the same VPC but denies traffic flow to entities outside the VPC. *Route tables*—which contain routing rules and permissions—are managed by a *router*, which remembers the IP address of devices in the VPC and allows or denies traffic between them.

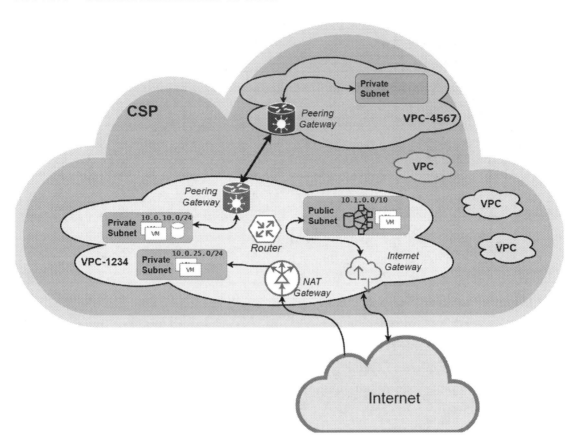

**Figure 9-2.**  *Virtual Private Clouds on a CSP*

Direct communication with entities outside the VPC needs special devices, termed gateways. A subnet communicating with the Internet, a public-facing HTTP load balancer, for instance, requires an *Internet gateway*. Some CSPs differentiate between a subnet that uses an Internet gateway as a *public subnet*; they also restrict the number of such public subnets. Every other subnet in the VPC becomes a *private subnet*. These CSPs require a particular *NAT gateway* to allow traffic from the Internet to flow into private subnets. In the Energence Home Platform setup on such clouds, the metering-system would need a NAT gateway to bring readings in. The applications or load balancers that open up to the Internet can take on a public IP—either temporarily or permanently, based on necessity. In a cloud environment with ephemeral IP addresses, the standard practice is to associate a DNS name to these IP addresses and abstracting the underlying IPs.

An enterprise such as Energence will own multiple accounts (and hence many VPCs), one for each of its departments; thus, it needs communication between different VPCs. This concept of connecting different VPCs is termed *VPC peering*. Accessing

Home Platform services in VPC-1234 from the VPC hosting various Energence portals needs a peering between the two VPCs. A *peering gateway* establishes and controls communication between two VPCs. VPC peering is heavily used by PaaS systems as well. For instance, the managed PaaS services used by a user gets created and maintained on the CSP's VPC; that CSP's VPC gets peered with the user's VPC, and traffic is secured by restricting origins, ports, and protocols of communication between the two VPCs. Peering controls the blast radius of an infiltration. A compromised VPC will disallow intruders to access other VPCs.

Understanding the concept of VPC is paramount for development teams to protect their services and assets on the cloud. Fortunately, CSPs provide great tools, dashboards, and guidelines to achieve this. Some basic principles we discussed earlier in securing microservices still apply. Restricting the public-facing endpoints reduces the attack surface. Whitelisting IPs, aka allow-listing of IPs, to limit accessibility is another excellent precaution to take. Whitelisting IPs for some areas is possible: for instance, Energence's partner-portal can restrict access to only a few IP ranges that their partners own. It is a limited set that can be predetermined. However, the user-portal cannot avail the same advantage, especially when Energence wants to go global.

# API Gateways and Load Balancers

CSPs typically offer two different ways to expose services to the Internet: *API gateways*, which can handle REST+HTTPS type of traffic, and *load balancers*, which work with communications at the TCP layer. A load balancer's primary purpose is to enable the scalability of HTTP endpoints.[9] Microservices architectures use load balancers *to distribute requests to the many replicas of a microservice*. API gateways are extensions of load balancers, with sophistication *to authorize payloads, and route traffic based on the request's content and context*.

---

[9]Load balancers can work at layer 4 as well, allowing TCP and UDP communication to route between multiple socket-servers. However, for microservices discussion, we focus on layer-7 capabilities of load balancers.

# Load Balancers

Load balancers allow configuring a target set of resources (services, in our case) against a global endpoint. Load balancers resolve requests to any of the configured services, based on several configurable patterns, such as round-robin, geographical affinity, and even-loading. Load balancers also detect unhealthy endpoints and remove them from the pool until they become healthy again.

Load balancers create an environment of improved service availability and elasticity. Having a load balancer fronting the services conduces elasticity and scalability, the two positive benefits of a microservices architecture. Load balancers enable newer instances to start up and take traffic in times of increased traffic, thus enabling elasticity. Similarly, it avoids overburdening a small set of service instances by evening out the traffic load. Load balancers are usually regional resources that can redirect traffic across availability zones—thus ensuring high availability.

Load balancers usually get plugged into the VPCs, thus having full access to the routing tables and security settings of the VPC. Load balancers can be both Internet-facing, redirecting traffic from the external world, or internal-facing—routing traffic from clients within the VPC. Load balancers are also well-connected to the CSP's PaaS and FaaS offerings, thus enabling traffic routing to such endpoints.

Choosing load balancers for a global or multi-region solution will require an added *global load balancer*. In such a setup, a global load balancer will front the regional load balancers and will route traffic based on rules. This type of load balancer improves the global availability of applications.

Global load balancers also speed up communication between the clients and the services in the destination region. Without a global load balancer, the network traffic might take multiple hops on the CSP's network before reaching the destination pool of services, which affects the performance and throughput of services. If the global load balancer is fronting a service that is available across multiple regions, it can detect the closest region of service availability and route the request.

## LOAD BALANCERS IN TOP CLOUD PROVIDERS

When enterprises move to cloud, there is a need for balancing traffic loads on horizontally scalable and potentially geographically distributed solution infrastructure. In here, it is important to know that products are offered in two flavors, a global/multi-region load balancer and a regional load balancer. For instance, AWS's Global Accelerator,[10] Azure's Traffic Manager,[11] and GCP's GLB (Global Load Balancer)[12] all offer load balancing across various regions. Within a region, AWS's ELB (Elastic Load Balancer),[13] Azure's Load Balancer,[14] and GCP's ILB (Internal Load Balancer)[15] can manage load balancing. Global load balancers tend to be more expensive than regional load balancers.

# API Gateways

APIs have changed the way business and technology function. APIs enable the easy flow of well-defined information. Businesses are aggressively retiring their eons-old processes such as file exchanges, SMTP-based messaging, EDI[16] with APIs. Microservices architecture of their applications exposes hundreds, if not thousands, of API endpoints for external use. Managing this scale of APIs efficiently, along with their evolution and security, requires leveraging CSP's API gateways, which are PaaS solutions that offer management of API, along with securing, monitoring, throttling, and metering them.

API gateways are also extremely beneficial for routing requests to the right pool of microservice endpoints. We can relate to the discussion we had about partitioned databases in the chapter on data stores on the cloud. We realized how an application might be a global application, but individual instances attempt to access a part of the data. Let us consider the billing domain of the Energence Home Platform. The billing system might have partitioned itself into various regions, each region holding accounts

---

[10]https://aws.amazon.com/global-accelerator

[11]https://azure.microsoft.com/en-us/services/traffic-manager/

[12]https://cloud.google.com/load-balancing/

[13]https://aws.amazon.com/elasticloadbalancing/

[14]https://azure.microsoft.com/en-us/services/load-balancer/

[15]https://cloud.google.com/load-balancing/docs/internal/

[16]Many enterprises rely on getting data from their business partners using SMTP-based messaging (automated emails, for instance), or EDI (electronic data interchange) process that is similar to fax transmission.

of customers in that geography. Let us assume that the billing system runs in every region, with its data store being a locally partitioned NoSQL store. In this case, load balancers and API gateways are valuable assets; they can route the requests to the right region where the microservice and its data exist.

Apart from routing, API gateways offer all features of load balancer concerning REST/HTTPS traffic. Using an API gateway ensures clean architecture, as it provides ways to

1. **Decouple clients from the actual implementation**: The clients do not need to know the destination of their service calls or the details of endpoints.

2. **Monitor usage of services, potentially for billing**: Energence's attempt to monetize their services, like many other businesses changing their model of providing services, relies on the ability to monitor the usage of services by clients.

3. **Rate-limiting based on client levels**: Along with monitoring usage, it is essential to limit the requests by clients based on their service agreements.

They can provide security by

1. Enforcing authentication at the periphery

2. Controlling access by providing authorization policies

3. Throttling request traffic and thus providing defense against malicious attacks such as DoS attacks

API gateways exist at the periphery and can handle various types of clients. We can also configure them as reverse proxies to *load-balance traffic* between multiple instances of services. As shown in Figure 9-2, API gateways can manage *peripheral authentication*: client requests are checked for authentication tokens and are redirected to the standard authentication service when tokens are missing/invalid. Upon successfully validating the token against authorization policies, API gateways *route the request* directly to the services configured against the specific API. API gateways can also *throttle traffic flow* based on configuration. Clients, or classes of clients, can be configured to an allowed rate (requests-per-second, for instance).

API gateways offer plenty of features compared to a load *balancer. However, API gateways are expensive to use*. Charges accrue based on (a) number of APIs configured and (b) the number of requests made to the gateway. Architects need to standardize when an API requires an API gateway. In general, API gateways make sense for monetized APIs. These APIs generate cash, and also the paying customers expect sophisticated functionality offered by an API gateway. Similarly, APIs whose client systems are external to the enterprise might need hosting on an API gateway.

---

API gateways are perfect for fronting a collection of services used by external entities, such as public-facing services and partner services. Load balancers are excellent options for exposing services to an enterprise's internal clients.

---

### API GATEWAYS IN TOP CLOUD PROVIDERS

AWS's offering Amazon API Gateway[17] and Azure's Azure API Management[18] are in-built offerings. GCP has Cloud Endpoints[19] that provide an nginx proxy and support OpenAPI spec. Interestingly, many enterprises use Apigee[20] (now owned by Google), a more cloud agnostic full API life cycle management tool.

# IAM of CSPs

Enterprises that are not born and built on the cloud have well-established IAA mechanisms on-prem. They often have federated authentication systems in place, which allow single sign-on. However, CSPs have their own IAM (identity and access management) in place, which is leveraged by all their services. It is impossible to decouple a CSP's IAM from its services effortlessly, and avoiding such endeavors is the best course of action. However, CSPs can easily integrate with on-prem IAA mechanisms if they conform to open standards such as OAuth2.0.

---

[17]https://aws.amazon.com/api-gateway/

[18]https://azure.microsoft.com/en-us/services/api-management/

[19]https://cloud.google.com/endpoints/

[20]https://cloud.google.com/apigee/

Even if an enterprise's IAM does not conform to open standards, it might still be possible to integrate with CSPs with one of the two possible options. The first option is to continue maintaining all authentication and authorization information on the existing infrastructure, but *mirror it to the cloud's IAM*. This mirroring could be a synchronization job, scheduled to execute periodically. However, this approach is cumbersome. Maintaining CSP roles or mapping enterprise roles/claims/other authorization schemes can quickly become unmanageable. The second option is to allow services to handle security by *using enterprise IAA, situated on-prem* (outside the cloud). The second option limits us from leveraging peripheral authentication and authorization provided by CSP services. It also adds overhead to service development and its performance.

# Securing Inter-Service Communication

In a microservices architecture, the connectivity between various microservices tends to be large and complex. Lack of transparency of cloud infrastructure prompts enterprises to deem securing communication between microservices critical. One of the standard ways to do this is via MTLS (mutual transport layer security). Mutual TLS enforces both client and server to authenticate each other. TLS (transport layer security) is a standard that protects communication over TCP connections. TLS enforces authentication and session key exchange using a strong asymmetric key encryption. Once authenticated and a session key (symmetric key) obtained, all communication gets encrypted with the session key.

To stand up an MTLS infrastructure, we have to set up a few fundamental entities. Asymmetric keys are usually digital certificates, which means a certificate authority is required. To reduce the exploit windows, we need to rotate security certificates frequently. We need a method, such as SCEP (Simple Certification Enrollment Protocol), to distribute new certificates to services. We also need a setup to issue identities to various service entities.

The most optimal way to implement an MTLS infrastructure on the cloud is via a service mesh. Service meshes allow identity and certificate management, MTLS authentication, policy enforcement, and authorization. We discussed the various features offered by service meshes in an earlier section on service meshes.

# Processing Integrity

In the earlier sections, we discussed securing the traffic flow into microservices environments. In this section, we will discuss securing the computational resources. Securing the VMs and containers that host the microservices environment is equally important. This act of ensuring the security of VMs and containers expands to both the runtimes and the binary images.

# Trusted Binaries

In earlier chapters, we discussed how automated build pipelines were an efficient way to manage the life cycle of microservices. The build pipelines check out the source code, compile it, run it through a series of checks, and finally generate container (or VM) images. These images are later used to create running instances of microservices.

Auditing the binary images, tracking their source, and ensuring no malcontent exists is essential. The build process of binary images of VMs and containers involves layering application binaries on top of an existing standard image. Typically, many of these standard binaries are imported into enterprises. In the open source world, many of these binaries could "slip in" from the public domain. Given this scenario, it becomes imperative to **verify the validity and availability of base binaries**. Enterprises need to set up a process to validate the base binary for authenticity. Every microservice binary image needs to go through such a check as part of the build cycle. This is a common threat for enterprises that deploy containers to the cloud. Malicious hackers taint binaries and exploit the computing capacity for their personal use. Cryptojacking, where hackers use someone else's compute to run their crypromining processes, is a significant and common threat. Enterprises regularly uncover that their containers are compromised and are mining bitcoins for a hacker[21].

The requirement of ensuring a clean container image is never repeated enough. The following are some of the recommended checks to ensure a safe and clean container image. Guaranteeing a clean container image is built on top of a trusted image, requiring auditing of the build process and at runtime. Development teams need to ensure that unnecessary components and libraries do not get bundled with the containers. Making sure that only the certified packages get into the container image is critical. Several image

---

[21]Cryptojacking worms such as 'Graboid', 'Cetus', spread through infected binaries.

scanning tools and services[22] are available, many of which are open-source. An often overlooked check by development teams is to confirm that the container image does not contain any sensitive information. Often, sensitive information such as passwords, connection parameters, network topology, tokens, or public/private key pairs get bundled into the container. Having containers embedded with sensitive information in a compromised container registry craters the many layers of defense in place against intruders. It is important to check containers for any information that can be used to exploit the security layeres during the CI/CD process. Such precautions also safeguard against hackers who could exploit the collocated container runtimes.

It is crucial to enforce checks on binaries to ensure the integrity of root and base images as part of the CI/CD process. We discussed such changes to pipelines earlier, under the *DevSecOps* section. It is also essential to have these checks inside the container management platform as well.

# Trusted Execution

A huge concern for enterprises is the confidentiality and integrity of execution environments. On a cloud platform, the risks exist in compromises to compute infrastructure. CSPs set up isolation between virtual machines of various tenants, possibly running on a single host machine. Failure in isolation is a severe event, where these control barriers break down. In such an event, an *exploit of a lower level host machine could result in a compromise of all virtual machines on that host*. This breakdown affects any enterprise's resources, even if they have secured connectivity between their assets. Worse, such failures could affect the PaaS and SaaS services of CSPs as well. Malfunctions of this nature are a frightening cause of concern for enterprises that run sensitive workloads, such as workloads containing PII or PCI data[23], on the cloud.

## Proactive Container Security

Containers mitigate a few of the problems, especially the ones based on immutable instances. Rebooting all running instances will eliminate any tainted ones. However, the container infrastructure poses additional challenges. *Containers leverage the host*

---

[22]Trivy, Anchore, Clair are some popular container image scanning tools.

[23]Securing PII (personally identifiable data) and PCI (payment card industry) data are vital areas of data compliance and legal responsibilities of enterprises.

*kernel directly, which is a critical concern*—the use of a compromised container could attack other entities on the host with ease. This concern can be mitigated by hardening kernels—specifically by isolating processes and securing host services used by the containers. Hardening kernels is an area of active research and is beyond the scope of this book. Interested readers are encouraged to explore this topic.

Containers running on an iCaaS setup are not devoid of concerns. Popular cluster management software such as Kubernetes is often configured without stringent security requirements. Well-documented cases exist[24], where hackers capitalized on the vulnerability of a single container's access rights in a cluster to infect and take over the entire container management cluster. Such iCaaS platforms also tend to be complicated, with many open, configurable, and well-documented endpoints, which give a larger attack-surface for malicious intruders. Even though copious cautions against vulnerabilities are listed by providers, the lack of knowledgeable engineers to manage these cluster management solutions are a serious concern.

Some fundamental preventive measures are highly beneficial for securing a container-based microservices infrastructure. Containers, at the core, are simply a group of processes that are artificially bundled into a group and restricted access. This artificial grouping means that every container process that runs on that machine is at the same level. Some necessary measures to prevent breaches:

1. **Partitioning container infrastructure on the host machine:** The resources container processes have access to are separated. For instance, folders used by the container software are strictly cordoned off, possibly even on a separate mount. Regular auditing of these folders is vital to detect breaches at the earliest.

2. **Ensuring all containers are hardened and audited before launching:** This just-in-time check is another safeguard against compromised container registries.

---

[24]In mid 2020, a hacker group "TeamTNT" used infected Docker containers to retrieve CSP's credentials and infected a large number of business systems. Similarly, malware such as 'WannaMine' (2017) and 'Graboid' (2019), found in infected containers, have caused security breaches.

3. **Restricting the network traffic to and from containers is advised**: The type of traffic, routes, and protocols used by the container are held in check at the host's bridge. For instance, ensuring only TLS is made available for communication, and on non-standard ports, reduces the chances of intrusion.

4. **Containers use control-groups, aka c-groups, on hosts to isolate themselves**: The membership of a particular c-group defines available access to various resources on the host—CPU, memory, disk, network, etc. It is mandatory to monitor these c-groups, along with the resources and access privileges the c-groups are assigned.

5. **Correct settings on the host system in terms of the capabilities of processes is critical**: These settings apply to process priorities, resource limits, access to devices, and privileged commands, to name a few. Restricting this disables containers from exploiting the host system for malicious intent.

# TEEs

A strategy that has gained popularity is using TEEs—short for *trusted execution environments*—which guarantee confidentiality and integrity of execution environments. TEE *"is a tamper-resistant processing environment that runs on a separation kernel" (Sabt, Achemlal, & Bouabdallah, 2015)*. TEEs encrypt data in memory as it is loaded and propagated in an encrypted format. TEEs also encrypt the entire memory of the virtual machine using separate keys for each virtual machine on the host system, thus disallowing memory reads across. TEEs abstract communication interface to underlying hardware to ensure sources and sink of virtual machines are secure and trusted.

TEE is a very new concept with many challenges, and a large amount of work is underway. Standardization in the implementation of TEEs is still lacking. Many implementation proposals depend on the characteristics of the underlying hardware. CSPs are also hesitant about incurring the extra cost involved in rolling out TEEs. CSPs will have to change many of their existing virtualization techniques to adopt, and they might have to change again when standards are defined. However, with an increasing number of secure workloads moving to the cloud, TEEs become a requirement. Readers are urged to read the NIST Cybersecurity White Papers, especially the ones focused on hardware-enabled security for server platforms (Bartock, et al., 2020).

Ensuring cluster and container security is paramount. Center for Internet Security has benchmark documentation and tools that help engineering teams run diagnostic tests and benchmarks as part of their build pipelines.

# Availability

*Nothing travels faster than the speed of light with the possible exception of bad news, which obeys its own special laws.*

—Douglas Adams, *Mostly Harmless* (1992)

Unfortunately, it is common to neglect the importance of availability as a security requirement; it is often considered an architectural embellishment. One of the main reasons is that although the high availability of services is a highly desirable trait, it is a highly ambitious one. **The CAP theorem encumbers high availability**: attempts to *increase availability by replication and partition invariably lead to consistency challenges.* Two disjoint sets of requirements enterprises face when moving to the cloud are *disaster recovery* and *global availability*.

Major CSPs build networks that span the entire globe. However, CSPs divide their global networks into regions, conforming geographical areas. We discussed the impact of the CAP theorem in our earlier chapters—CSPs offer highly available multi-availability-zone solutions for most of their services. Services built on regional resources have a high degree of availability, often 99.95% to 99.99% availability. This level of sophistication is sufficient for many applications to maintain business continuity; however, there are applications, such as web storefronts, which find it insufficient. Catastrophic failure of a region is possible; some CSPs have experienced outages that have spanned multiple hours. Extended outages are a concern for enterprises that need business continuity to a high degree.

There are two possible solutions to mitigate this:

1. *We implement a disaster recovery process and move the entire workload to a different region.*

2. *We create a multi-region or global solution that is immune to such failures.*

# Disaster Recovery (DR)

When architectures built on the cloud use regional resources, architects need to plan for regional outages. Regional failures are rare; the rarity of these incidences means CSPs take a long time to recover. The ability to transfer workloads to a different region is needed to maintain business continuity. Disaster recovery on the cloud is prohibitively expensive, exceptionally burdensome, and mindbogglingly labor-intensive. Disaster recovery is effective when the cost involved has to outweigh the loss incurred in losing a region.

The effectiveness of DR in the cloud is dependent on a few key factors. It is essential to define **RPO** (*recovery point objective*) and **RTO** (*recovery time objective*) for failovers. RTO of a service is the *measure of time taken to bring the service back online*, and RPO is simply a *measure of data loss during that time*. Many techniques to lower RTO and RPO exist, with varying degrees of difficulty and cost. It is possible to *continuously run a small-scale replica* of infrastructure in another region, which is coordinated with the active infrastructure to attempt a *hot failover*. This proposition yields a very low RPO and RTO, but an expensive one. We are reserving replica infrastructure, which is continuously running without load. Replicas double up cloud costs. Another choice is a *cold failover*, where we spin up the other region after detecting a failure. The data is replicated to the DR region in the cold failover option as well. Though a cheaper option, it could result in longer RTO and higher RPO. As we discussed in "Infrastructure as Code" section of our earlier chapter on process changes, scripting the creation and teardown of infrastructure helps speed up the cold failover process.

When a region fails, the failure could be for multiple reasons:

1. *A vital resource,* **such as container orchestration service,** *might fail,* **crippling or bringing down applications**: Surprisingly, this is a more straightforward scenario to handle. The solution is to stand up an equivalent infrastructure in another region and reroute traffic.

2. **A network glitch might take the entire region offline**: In this dire scenario, applications might still be functioning, but are unable to communicate with the Internet. Network losses pose a considerable problem: applications are still available but are disconnected. If the cause of network glitch is deterministic, we need to set up in a new region and the unresponsive region taken out.

When we lose specific resources within a region, even if a complete shutdown of those resources, the blast radius is small. The region is still accessible—which provides a window for failing over to another region and gracefully shutdown resources. Note that it is possible to determine the source of failure in this case: DevOps (or DevSecOps) teams should plan to script the recovery process from the scenario for higher accuracy and speed.

When we attempt to failover to another region upon a network glitch, we might encounter severe challenges based on the architecture. For instance, severe side effects arise if *applications are using global resources*. Once the region recovers, global resources might try to sync—resulting in irrecoverable errors or corrupted data. Messaging is an excellent example of a sensitive global resource. When employed, a failed region might queue up messages on its local replica of global queues and topics. When the old region recovers, it attempts to rejoin the CSP's global network and republish all the old messages. Global nature of messaging causes these messages to appear in the new region, leading to data corruption. Architects need to craft solutions around such problems, by using namespace/labeling techniques, or by building applications to handle such errors.

Architects should begin the DR discussion with the mindset that DR setup is expensive: in terms of engineering hours, dollars for extra capacity, and maintenance. Engineering efforts are required when disaster happens, and also for frequent **DR testing**. For effective DR testing, automated scripts should create the equivalent infrastructure in a new region and divert production traffic. Simulating actual scenarios—of a lost region, unresponsive network, failed resources—are paramount for a successful DR test. Periodical DR testing ensures that the alternate setup is functional and viable for a failover. Architects need to be judicious in ensuring the efforts bear enough returns. Creating DR for applications makes sense only for applications that cannot be offline for a few hours.

# Multi-region Solutions

**Multi-region solutions are best suited for *applications that can truly leverage the locality of usage.*** Consider the application SmartMeter system from our earlier discussion, which collects data from smart meters in various geographic boundaries. For the SmartMeter system, regional copies can provide low response times and high performance because of proximity. However, running such applications—especially when they involve state—as truly multi-region needs a lot of upfront future-proofing.

Using multi-region architecture for high availability is acceptable in some instances. For ensuring *high availability*—anything beyond three-and-a-half nines—architects can look at multi-region solutions. The other common reason for using a multi-region deployment is local laws governing areas of service. EU, for instance, has strict rules of where data lives. China has heavy restrictions on what data can leave China's boundaries. Such situations warranty deploying solutions locally in CSP's regions targeted for those countries.

The central principle of short response times is based *partly on good architecture and partly on physics.* Imagine Energence has expanded operations to Australia, and their Home Platform is now serving users in Australia. Continuing to run applications from the Washington DC data center will mean anywhere between 100ms to 300ms in ping times alone. No matter how performant the applications are, the communication overhead is tremendous: there is no way to beat the speed of light. Add to that any factor of chattiness, performance suffers terribly. This communication limitation means Energence must roll out their applications in CSP's Australia regions.

To run in multi-region, the required services—compute, storage, and connectivity—are managed at a global level. This global spanning infrastructure means compute clusters run in multiple regions, with storage and connectivity established across them.

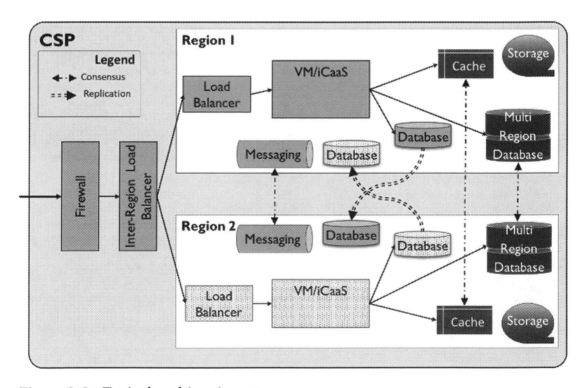

***Figure 9-3.*** *Typical multi-region setup*

Though this is a broad area with no standardization across CSPs, we can conceptualize such an architecture. It is possible to front multiple regional container orchestration clusters with a global load balancer and run them in multiple regions. If the applications are stateless, the clusters that receive the traffic to top-level services will continue to leverage regional services and regional datastores. We discussed datastores that are global datastores, which ensure data gets replicated to multiple regions. A multi-region solution is an arduous undertaking, and architects need to do a tremendous amount of upfront work.

# Summary

The security of any architecture is an activity that begins early in the life cycle. The concepts of CIA—confidentiality, integrity, and availability—define the security triad. It is important to reduce the attack surface by exposing only the top-level services that face the external world. Enforcing strong security policies around access control also adds another layer of security. Enterprises that are building cloud-native applications could leverage CSP's security mechanisms. However, enterprises with existing security infrastructure need to adopt open security standards to ease the integration of their IAA mechanism with CSP's IAMs.

Apart from securing communication, due to the opaqueness of underlying cloud infrastructure, enterprises that run sensitive workloads might evaluate the integrity of processing and data on the cloud. Availability on the cloud is decided by cost and is best suited for applications that really need more than four-nine availability. Running applications in multiple regions, or running in one region and quickly failing over to other regions, allow very high availability. Considerable planning and prudence are required from architects to evaluate and ensure such implementations are feasible.

# Points to Ponder

1. What new threats materialize as enterprises move to microservices architecture?

2. Is the opaqueness of cloud infrastructure good or bad? What do we lose, and what do we gain?

3. How do we decide the level of trust needed for each application? Can some principles guide this selection?

4. How do security threats vary from IaaS/iCaaS to PaaS to SaaS models?

5. What is the tipping point for an enterprise to enable the multi-cloud option, or a cloud-bursting option (expanding from on-prem to cloud when capacity is needed)? What makes this effort worthwhile?

# Further Related Reading

**RFC 6749** – OAuth2 specification, SAML2.0 specification, and OpenID specification.

**Building the Infrastructure for Cloud Security** by Yeluri et al. (Yeluri & Castro-Leon, 2014).

Ph.D. thesis of Tetiana Yarygina on microservices security (Yarygina, 2018).

# CHAPTER 10

# Microservices, Here and Beyond

*I want to stay as close to the edge as I can without going over. Out on the edge you see all kinds of things you can't see from the center.*

—Kurt Vonnegut, *Player Piano* (1952)

The first rule of soothsaying is to be abstract, generic, and futuristic. Our immediate predictions are invariably wrong: the year 2020 exemplifies the fallibility of our short-term plans. Also, to understand the future, we need to know how we got here and which human factors got us here. Fiction writers of the nineteenth century had predicted that we would build ways to share information globally. By the beginning of the twentieth century, they foresaw machines that would be small and commonplace by the end of the century. Most of these predictions—the true ones—were based on extrapolating the prevailing trends in scientific research and inventions, and also based on which ones have historically succeeded. The common underlying themes that lead to improvements remain the same: *creativity*, *necessity*, or *laziness*.

A useful prediction foresees two aspects: *what* will be the changes and *when* will they happen. New ideas in technology see varying speeds of successful adoptions. Some ideas become the norm within a few years, some ideas stay theoretical for decades, and some others take decades of churn before becoming mainstream. Consider how the programming community immediately embraced the concepts of procedural/functional programming in the early 1950s. However, distributed systems stayed mostly theoretical until the late 1970s. Consider the evolution of object-oriented design: it was conceived in the late 1960s but formalized only in the early 1990s. The current trend of microservices growth does not fit any of these models. Though microservices architecture will

© Chandra Rajasekharaiah 2021
C. Rajasekharaiah, *Cloud-Based Microservices*, https://doi.org/10.1007/978-1-4842-6564-2_10

continue to see wider adoption, *we lack an overarching theory, standardized tooling, and community consensus on techniques*—the missing links to success. We will continue to implement new systems with microservices architectures, with results ranging anywhere between phenomenal successes and appalling failures.

It is possible to foresee the patterns and veins of changes in the microservices field. Large amounts of investments, research, and workforce mobilization will imperatively happen in this field—increasing the efforts in the area. There will be both upsides and downsides on this journey. There will be a tremendous focus on **automation**, as development communities and enterprises alike will try to devise methods to cut down development overhead. We will see fantastic new ideas and theories in specific academic fields, such as distributed computing, consensus theory, to name a few. However, many product and service companies will see opportunities for new "frameworks" and "platforms"—or some other variation of microservices snake oil.

Automation will change many software engineering **processes**, the way engineers learn, interact, and work. We will see new collaboration tools and learning platforms for engineers. Processes will evolve to become more agile. The focus will shift to *continuous experimentation of ideas, rather than time-bound massive production deployments*. However, enterprises will misunderstand this movement and will foolishly attempt to cram more people and more work into the processes. New variations of agile methodology will be born, which will try to track engineers' efforts in silly metrics—such as hours, feature-points, story-points—without following the underlying spirit of agility. New ridiculous ideas such as colocation of engineers, pod seating, and war rooms will become abundant—though health concerns appear to be nipping them at the bud.

# Forecasts and Trends

The field of cloud-based microservices will undergo a lot of transformation in the coming years. The paradigm of cloud, though has matured for more than a decade, is still undergoing drastic changes regularly. Businesses will continue to invest time and effort into this architecture. Engineers will continue to discover better ways to build these architectures. Though the playing field seems to be very volatile, we can forecast trends and shifts based on the general direction of changes.

# Integration of Microservices

Enterprises that use microservices architecture will accrue a large collection of foundational microservices. They will spend more time integrating microservices to build new functionality. We discussed some of the associated challenges and solutions in Chapters 3 and 4. The enterprises will spend more time in the maintenance of microservices and focus on non-functional aspects such as speed, throughput, and precision.

The need to focus on improving microservices will create a demand for new tools and improved processes in the automation of testing. With reasonable standardization in the definition of microservices, it is possible to devise constructs to automate testing. Enterprises might build or adopt tools that validate the accuracy of various actions on data. A simplistic example tool would, given a microservice and its resource, automatically test if operations provide consistent and expected results. The test tool might run all four REST actions—PUT, POST, GET, and DELETE—in various sequences to ensure the changes in data are correct.

The need for faster responses from REST services challenges us to look at the communication and composition of information exchanged. With HTTP 2+, we switch to binary-encoding and compression of frames; hence, the message exchanges can be concise for communication and precise for design. This change enables building microservices with gRPC with HTTP2, significantly speeding up the performance of microservice architecture. It is also important to note that most container orchestrations and service meshes are already HTTP2 compliant.

# Automation of Support and Operations

A field that is "ripe for standardization" is DevOps for microservices. If we succeed in deriving a standard convention for microservices development life cycle, we can turn it into service. We can start by automating operations such as build-pipeline creation, static checking, contract testing, containerization, deployment, service mesh setup, and security testing. Once automated, if we add the capability to run using a standard language, we can open this up for self-service. With this approach, enterprises write business-specific code and a configuration file that configures the DevOps (or DevSecOps) process.

# Standardization of Compute Options

Containerization and container orchestration have found standardization. CSPs (cloud service providers) offer similar options for most of their services, which is a unique advantage for enterprises. Enterprises can adhere to open standards and expect more portability across CSPs. Platform concepts such as service meshes will gain popularity, and efforts such as OCI (Open Container Initiative) and CNCF (Cloud Native Computing Foundation) will attempt to standardize the various components that compose service meshes. We will continue to see an uptick in the adoption of service meshes. Standardization such as these will provide enterprises and developers to focus less on infrastructure and more on business-related problems.

# Cloud-Bursting, Multi-Cloud, Cloud Agnosticism

In our case study about Energence, one of the critical requirements was elasticity, so that enterprises can manage seasonal and burst workloads. *Cloud-bursting* is a popular technique that can benefit enterprises with existing data centers. When enterprises go beyond their current data center capacity, it is advantageous for enterprises to offload the excess load to the cloud. Cloud-bursting is this very technique where an additional resource pool on the cloud is temporarily acquired to handle the extra load. Another nascent area, which enterprises crave for, is *multi-cloud infrastructure*. In a multi-cloud infrastructure, enterprises run their loads across multiple clouds. A large amount of research is underway to devise ways to leverage resources from various CSPs. Multi-cloud is attractive, as enterprises can "shop" multiple CSPs and spend their dollars wisely. However, the engineering communities are still solidifying the concepts that address the lack of standardization across CSPs.

Enterprises pursuing multi-cloud infrastructure traditionally faced challenges in finding talent that is conversant with multiple clouds. However, ideas such as containerization, container orchestration, and service mesh are making it easy and transparent to transfer the compute workloads across CSPs. Ideas such as HCI (hypercloud infrastructure) are transforming on-prem infrastructure to match the cloud infrastructure. Somewhere in the future, we might find ourselves where multi-cloud is a norm. In the interim, interested enterprises could build solutions in a cloud-agnostic way, without using cloud-native services.

# Changing Security Landscape

We have built our security infrastructure based on the relation between the size of encryption-keys and the necessary computing power to break it. Using a regular computer, sessions encrypted with small session-keys—say, a few tens of bits—can be compromised. As the size of the session-key increases, computation time/power increases exponentially. For instance, a SHA key size of 80 bits was considered the limit of infeasibility in the 1990s. This is no longer a safe limit for a session key in 2020. In 2020, bitcoin miners hashed at 140M hashes/second, pushing it close to the required flops for a successful brute-force attack. This relation is the basis of all modern cryptographic standards. In this information age, countries often get into cyberwars and exploits. When governments with supercomputers engage in breaking security, it becomes exceedingly difficult to guarantee the safety of data. With the advent of quantum computers, brute-force techniques to break foundational encryption techniques such as RSA, ECDSA, DSA take a much shorter time. These threats, along with revolutionary scientific advances, are real and imminent. We realize these developments will shake the foundation of the security domain and will force us to rethink our current security infrastructure setup.

# Alternate Thoughts

We spend the entire book discussing why microservices architecture is the best method to build software, how it is best suited to move to the cloud, and what benefits enterprises like Energence can reap. At this juncture, we need to stop to answer two questions for non-believers:

1.   Microservices architecture is a nascent domain; will it stay?

2.   In this case, is the newer architecture technique better? Has microservices architecture proved its worth already?

We argued that the answer to these questions is a resounding "yes," and have provided enough proof throughout this book. To not blindside ourselves with any shortcomings and ensure our treatment is thorough, it is better to look at opposing points of view.

# Monoliths are Dead; Long Live the Monolith

Though I am an ardent proponent of microservices, *I cannot but agree that monoliths are not dead yet.* There are certainly instances and reasons where engineers might prefer monoliths over microservices.

Vendors continue to sell many standard enterprise solutions as products, which tend to monolithic for multiple reasons. Monolithic deliverables are easy to install and configure in the enterprises where a majority of applications run on-prem. Monolithic applications guarantee complete ownership of the domain. Sharing ownership of a domain is frowned upon by vendors to avoid competition and to reduce integration complexity. However, some vendors are moving to a service model; such moves are indeed into microservices-based architecture.

Many modular and well-designed monoliths have outperformed microservices architecture in speed, accuracy, and ease of maintenance. Monolithic architectures also enjoy support from industry leaders in terms of platforms. *The application platforms also evolve*, and these platforms may handle the burden of breaking the monolith into microservices; they might even do it at runtime!

An alternate school of thought contends that the success of microservices architecture is due to the *shift of engineering talent*. Talented engineers who used to build great monoliths are now invested in microservices architectures. *The question of whether success is attributed to smart engineers or to better architecture remains.*

# HCI or the Comeback of On-Prem

Any data center comprises three layers: compute, storage, and network. First, there is a need for racks of computational hardware, such as blades or machines with CPUs and GPUs. Next, there is a need for storage, hard drives, network drives, tape stores, etc., accessed via SANs (storage access network). Finally, the data center has networking requirement—routers, switches, firewalls, among many other—the specialized hardware that allows fast and secure communication between computes and with the external world. Over the years, many small progressive steps pushed for the simplicity of managing these three aspects of data center. First, the advent of hypervisor saw the creation of virtual machines carved out of bare metal servers. The virtual machines used the compute of the bare metals and connected to storage using SANs. The way to scale out was to add storage and compute blades. Then, sometime in 2015, Cisco, EMC, and VMW got together and provided software that merges all three layers into one. This single software solution was called the converged infrastructure, managing all the three layers by itself.

We discussed the movement to hybrid and multi-clouds. An excellent enabler for multi-cloud and hybrid-cloud infrastructure is the *hyper-convergent infrastructure*, aka HCI. HCI is an incredible opportunity for enterprises that are about to make a cloud journey but might want to seek equivalence in their data center infrastructure and cloud infrastructure. This desire for similarity could stem from a variety of reasons. The first scenario is when enterprises have a *mixture of on-prem and cloud*. For instance, many traditional enterprises that have existing data centers often use the cloud for application development. The development team uses the power of the cloud and automate their entire infrastructure. This effort cannot work on-prem, as the sophistication does not exist in their own data centers. The second scenario is when *enterprises are interested in cloud-bursting*. The ability to use a similar script setup, which can create on-prem and cloud-based resources without rework, is a great benefit. Requirements such as these bring us to the world of HCI.

For enterprises with an existing hardware footprint, HCI also offers the capability to reduce their cloud needs. Many enterprises suffer from a lack of elasticity: though they have enough hardware for peak, they cannot quickly divert their loads to the available hardware.

# In Closing

> *Any intelligent fool can make things bigger, more complex, and more violent. It takes a touch of genius — and a lot of courage to move in the opposite direction.*
>
> —Ernst F. Schumacher (1911–1977)

**Good microservices architecture is difficult to attain**. It is unbelievably hard to correctly demarcate the domains and their dependencies in a future-proof way. It is demanding because it requires us to correctly apply distributed computing, concurrency control, consistency theory, and discrete math. When we extend this already difficult journey to the cloud, we reach the place where only thinkers and dreamers survive. Here every decision has an enormous impact. We are no longer walking with our pets in a garden, but we are in the wilderness guarding our livestock.

The good news is, **microservices architecture is a prolific way to build modern software systems**. It sets us—architects, engineers, and enterprises—up for success. With enough experience, efforts, and errors, getting the architecture becomes second nature. The first best step is to know the opportunities and pitfalls, which was the target content of the book. I hope the readers of this book advanced their knowledge in microservices architecture—whichever field they work in, whatever technology they use. I wish them great success in their endeavors.

# APPENDIX

# Comparison of Cloud Service Providers

| Service | AWS | Azure | GCP |
|---|---|---|---|
| **Connectivity** | | | |
| **Edge Locations** | Edge Networks | POPs | POPs |
| **VPN Connectivity** | PrivateLink | Virtual Network | Cloud VPN |
| **Fiber Optic** | Direct Connect | Express Route | Interlink |
| **DNS Service** | Route 53 | Azure DNS | Cloud DNS |
| **CDN** | Cloudfront | Azure CDN | Cloud CDN |
| **Firewall** | WAF | Azure Firewall | CloudArmor |
| **Multi-Region LB** | Global Accelerator | Traffic Manager | GLB |
| **Regional LB** | ELB | Load Balancer | ILB |
| **Compute** | | | |
| **VMs** | EC2 | Azure VMs | Cloud Compute |
| **Proprietary iCaaS** | Elastic Container Service | Azure Container Service | |
| **Kubernetes** | ECS for Kubernetes | Azure Kubernetes Service | GKE |
| **PaaS iCaaS** | Fargate | Azure Server Fabric | |

(*continued*)

211

© Chandra Rajasekharaiah 2021
C. Rajasekharaiah, *Cloud-Based Microservices*, https://doi.org/10.1007/978-1-4842-6564-2

| Service | AWS | Azure | GCP |
|---|---|---|---|
| **PaaS App Server** | AWS Beanstalk | Azure Web Apps, Azure App Service, Azure Cloud Service | AppEngine, AppEngine Flex |
| **FaaS/Serverless** | AWS Lambda | Azure Functions | Cloud Functions |
| **Kubernetes FaaS** | | | kNative |
| **Integration** | | | |
| **Open Source (ActiveMQ)** | Amazon MQ | | |
| **P2P Messaging** | Amazon SQS | Azure Event Grid | |
| **Messaging Topics** | AWS SNS | Azure Service Bus | Cloud Pub/Sub |
| **API Gateways** | Amazon API Gateway | Azure API Management | Cloud Endpoints Apigee |
| **Databases and Datastores** | | | |
| **Open Source DB**[1] | Amazon RDS | Azure Database | CloudSQL |
| **BYOL/Commercial** | Oracle, SQLServer | SQLServer | |
| **Closed Source DB** | AuroraDB | | *Cloud Spanner*[2] |
| **NoSQL Store** | DynamoDB | CosmoDB | BigTable |
| **Document DB** | Amazon DocumentDB | CosmoDB, Azure Table Storage | Cloud Datastore |

*(continued)*

[1]MySQL, PostgreSQL, and MariaDB are offered as managed databases in AWS's Amazon RDS. Azure Database is also available in MySQL, Postgres, and MariaDB variations. GCP's CloudSQL offers MySQL and PostgresQL variants, no MariaDB.

[2]GCP's CloudSpanner, which is a closed source and pseudo RDBMS. Largely built-off of BigTable ideas, it is a distributed, partially SQL compliant (no relations or referential integrity) multi-region transactional database.

| Service | AWS | Azure | GCP |
| --- | --- | --- | --- |
| **Timeseries DB** | Amazon Timestream | Azure Time Series Insights | |
| **BlockChain Ledger** | QLDB | | |
| **Caching—Redis as a Service** | Amazon Elasticache | Azure Cache for Redis | Cloud Memorystore |
| **Data Warehousing** | Amazon Redshift | SQL Data Warehouse | BigQuery |
| **Bulk Storage Options** | | | |
| **Frequent access** | S3 Standard | Hot Blob Storage | Cloud Storage Standard |
| **Rapid Read** | S3 I/A, S3 Z-I/A | Cool Blob Storage | Cloud Storage Nearline |
| **Low-cost** | S3 Glacier | Blob Archive Storage | Cloud Storage Coldline |

# Bibliography

Abbott, M. L. (2009). The art of scalability: Scalable web architecture, processes, and organizations for the modern enterprise. Pearson Education.

Ajoux, P., Bronson, N., Kumar, S., Lloyd, W., & Veeraraghavan, K. (2015). Challenges to adopting stronger consistency at scale. *15th Workshop on Hot Topics in Operating Systems (HotOS {XV}).* Kartause Ittingen, Switzerland: {USENIX} Association. Retrieved from `https://www.usenix.org/conference/hotos15/workshop-program/presentation/ajoux`

Amiri, A., Krieger, C., Zdun, U., & Leymann, F. (2019). Dynamic Data Routing Decisions for Compliant Data Handling in Service-and Cloud-Based Architectures: A Performance Analysis. *2019 IEEE International Conference on Services Computing (SCC)* (pp. 215--219). IEEE.

Atkinson, C., & Groß, H.-g. (2002). Built-in Contract Testing in Model-driven, ComponentBased Development. *In ICSR-7 Workshop on ComponentBased Development Processes.* Citeseer.

Baldini, I., Castro, P., Chang, K., Cheng, P., Fink, S., Ishakian, V., . . . Suter, P. (2017). Serverless computing: Current trends and open problems. *Research Advances in Cloud Computing,* 1--20.

Bartock, M., Souppaya, M., Savino, R., Knoll, T., Shetty, U., Cherfaoui, M., Scarfone, K. (2020, April 28). Hardware-Enabled Security for Server Platforms: Enabling a Layered Approach to Platform Security for Cloud and Edge Computing Use Cases (Draft). National Institute of Standards and Technology.

Brewer, E. A. (2000). Towards robust distributed systems. PODC Key Note. 7. Portland: PODC.

Buxton, J. N., & Randell, B. (1969). Software engineering techniques. *Report of a Conference Sponsored by the NATO Science Committee.* Rome, Italy: NATO Science Committee.

© Chandra Rajasekharaiah 2021
C. Rajasekharaiah, *Cloud-Based Microservices*, https://doi.org/10.1007/978-1-4842-6564-2

Dattatreya Nadig, N. (2019). Testing Resilience of Envoy Service Proxy with Microservices. STOCKHOLM, SWEDEN: KTH ROYAL INSTITUTE OF TECHNOLOGY.

Deutsch, P. (1994). The eight fallacies of distributed computing (on Wayback Machine). *Oracle Blogs*. Retrieved from https://web.archive.org/web/20160909234753/https://blogs.oracle.com/jag/resource/Fallacies.html

Dijkstra, E. W. (1968, March). Go To Statement Considered Harmful. *Communications of the ACM, 11*(3), 147-148. doi:10.1145/362929.362947

Dragoni, N., Giallorenzo, S., Lafuente, A. L., Mazzara, M., Montesi, F., Mustafin, R., & Safina, L. (2017). Microservices: yesterday, today, and tomorrow. *Present and ulterior software engineering*, 195-216.

El Malki, A., & Zdun, U. (2019). Guiding Architectural Decision Making on Service Mesh Based Microservice Architectures. *European Conference on Software Architecture* (pp. 3-19). Springer.

Erl, T. (2005). Service-Oriented Architecture: Concepts, Technology, and Design. In T. Erl, *Service-Oriented Architecture: Concepts, Technology, and Design.* Pearson Education.

Evans, E. (2004). *Domain-Driven Design: Tackling Complexity in the Heart of Software.* Addison-Wesley. Retrieved 4 10, 2020, from http://dddcommunity.org/book/evans_2003/

Feathers, M. (2004). *Working Effectively with Legacy Code.* Pearson Education.

Felter, W., Ferreira, A., Rajamony, R., & Rubio, J. (2015). An updated performance comparison of virtual machines and linux containers. *2015 IEEE international symposium on performance analysis of systems and software (ISPASS)* (pp. 171--172). IEEE.

Fielding, R. T. (2000). *Architectural Styles and the Design of Network-based Software Architectures.* University of California, Irvine. Retrieved 4 10, 2020, from http://www.ics.uci.edu/~fielding/pubs/dissertation/top.htm

Foote, B., & Yoder, J. (1997). Big Ball of Mud. *Pattern Languages of Program Design*, 4, 654--692

Gao, X., Gu, Z., Kayaalp, M., Pendarakis, D., & Wang, H. (2017). ContainerLeaks: Emerging security threats of information leakages in container clouds. *2017 47th Annual IEEE/IFIP International Conference on Dependable Systems and Networks (DSN)* (pp. 237--248). IEEE.

Garcia-Molina, H., & Salem, K. (1987). Sagas. *Proceedings of the 1987 ACM SIGMOD International Conference on Management of Data.* 16, pp. 249--259. SIGMOD '87.

Gartner. (2020, July 23). *Gartner Forecasts Worldwide Public Cloud Revenue to Grow 6.3% in 2020*. Retrieved from `https://www.gartner.com/en/newsroom/press-releases/2020-07-23-gartner-forecasts-worldwide-public-cloud-revenue-to-grow-6point3-percent-in-2020`.

Grama, A. Y., Gupta, A., & Kumar, V. (1993). Isoefficiency Function: A Scalability Metric for Parallel Algorithms and Architectures. *IEEE Parallel & Distributed Technology: Systems & Applications*, 1(3), pp. 12-21.

Hightower, K., Burns, B., & Beda, J. (2017). *Kubernetes: up and running: dive into the future of infrastructure*. O'Reilly Media, Inc.

How, M. (2020). *The Modern Data Warehouse in Azure: Building with Speed and Agility on Microsoft's Cloud Platform*. Apress.

Humble, J., & Farley, D. (2010). *Continuous Delivery: Reliable Software Releases through Build, Test, and Deployment Automation*. Pearson Education.

Humble, J., & Molesky, J. (2011). Why enterprises must adopt devops to enable continuous delivery. *Cutter IT Journal, 24*(8), 6--13.

Iglesias, C. A., & Garijo, M. (2010). Microservices - Lightweight Service Descriptions for REST Architectural Style. *ICAART (1)*, (pp. 576--579).

Kepes, B. (2011). Cloudonomics: The Economics of Cloud Computing. *Diversity Limited*, 181.

Kim, G., Humble, J., Debois, P., & Willis, J. (2016). *The DevOps Handbook:: How to Create World-Class Agility, Reliability, and Security in Technology Organizations*. IT Revolution.

Kleppman. (2017). Designing data-intensive applications: *The big ideas behind reliable, scalable, and maintainable systems*. O'Reilly Media, Inc.

Lamport, L. (1978, July). Time, Clocks, and the Ordering of Events in a Distributed System. *Commun. ACM, 21*(7), 558–565. doi:10.1145/359545.359563

Lamport, L. (1998). The part-time parliament. *ACM Transactions on Computer Systems, 16*(2), 133--169.

Lamport, L. (2001). Paxos Made Simple.

Larsson, L., Tärneberg, W., Klein, C., Elmroth, E., & Kihl, M. (2020). Impact of etcd deployment on Kubernetes, Istio, and application performance. *arxiv, preprint arXiv:2004.00372*.

Lewis, J., & Fowler, M. (2014, March 25). *Microservices.* Retrieved from Martin Folwer. com: `http://martinfowler.com/articles/microservices.html`

Li, Z., Kihl, M., Lu, Q., & Andersson, J. A. (2017). Performance overhead comparison between hypervisor and container based virtualization. *2017 IEEE 31st International Conference on Advanced Information Networking and Applications (AINA)* (pp. 955--962). IEEE.

Lynch, N. A. (1996). *Distributed Algorithms.* San Francisco, CA, USA: Morgan Kaufmann Publishers Inc.

Marston, S., Li, Z., Bandyopadhyay, S., Zhang, J., & Ghalsasi, A. (2011). Cloud computing—The business perspective. *Decision support systems*, 51(1), 176--189.

McCarthy, J. (1978, August). History of Lisp. *SIGPLAN Not.*, 217–223. doi:10.1145/960118.808387

Moss, J. E. (1981). *Nested Transactions: An Approach to Reliable Distributed Computing.* MASSACHUSETTS INST OF TECH CAMBRIDGE LAB FOR COMPUTER SCIENCE.

Myrbakken, H., & Colomo-Palacios, R. (2017). DevSecOps: a multivocal literature review. *International Conference on Software Process Improvement and Capability Determination* (pp. 17--29). Springer.

Neuman, B. C. (1994). Scale in Distributed Systems. *IEEE Computer Society*, 463--489.

Newman, S. (2015). *Building Microservices* (1st ed.). O'Reilly Media, Inc.

NIST, SP. (2012). 800-145: The NIST definition of cloud computing.

Pease, M., Shostak, R., & Lamport, L. (1980). Reaching agreement in the presence of faults. *Journal of the ACM (JACM), 27*(2), 228--234.

Preston-Werner, T. (2013 ). Semantic Versioning 2.0.0. *Semantic Versioning. Available: https://semver.org/.*

Raho, M., Spyridakis, A., Paolino, M., & Raho, D. (2015). Kvm, xen and docker: A performance analysis for arm based nfv and cloud computing. *2015 IEEE 3rd Workshop on Advances in Information, Electronic and Electrical Engineering (AIEEE)*, 1-8.

Reed, D. P. (1978). Naming and synchronization in a decentralized computer system. Massachusetts Institute of Technology.

Sabt, M., Achemlal, M., & Bouabdallah, A. (2015). Trusted execution environment: what it is, and what it is not. *2015 IEEE Trustcom/BigDataSE/ISPA. 1*, pp. 57--64. IEEE.

Sadalage, P. J., & Fowler, M. (2012). *NoSQL Distilled: A Brief Guide to the Emerging World of Polyglot Persistence.* Addison-Wesley Professional.

Sampaio, A. R., Kadiyala, H., Hu, B., Steinbacher, J., Erwin, T., Rosa, N., ... Rubin, J. (2017). Supporting microservice evolution. *2017 IEEE International Conference on Software Maintenance and Evolution (ICSME)* (pp. 539--543). IEEE.

Schiel, C., Lind, P. G., & Maass, P. (2017). Resilience of electricity grids against transmission line overloads under wind power injection at different nodes. *Scientific Reports, 7*(1), 1-11.

Schultz, C., Braunreuther, S., & Reinhart, G. (2016, 12). Method for an Energy-oriented Production Control. *Procedia CIRP, 48*, 248-253. doi:10.1016/j.procir.2016.04.058

Seo, K.-T., Hwang, H.-S., Moon, I.-Y., Kwon, O.-Y., & Kim, B.-J. (2014). Performance comparison analysis of linux container and virtual machine for building cloud. *Advanced Science and Technology Letters, 66*(Networking and Communication 2014), 105-111.

Sharma, R., & Singh, A. (2019). *Rahul Getting Started with Istio Service Mesh: Manage Microservices in Kubernetes.* Apress.

Sigelman, B. H., Barroso, L., re, Burrows, M., Stephenson, P., Plakal, M., . . . Shanbhag, C. (2010). Dapper, a large-scale distributed systems tracing infrastructure.

Sridharan, C. (2018). *Distributed Systems Observability.* O'Reilly Media, Inc.

Strauss, D. (2013, June 17). The future cloud is container, not virtual machines. *Linux Journal, 2013*(5), 228. Retrieved from `https://www.linuxjournal.com/content/containers%E2%80%94not-virtual-machines%E2%80%94are-future-cloud`

Turnbull, J. (2014). *The Docker Book: Containerization is the new virtualization.* James Turnbull.

Wiggins, A. (2012). `http://12factor.net`.

Wu, C., Buyya, R., & Ramamohanarao, K. (2019). Cloud pricing models: Taxonomy, survey, and interdisciplinary challenges. *ACM Computing Surveys (CSUR), 52*(6), 1--36.

Yarygina, T. (2018). Exploring Microservice Security. The University of Bergen.

Yeluri, R., & Castro-Leon, E. (2014). *Building the Infrastructure for Cloud Security: A Solutions View.* Springer Nature.

Yu, X., Joshi, P., Xu, J., Jin, G., Zhang, H., & Jiang, G. (2016). Cloudseer: Workflow monitoring of cloud infrastructures via interleaved logs. *ACM SIGARCH Computer Architecture News, 44*(2), 489--502.

Zhang, G., Ren, K., Ahn, J.-S., & Ben-Romdhane, S. (2019). GRIT: Consistent Distributed Transactions Across Polyglot Microservices with Multiple Databases. *2019 IEEE 35th International Conference on Data Engineering (ICDE),* (pp. 2024--2027).

# Afterword

An enormous amount of work is happening in the software development field today. The 2010s saw a significant shift in enterprises toward building distributed architectures. There were efforts in both modernizing software stacks and in developing new systems. Most modern technology enterprises adopted microservices architecture as the standard for modernization efforts. Microservices architecture demonstrated the ease of scaling, inbuilt elasticity, and reduction in time-to-market of business features. Microservices architecture is also a sane way of building distributed systems.

Distributed architectures are at the forefront today because of two reasons: global economies and the advent of the cloud. The customer base enterprise has access to is no longer local. They can reach global consumers and offer services and goods. The idea of enterprises renting out infrastructure that they need, and paying only for what they use, is a real option. Instead of maintaining massive data centers, they can rent from a catalog of services a cloud service provider offers. These developments in the field have made the knowledge of cloud-based microservices architecture paramount for engineers and architects.

Advancing the field of cloud-based microservices requires published literature. Most of the materials available on this topic are grey literature, covering a specific item, or focusing on a particular technology. The minimal content that *is* available discusses academic viewpoints of cloud-based microservices, or a patent, or a discovery of a custom solution. I wrote this book to share my experience and perspective on the subject, in a technology-agnostic manner. The book intends to provide a complete view of starting from a monolith, moving to microservices, porting to the cloud, and adopting changes. I hope that this book, and future books on this topic, will initiate discussions and advance and standardize the field.

221
© Chandra Rajasekharaiah 2021
C. Rajasekharaiah, *Cloud-Based Microservices*, https://doi.org/10.1007/978-1-4842-6564-2

# Index

## A

Agility, 38, 39, 41
Asteroid Mining, 31, 32, 34, 35
Automation, 60, 70, 84, 204
Autopay transaction, 45

## B

Business logic, 44, 46, 47

## C

CAP theorem
    definition, 161
    distributed consensus, 170, 171
    NoSQL databases, 165–167
    quorum-based
        transactions, 167, 169
    relational databases, CA, 163
    shared/distributed, 164
    types, 162
Choreography technique, 19
Cloud-bursting, 202, 206, 209
Cloud computing, 97, 98
    business opportunities, 100
    compute, 106, 107
    cost analysis, 110–113
    databases/traditional datastores, 108
    datastores, 109, 110
    definition, 98

    emergences, 114–116
    financial gains, 98, 99
    integration, 108
    microservices, setup, 103, 104
    networking/connectivity, 104–106
    prerequisites, 102
    technology gains, 101
Cloud Native Computing Foundation
    (CNCF), 122, 206
Cloud service providers (CSPs), 97, 183
Consumer Portal, 5, 6
Containerization
    container image, 122
    emergences cloud setup, 150, 151
    microservices, 123–125
    orchestration, 125–127, 129–131
    PaaS, 141
    virtualization, 120, 121
Continuous delivery (CD)
    delivery techniques, 90–92
    infrastructure as code, 90
Continuous integration (CI), 84
    automated testing, 87
    ephemerality, 89
    factors/reasons, 88
    non-production environments, 85, 86
    performance testing, 87, 88
Contract testing, 77, 78
Cross-organizational
    transactions, 19, 20

© Chandra Rajasekharaiah 2021
C. Rajasekharaiah, *Cloud-Based Microservices*, https://doi.org/10.1007/978-1-4842-6564-2

# D

DBaaS
    CAP, 161
    CSPs, 155
    NoSQL databases, 158–160
    relational databases, 156, 157
Demand Planner, 5, 6
DevSecOps, 92, 93, 95, 194
Disaster recovery (DR), 197–199
Distributed architectures, 117, 221
Distributed transactions, 47
    choreographed domains, 49
    composite data, 53
    data exchange, 51, 52
    dread-difficulty, 56
    failures/faults, 54, 55
    monoliths *vs.* microservices, 49
    orchestrated domains, 48
    overall state, 50, 51
    sharding, 52, 53
Distribution system
        operator (DSO), 1

# E

Elasticity, 37, 38
Energence, 1
    abilities, 2
    changes, 94
    collected data, 4
    data connectivity setup, 4
    energy distribution setup, 2
    goals, 39
    growth opportunities, 8, 9
    hardware/software, 5
    home platform, 7, 8
    software needs, 5
Energence Home Platform, 6

Enterprise-service-buses (ESBs), 131
Extract, transform,
        load (ETL), 68

# F

Fisher's scale cube, 37
Forecast Platform, 6

# G

Global state
    always-listening option, 70, 71
    centralized view, 72, 73
    domain surface, 67, 68
    intermittent-peek option, 69
    observability, 74–76
    OTA, 66, 67
Google Cloud Platform (GCP), 121
Graphics processing unit (GPU), 120

# H

Home Platform, 6, 42, 44, 54, 66

# I, J, K

Identifying and classifying
        challenges, 42, 43
Identity and access management (IAM),
    184, 191
Incremental architectures, 34
Integration services
    Maas, 142, 143
    point-to-point messaging, 143–145
    publish-subscribe messaging, 145–147
    streaming/distributed commit logs,
        147, 148, 150

# L

Log aggregation, 75
Logging, 74–76

# M

Metrics, 3, 75
Microservices
    automation, 205
    changing security
        landscape, 207
    cloud-bursting/multi-cloud/cloud
        agnosticism, 206
    compute options, 206
    HCI, 208
    monolith, 208
    reducing, burden
        maintenance, 205
Microservices architecture
    characteristics, 16
    choreography, 19
    CI/CD, 83, 84
    fail, 83
    implementing, 16–19
    orchestration, 19
    origins, 13, 14
Microservices migration, 21
    architecture, 27, 28
    financial implications, 29
    modules into submodules, 24–26
    monolith into modules, 21–23
    systemic implications, 29
    transition architecture, 28
Microservices-native solution
    designing, 34, 35
    interdomain communication, 32
    subdomains, 33, 34
    top-level domains, 31, 32

# N

Normalized-message-routers (NMRs), 131

# O

Online analytics processing (OLAP)
    datastores
    data movement, 174, 175
    data warehouses, 172
    enterprises, 172
Open Container Initiative (OCI), 121, 206
Over-the-air (OTA), 66

# P, Q

Partner Portal, 6
Point-to-point messaging, 143
Proxy/sidecar, 132

# R

Recovery point objective (RPO), 198
Recovery time objective (RTO), 163, 198

# S

Sagas, 63
    compensating transactions inline, 64
    compensating transactions offline, 64
    ignore errors, 63
    implementation, 65
Scalability, 35, 36
Securing microservices
    API gateways/load balancers, 187–190
    attack surface, 181
    availability, 197–201
    cloud deployment setup, 179, 180
    IAM, CSPs, 191, 192

Securing microservices (*cont.*)
    inter-service communication, 192
    outgoing communication, 183
    processing integrity, 193, 194, 196
    services, 182
    VPC, 184, 186, 187
Service catalog, 59–61
Service-level agreements (SLAs), 100, 163
Service meshes
    challenges,state of art, 138
    definition, 131
    establishing/securing communication,
        135, 136
    Faas aka serverless, 138, 139
    microservices architecture, 133

    observability, 136, 137
    SOA, 131
    traffic management, traffic control, and
        traffic shaping, 134, 135
Service-oriented architecture (SOA), 15
Sharding, 52, 53
Software development process, 81

## T, U

Tracing, 74–76, 136

## V, W, X, Y, Z

Virtual machines (VMs), 106, 138, 151

Printed in the United States
By Bookmasters